COASTAL RESOURCES MANAGEMENT
Institutions and Programs

JOSEPH M. HEIKOFF

Professor of Public Administration
Graduate School of Public Affairs
State University of New York at Albany

ANN ARBOR SCIENCE
PUBLISHERS INC
P.O. BOX 1425 • ANN ARBOR, MICH. 48106

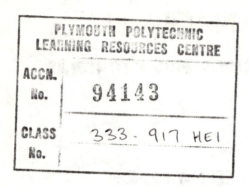
Library of Congress Catalog Card No. 76-050986
ISBN 0-250-40157-6

This research was sponsored by the New York Sea Grant Institute under a
grant from the Office of Sea Grant, National Oceanic and Atmospheric Administration (NOAA), U.S. Department of Commerce. The U.S. Government
is authorized to produce and distribute reprints for governmental purposes
notwithstanding any copyright notation appearing hereon.

 New York Sea Grant Institute
Albany 1977

COASTAL RESOURCES
MANAGEMENT
Institutions and Programs

PREFACE

Coastal zone management as a distinct field of government attained some degree of widespread public attention when Congress passed the Coastal Zone Management Act of 1972. This law encourages states to develop coastal resources management programs that will conform to national policies and meet specified performance criteria. Some coastal states including Maine, Rhode Island and Washington, enacted coastal management programs before Congress got around to it. This study presents an account of these early efforts and focuses on the institutional structures that were devised to take program management responsibility. No attempt was made to attain comprehensive coverage of coastal zone management in the United States. Many states are still in the program development stage, and at this time only the Washington coastal program has received formal approval by the federal government through the Secretary of Commerce. Nevertheless, the three state programs summarized here have been in operation since 1971. Some useful information can perhaps be derived from these early experiences with coastal resources management.

Joseph M. Heikoff
Albany, New York

ACKNOWLEDGMENTS

This survey could not possibly have been accomplished without the cooperation of staff members in the state agencies who freely provided information and took time to read manuscript drafts. For taking time from very busy shcedules their assistance is gratefully acknowledged: In Maine, R. Alec Giffen, supervisor, Resource Planning Division, and Rob Elder; in Rhode Island, Daniel Varin, chief of the Statewide Planning Program, and Lee R. Whitaker; in Washington, D. Rodney Mack, head of the Shorelands Division, Department of Ecology, and Don Peterson.

I am grateful also to the New York Sea Grant Institute director, Dr. Donald F. Squires, and members of the editorial and administrative staffs. Their financial support and management assistance made this study possible. Neither they nor the state officials listed above are responsible for its deficiencies.

Typing and retyping manuscript drafts was ably accomplished by the secretarial pool of the Graduate School of Public Affairs supervised by Ann Wright and Donna Parker.

— JMH

FOR

ROSE AND REUBEN

IN MEMORIAM

Do you think you can take over the universe
    and improve it?
I do not believe it can be done.

The universe is sacred.
You cannot improve it.
If you try to change it, you will ruin it.
If you try to hold it, you will lose it.

Lao Tsu, *Tao Te Ching*, 29

CONTENTS

PART V ANALYSIS

ILLUSTRATIONS

PART I

THE FEDERAL PROGRAM

CHAPTER I

INTRODUCTION

Industrialization of the American economy brought unparalleled prosperity to most of the nation. It also fostered the urbanization of about three-fourths of the population, most of it concentrated in metropolitan areas along the marine coasts and the shores of the Great Lakes. Economic development was not without costs to the environment. Industry, transportation and energy production seek waterfront locations in competition with residential development and its associated demands for recreation facilities. To satisfy development pressures on coastal sites, wetlands have been filled, sand dunes leveled and barrier beaches crowded with second homes and resorts; and shorefronts have been polluted by municipal and industrial effluents and surface drainage. Offshore drilling for oil and refining and transportation of petroleum products pose new threats to the coastal environment.

Society has been ready to accept the environmental costs of economic benefits up to a point. In recent years, however, it has become evident that environmental values have been destroyed out of proportion to the economic advantages derived from resources exploitation. Conservation of unique and fragile environments and careful planning of future development have become policy issues of serious public concern.

Current concern about the environment stems from the evidence that exploitation of environmental resources—as sources of raw materials and as sinks for waste products—has resulted in serious depletion of nonrenewable resources and in hazards to human health and to the entire biosphere. In the absence of human intervention, ecological systems come about and maintain themselves in

3

particular geomorphic and climatic environments by the evolutionary processes inherent in what we call the laws of nature. Propagation of individual species and ecological balance within the secular process of evolution seem to be nature's objectives. Human technological invasion of pristine territory diverts natural law from its own objectives and processes. Man cannot abolish or change the laws of nature in pursuing economic objectives. But human technology can harness and divert those laws, with unanticipated harmful as well as desired beneficial results.

Primitive societies were integral components of balanced ecological systems, for their technology was too weak to cause much change in the way the laws of nature operated. Primitive social orders established territories to assure food supplies; but human territoriality was no more disruptive of ecological systems than the territorial imperatives of other animals. Furthermore, tribal territories were regarded as common property held and defended for the benefit of all.

Serious disruption of ecological systems by man came with advancing technology, the invention of the concept of private property, and the struggle to gain and control wealth. Property and power, concepts that had no place in the laws of nature, required human laws to sanction and legitimate the appropriation and concentration into individual and corporate ownership of resources that had once "belonged" only to "nature."

Private property and economic specialization go together, requiring the establishment of markets for exchange. The market system fostered economic development, except in one important respect. Some kinds of resources—air and large water bodies for example—were not easily appropriated by individuals and remained common property. These are nonmarket resources, and their use is not restrained or regulated by the private market system. Hence the eventual pressure for public management of common property resources.[1]

Human law protected newly invented rights to the ownership and accumulation of property and power. The rights of nonproprietors were less clearly defined or vigorously protected. Abetted by human law in the interest of expanding property and power, proprietors intensified the application of technology to the exploitation of environmental resources and at the same time to the exploitation of the nonproprietors who were their dependents.

Legally legitimated exploitation of the environment came from two directions. Property rights conveyed the privilege of doing with one's property whatever one wanted, most often for maximizing profit in the short run, regardless of the long-run environmental consequences. Exploiters of land and natural resources for the expansion of their wealth and power were also able to acquire control of advancing technology. Since air and water were considered free of cost, the concept of economic progress favored their unlimited use as sinks for the waste products of production, transportation and consumption.

Not until the proprietors themselves could no longer escape the consequences of environmental degradation, either because it affected them personally or limited the productivity of their property and the marketability of its products, did human law begin to consider the rights of nonproprietors. This was only a gradual process, and the struggle for the definition and protection of societal rights as against proprietary rights in the environment seems only to have just begun.

We have known all along that the laws of nature cannot be abrogated by technology. Technology only imposes new patterns of costs and benefits on society arising from the inevitable consequences of new ways of the working out of the eternal laws of thermodynamics and biological processes. As technologically advanced societies experience intensifying problems of depleted resources, unbreathable air, undrinkable water, and uneatable food, the controllers of property and power may acquire a new respect for the laws of nature. They may eventually learn that there are limits to the conversion of resources in their natural state into private property for short-term exploitation. Perhaps these lessons may even be applied to revision of human laws to define and protect societal rights and guide the applications of technology into greater harmony with the operation of natural laws to stop, and perhaps reverse, environmental degradation, insult to the biosphere, and threat to human health.

Coastal zone management is only one recent manifestation of the recognition that human law must be modified to permit a redistribution of rights and privileges between individual and corporate proprietors and the rest of society. Untrammeled conversion of the coastal environment from its "natural" state for the short-term benefit of proprietors can no longer be permitted, for the environmental consequences are no longer bearable by the whole society. The political problem posed by this recognition is how to redefine proprietary and communal rights and how to trade off environmental protection against economic advantage. The managerial problem is to provide reliable information to the political decision-makers so that they may equitably solve the political problem and then regulate the future use and development of coastal resources to solve the environmental problem. The objective appears to be the establishment of harmony between human and natural law so that regeneration and renewal may replace destruction and depletion.

It has been suggested that the following functions are required for effective environmental management and control:[2]

1. Selective and continuous monitoring of the environment to identify problem areas and to provide a data base for projections and time series comparisons;
2. Research and planning to anticipate emerging problems and to counter them by technical and policy innovations;
3. Identification and consideration of differences in value preferences in determining the public interests in policy making;
4. Development of standards and criteria as general guidelines to regulation policy;
5. Coordination of activities of agencies having major and 'peripheral' responsibility for resources management;
6. Establishment of necessary administrative and control mechanisms;
7. Generation of adequate funding.

One manifestation of concern at the national level for the coastal environment is the Coastal Zone Management Act of 1972. Two of the reasons Congress gave for legislating in this field relate to what it perceived to be deficiencies in environmental resources management institutions in state and local government:

[First] In light of competing demands and the urgent need to protect and to give high priority to natural systems in the coastal zone, present state and local institutional arrangements for planning and regulating land and water uses in such areas are inadequate . . .

[Second] The key to more effective protection and use of the land and water resources of the coastal zone is to encourage the states to exercise their full authority over the lands and waters in the coastal zone by assisting the states, in cooperation with federal and local governments and other vitally affected interests in developing land and water use programs for the coastal zone, including unified policies, criteria, standards, methods, and processes for dealing with land and water use decisions of more than local significance.[3]

By this Act, Congress encourages the coastal states to retrieve some of their powers for development control and resource management. If states do so, they may supervise and influence local land and water use decisions that have an impact beyond the boundaries of single municipal jurisdictions.

Coastal zone management has been given particular visibility by the federal Coastal Zone Management Act. Although this program deals with only one aspect of environmental resources management, federal government attention to it and the financial resources made available have encouraged coastal states to embark on program development for coastal management following federal guidelines.

INTERGOVERNMENTAL RELATIONS
IN THE COASTAL ZONE

Effective coastal resources management involves participation by all levels of government. The state has basic responsibility for the social and economic welfare of its citizens and the protection of their environment. It is also the constitutional repository for powers to regulate private activities that affect the environment and to establish programs for public works and services to conserve and protect it. In response to the tradition of local self-determination in this country, states have also come to share these powers

with county and municipal governments. Home rule and local
authority for regulating land use, for example, are accepted and
deeply entrenched features of our governmental system. On the
national level, responsibilities for navigation and protection of the
shore against the ravages of storms and erosion have long involved
the federal government in coastal problems.

The Coastal Zone Management Act has offered federal financial
aid to state and local governments to assure wise use and conservation of lands and waters in the coastal zone. Coastal management,
as conceived in the federal Act, involves these major operations:

1. Identification of the boundaries of the coastal management
   zone;
2. Definition and identification of land and water uses that have
   a significant impact on coastal waters and that will be permitted in the coastal zone;
3. Designation and inventory of areas of particular environmental concern;
4. Setting priorities for uses, especially those of regional, statewide, or national significance, in particular areas of the
   coastal zone;
5. Establishing procedures and organizational structure for
   managing the coastal zone.

The last task is the focus of this discussion. Its significance lies
in the fact that the coastal management organization is the
vehicle for carrying out all of the other aspects of program development and implementation. It has already been noted that
managing intergovernmental relations is crucial to the management of coastal resources, because powers, responsibility and
financial commitments must be shared by state, local and federal
governments. Provision must also be made for citizen participation in management decisions and implementation of coastal zone
policies. Effective management of coastal resources will be determined to a large extent by the effectiveness of the state management organization in carrying out its implementation tasks and
eliciting the cooperation and participation of federal and local
agencies as well as gaining citizen support for the state program.

MANAGEMENT STRUCTURE AND
PROGRAM EFFECTIVENESS

Approaches to Coastal Zone Management

Theories of governmental organization are the product of long experience in public management, and they offer useful general guidelines. They must be adapted, however, to the particular functions and responsibilities an organization is expected to perform. Perhaps the first step in making this adaptation for a coastal management organization is to analyze the state's conceptual approach to coastal resources management. The nature of the coastal program, its management objectives, and the kinds of tasks and operations it would be expected to carry out would presumably determine, to some extent, the appropriate kind of management structure. The nature of the management roles assigned to state and local agencies and the way in which regulatory powers are shared between these government levels would be especially significant.

Management Structure

Determining a state's approach to coastal resources management provides a background for analyzing the organizational structure established to implement it. Such an analysis would include delineation of the characteristics of the structure, the legislative foundation for it, and its relation to existing state and local agencies, especially those concerned with land use, public works, environmental protection and resources management. If relevant information can be found about the political environment of the coastal management program, the analysis would include the effects on it of the attitudes of the governor and key state legislators as reflected in administrative and legislative actions. Political factors also include the attitudes of local governments toward the state program, especially as they might perceive its effect on diminishing local autonomy and power over land development regulation.

Program Effectiveness

It is not enough simply to describe coastal zone management institutions in various states but one must also seek empirical evidence of the influence that different approaches to the management process and management structure may have on the effectiveness of the coastal zone program. To do this it will first be necessary to identify criteria of effective resources management. If it is not possible to identify measures of management effectiveness, then there is no way of evaluating the effect that the variables of management structure, legal foundation for the program, financial commitment or popular support have on the relative operational success of the coastal resources management program.

Having identified criteria of effective coastal zone management, it may then be possible to evaluate different approaches to institutionalizing state management responsibility. The question is whether organizational structure makes any serious difference to the success of the coastal program. It is quite possible that positive correlations between management success and institutional structure will not be found. Because there are intervening variables, such as political and popular support for the program, its funding, and the technical and managerial capabilities of its personnel, it would be difficult to demonstrate that organizational features *per se* are responsible for success or failure in resources management. Equally important, perhaps, are the attitudes of legislators, bureaucrats, business executives, property owners and voters. If they favor environmental management, there may be good chances for successful programs regardless of the institutional structure.

What it may be feasible to demonstrate empirically are institutional *obstacles* to effective management. The term 'institutional' is used broadly here to include organizational structure, legal foundation, funding, personnel skills and popular support. Experience may indicate that awkward organizational arrangements create obstacles to policy and program coordination and to effective management. The results of such a study may, therefore, more validly be used to identify what should *not* be done rather than to make recommendations about what should be done.

ENVIRONMENTAL MANAGEMENT
COORDINATION STATEWIDE

It has been noted that coastal zone management is one aspect of state responsibility for environmental resources conservation and protection. Its legal and administrative separation from other environmental concerns by the Coastal Zone Management Act of 1972 points up the problem of intergovernmental relations and intragovernmental coordination in environmental management. There has been a fragmented approach to environmental legislation and programs. Separate acts deal with freshwater and tidal wetlands, wild and recreational rivers, regional park reservations, shore protection, wildlife reservations, and general land use regulation. If separate administrative organizations were established for each program, the bureaucratic thicket would become impenetrable.

The fragmented approach may, however, be most appropriate for present circumstances. It permits environmental issues to be identified, studied, and debated by the various constituencies and legislators concerned with each one. The process is incremental and evolutionary, adapting environmental legislation to the pace of public awareness of the issues and acceptance of governmental intervention. Nevertheless, this approach may create administrative problems for the general area of public responsibility for environmental management. Fragmented programs assigned to different state agencies may create a bureaucratic jungle. If the bureaucratic apparatus becomes unmanageable, the chances for success in environmental resources management itself are reduced.

There appear to be no simple administrative solutions to the problem of governmental organization, which becomes increasingly complex as the scope of public responsibility for social, economic, and environmental welfare expands. Some states have taken the approach of establishing massive superagencies that consolidate environmental resources conservation with pollution control; others have established separate agencies for these functions. Some states prefer separate coastal zone management commissions; others have integrated coastal and inland resources management. The administrative and political problem is how to create coherent

integrate

environmental policies and programs that will complement and reinforce each other to successfully maintain healthy ecological systems and at the same time support viable regional and local economies.

Although the federal Coastal Zone Management Act focuses on a particular aspect of environmental resources management and requires participating states to designate coastal management agencies, it does not preclude the institutional integration of coastal and inland resources management. On the contrary, it is possible not only to effect such integration, but also to bring to environmental management statewide the perspectives of the coastal zone program. Some of the resource management procedures identified in the federal coastal program that may be applied beneficially statewide are as follows:

1. Designation of land and water uses of direct and significant impact on the environment;
2. Designation of areas of particular environmental concern;
3. Preparation of environmental resource inventories and atlases;
4. Formulation of state guidelines for the location of services and facilities of regional, statewide, and national significance;
5. Formulation of state guidelines for regional and local action for resources planning and management, particularly by regulation of land and water uses.

REFERENCES

[1] Russel, C. S. and A. V. Kneese. "Establishing Scientific, Technical, and Economic Basis for Coastal Zone Management," *Coastal Zone Management J.* 1:48–52 (Fall 1973).

[2] Spencer, W. H. *Environmental Management for Puget Sound* (Seattle, Washington: University of Washington, Division of Marine Resources, 1941), p. 4.

[3] "Coastal Zone Management Act of 1972," Sec. 302 (9) (h).

CHAPTER II

COASTAL ZONE MANAGEMENT PROGRAMS

The coastal zone is so complex ecologically, geomorphically, and in its man-made environmental structures that the technical features of a coastal zone management program may vary widely from state to state. Nevertheless, programs submitted to the Office of Coastal Zone Management (OCZM) and the Secretary of Commerce for approval, so that federal implementation grants may be made, must conform to provisions of the Coastal Zone Management Act of 1972 and the rules and regulations that supplement it.

One of the Congressional findings in the Act is that states should be encouraged

> ... to exercise their full authority over the lands and waters of the coastal zone by ... developing land and water use programs for the coastal zone, including unified policies, criteria, standards, methods, and processes for dealing with land and water use decisions of more than local significance.[1]

The key elements of this broad definition of a coastal zone management program are (a) that it should contain *unified* policies, standards and processes for managing coastal resources that are applicable statewide, and (b) that it should govern land and water uses of *more than local concern.* The state coastal management program should, therefore, focus on resource use and conservation to serve national, statewide and regional interests. Environmental decisions of purely local concern would presumably be left to local governments.

This dichotomy of "local" and "more than local" is one feature of a coastal management program that will arouse considerable controversy. By definition, perhaps, environmental matters of

13

local concern are those that do not go beyond the boundaries of local political jurisdictions. But determination of what may be permitted to happen to beaches or wetlands wholly within the legal purview of a municipal government may have implications for people outside that particular community. Should outsiders have access to the local beaches, for example? Should wetlands that provide habitats for migratory birds and spawning grounds for sport and commercial fisheries be allowed to be filled to serve purely local interests?

Another definition of coastal zone management programs is found in the Declaration of Policy section of the Federal Act. This states that the federal government should

> ... encourage and assist the states to exercise effectively their responsibilities in the coastal zone through the development and implementation of management programs to achieve wise use of the land and water resources of the coastal zone giving full consideration to ecological, cultural, historic, and esthetic values as well as to needs for economic development.[2]

This statement points up another area of policy conflict that will have to be resolved in the formulation of coastal management programs. The two objectives of protecting "ecological, cultural, historic, and esthetic values" and meeting "needs for economic development" that are yoked together here are not particularly compatible. Converting land, water bodies, and wetlands from their natural undeveloped state to use for some economic advantage, including use as a repository for wastes, is bound to have some effect on their air, water, land and biological characteristics. The management program will have to include procedures and criteria for determining the trade-offs between economic development and environmental degradation that will be considered acceptable.

A third source of potential controversy arising out of the coastal management program is the requirement for federal approval of state programs. The Coastal Zone Management Act contains this definition of the term management program:

> 'Management program' includes, but is not limited to, a comprehensive statement in words, maps, illustrations, or other media of communication, prepared and adopted by the state in accordance with the provisions of this title, setting forth objectives,

policies, and standards to guide public and private uses of lands
and waters in the coastal zone.[3]

This is a succinct definition, but it includes the phrase "in
accordance with the provisions of this title." This indicates that
the federal Office of Coastal Zone Management will be the arbiter
of the acceptability of state coastal management programs as a
condition for granting implementation funds. This is no different
from federal agency administration of other grant-in-aid programs,
for states must meet federal standards. Nevertheless, states that
elect to participate in the federal coastal zone program will have
to satisfy federal agencies that their management programs conform to the requirements of federal law and regulations.

That this is a real problem is indicated by federal energy agency
review of the first coastal zone management programs submitted
to OCZM. These agencies were not satisfied with simply reviewing
the management *process*. They also wanted to determine the content of the programs by requiring that sites be designated for
energy facilities.

> . . . with Maine, Washington and other states now beginning to
> submit their coastal management programs to the OCZM for
> review, this fledgling agency is in something of a dilemma. On
> the one hand, it does not want to overstep its statutory mandate
> by second-guessing states on matters such as energy planning.
> On the other hand, it is being pushed by the FEA (Federal
> Energy Administration) and other agencies to reject state plans
> that do not specifically provide for energy facility siting. In
> instances where the omission is clearly arbitrary, the OCZM
> will be on safe legal ground in complying with the agencies'
> demand. Absent such arbitrariness, the OCZM either will
> have to stretch the letter of the law (as it understands the
> law) and require program revisions, or it will have to reject
> the energy agencies' demands.[4]

MANAGEMENT PROGRAM
REQUIREMENTS

The Coastal Zone Management Act (Sec. 305) and the rules and
regulations promulgated by the Secretary of Commerce to implement it give detailed information about the criteria that will be

used for federal agency review of state coastal management programs.[5] In general, management programs should address the following points:

1. Major problems and issues within the coastal zone affecting it from outside;

2. Objectives for an interagency and intergovernmental management structure capable of identifying issues and problems, resolving conflicts, and efficiently administering regulations at the state and local levels;

3. Objectives of the management program for preserving, protecting, developing, restoring and enhancing the state's coastal zone;

4. Policies for protecting and conserving coastal zone natural systems, areas of cultural, historic, or scenic value, and renewable and nonrenewable resources; policies also for preserving, restoring, and economically developing selected coastal areas.[6]

Establishing Coastal Zone Boundaries

Because coastal zone management will have legal parameters based on the federal act and state legislation, a legally definable boundary of the state coastal zone will have to be an important feature in the management program. Conservationists are likely to favor an ample coastal zone while developers and local governments anxious for economic expansion will favor a narrower area subject to restrictions on development. Definition of the coastal zone will include the following procedures:

1. Determination of the inland boundary necessary to control uses of the shorelands that would have a direct and significant impact on the coastal waters;

2. Determination of the seaward boundary off the marine coasts and the shores of the Great Lakes;

3. Identification of intertidal areas, salt marshes, wetlands and beaches;

4. Identification of federally owned lands and those held in trust by the federal government, whose uses are not regulated by the state.[7]

Resources Inventory, Permissible Uses, and Areas of Particular Concern

The management program should show how the state has developed and applied a procedure for identifying land and water uses in the coastal zone that have a direct and significant impact on the coastal waters. An operational definition of "direct and significant impact" is required to show how various land and water uses affect the coastal waters. The program should also analyze the development capability of each type of resource and suitable uses that may be made of them; and the environmental impact of reasonable resource uses should be assessed.

To identify permissible uses of land and other resources in the coastal zone an inventory of its natural and man-made resources would have to be prepared. This would also provide the information base for designating and mapping areas of particular environmental concern. Some of these are areas whose uniqueness, vulnerability, or biological productivity require that they be carefully protected. Others are of particular concern because they are areas of urban concentration where there is great competition for use of land and water, or where exploitation of biological and mineral resources must be carefully managed.[8]

Priority of Uses, Regional Benefit, and National Interest

Some coastal areas are unique or environmentally fragile or hazardous, others are already developed or suitable for urbanization or intensive use, and still others are particularly suitable for certain uses because of their location or physical characteristics. For each type of area the management program should include broad policies or guidelines on relative priorities of use. Priority designations should range from high to low. High priorities might be given to particular uses in certain areas because they are appropriate and suitable for intensive development, or because the uses are of important regional or national interest. Low priorities might be assigned to intensive uses in environmentally fragile or hazardous areas, in order to discourage them.[9]

The coastal management program must pay particular attention to preservation or restoration of coastal resources. The program should, therefore, establish standards and criteria for designating areas for preservation because of their conservation, recreation, ecologic or aesthetic values. Areas so identified should be treated as areas of particular concern, and they should be ranked in order of priority for action as funds become available.[10]

As a complement to designating areas and priorities for protection or preservation, the management program must also develop and apply a method for determining uses of regional benefit; and it must assure that local land and water use controls do not arbitrarily or unreasonably restrict these uses. Many public services and infrastructure facilities, such as energy production and transmission, recreation, and transportation are important to a larger region than the single local government in which they may be most advantageously located. Local communities must therefore be persuaded by the state coastal management program to accept a fair share of social responsibility.

> Many local governments and states consider a variety of coastal uses undesirable, and they therefore exclude these uses from locating in areas within their jurisdiction. Notable examples are oil refineries, heavy industry, intensive recreation, power plants, oil extraction, solid waste disposal, off-shore oil terminals, low-income housing and airports.

> Assuming that these uses are expressions of social needs, and at least to some extent, must be located in the coastal zone, then states and local governments which already have accepted their 'fair share' of 'undesirable' uses should not necessarily be forced to bear the burden of accepting more, while other state or local governments which have less than their fair share should not necessarily continue to exclude 'undesirable' uses.[11]

The regional benefit of such uses may extend over part of the state, the whole state, or even the nation. Offshore petroleum extraction and onshore refining and transportation on a particular reach of the coast may be important components of a national policy to maintain adequate energy resources. National defense and aerospace programs also require coastal facilities in strategic locations.

LEGAL STATUS OF COASTAL ZONE MANAGEMENT PROGRAMS

One important objective of the Coastal Zone Management Act of 1972 is to ensure that the state coastal zone management program is more than just another planning document. The definition of "management program" in the Act insists that it be prepared and *adopted* by the state.

> The management program must demonstrate that it represents the official policy and objectives of the State. In general, this will require documentation in the management program that the State management entity has formally adopted the management program in accordance with either the rules or procedures established by statute, or in the absence of such law, administrative regulations.[12]

One of the required elements of a coastal management program is stated in Sec. 305 (b) of the Act:

> ... an identification of the means by which the state proposes to exert control over the land and water uses ... including a listing of relevant constitutional provisions, legislative enactments, regulations, and judicial decisions.

Such an account of the legal foundation of the management program would certainly indicate what powers and authority are available to the state, and to its jurisdictional subdivisions, to implement the program. Nevertheless, citing the legal tools available for program implementation may not be the same thing as formal adoption of the program by the state. This question arises: is indication of the legal status of the program sufficient, or does the federal Act require some formal legislative resolution adopting a specific document called the coastal zone management program?

Section 306 of the federal Act contains additional language referring to the legal status of the management program:

> (c) Prior to granting approval of a management program ... the Secretary shall find that:
>
> (1) The state has developed and adopted a management program for its coastal zone in accordance with rules and regulations promulgated by the Secretary ....

(3)   The state has held public hearings in the development of the management program.

(4)   The management program and any changes thereto
have been reviewed and approved by the Governor.

The adoption procedure must include a formal statement of
approval of the program by the governor, but a form of legislative
enactment is not specified by this provision of the federal Act.

What the rules and regulations say in a roundabout way is that
state and other agencies involved in carrying out the coastal management program must have police power authority to regulate land
and water uses, eminent domain power to acquire ownership or
interests in property, a designated lead agency to administer federal
coastal zone grants, and formal approval of the management program by the governor.

Interagency Coordination in
Coastal Program Development

The federal Act requires that the process of state development
and adoption of a coastal program offers ". . . the opportunity for
full participation by relevant federal agencies, state agencies, local
governments, regional organizations, port authorities and other interested parties, public and private . . ."[13] The intent of the Act
is to ensure that the state is aware of the full array of organized
public and private interests in the coastal zone, that it has provided
them with the opportunity to participate in development of the
coastal program, and that it will continue to consult and cooperate
with them. The management program should, therefore, include
a list of such agencies and organizations, the nature of their interest, and the opportunities afforded them to participate in the
development of the management program.

A specific form of coordination within the general requirement
of interorganizational participation relates to the coordination of
state plans for the coastal zone with the plans of local, regional
and interstate planning agencies.[14] These agencies are authorized
to prepare plans for the area of their jruisdictions by the provisions
of state laws. Their planning activities should not be ignored by
the state organization responsible for coastal management.

Moreover, the coastal management program may benefit from the planning capabilities and information made available by local, regional and other planning organizations.[15]

Briefly stated, these are the federal guidelines for coastal zone management program development or program planning that are incorporated in the Coastal Management Act of 1972 and the rules and regulations relating to it. The guidelines are general enough to allow for a variety of approaches to management programing by the states.

REFERENCES

[1]*Coastal Zone Management Act of 1972,* Sec. 302 (h).

[2]*Ibid.,* Sec. 303 (b).

[3]*Ibid.,* Sec. 302 (g).

[4]Carter, L. J. "Energy and the Coastal Zone: Pulling and Hauling Among the Feds," *Science* 188:1288 (1975).

[5]15 CFR Part 923, (January 9, 1975).

[6]*Ibid.,* Sec. 923.4.

[7]*Ibid.,* Sec. 923.11.

[8]*Ibid.,* Sec. 923.12, 923.13. See Also 15 CFR Part 920, Sec. 920.13, (November 29, 1973).

[9]*Ibid.,* Sec. 923.14.

[10]*Ibid.,* Sec. 923.16.

[11]Armstrong, J., *et al. Coastal Zone Management: The Process of Program Development* (Sandwich, Massachusetts: Coastal Zone Management Institute, 1974), p. 78.

[12]15 CFR Sec. 923.31 (b) (1), (January 9, 1975).

[13]*Coastal Zone Management Act of 1972,* Sec. 306 (c) (1).

[14]*Ibid.,* Sec. 306 (c) (2).

[15]15 CFR Sec. 923.32.

CHAPTER III

STATE LEGISLATIVE FOUNDATION AND MANAGEMENT STRUCTURE

The state coastal zone management institutional structure and its powers are established by state legislation. An important component of the state management program as prescribed by the guidelines in the federal Act is:

> . . . an identification of the means by which the state proposes
> to exert control over the land and water uses—including a
> listing of relevant constitutional provisions, legislative enact-
> ments, regulations, and judicial decisions.[1]

The objective of specifying the legal foundation for coastal management is to assess the state's capability for implementing the management program. Perhaps the most significant feature of the federal Act is its concern that coastal states will go beyond plan-making to actually carrying out their management programs. For this reason it requires that before the Secretary of Commerce may grant approval of a state management program he must be satisfied about these features relating to implementation:

1. The state has held public hearings in the development of the management program;
2. The management program has been reviewed and approved by the state governor;
3. The governor has designated a single agency to receive and administer grants for implementing the management program;
4. The state is organized to implement the management program;

23

5. The state has these powers necessary to implement the program:

   a) To administer land and water use regulations, to control development in order to ensure compliance with the management program, and to resolve conflicts among competitive uses. This is the police power.

   b) To acquire fee simple and less than fee simple interests in lands, waters, and other property through condemnations or other means when necessary to achieve conformance with the management program. This is the power of eminent domain.[2]

The Police Power

One of the required authorities is the police power. The governor's documentation must show "that the agencies and governments chosen by the State to administer the management program have the authority to administer land and water regulations, control development in accordance with the management program and resolve use conflicts."[3] The states are inherent repositories of the police power, so it should not be difficult for them to demonstrate that they are prepared to use it for coastal zone management. One of the administrative and political problems that will likely arise from the application of the police power in implementing coastal programs derives from the considerable delegation of this power to municipal governments by enabling legislation for zoning, subdivision controls, official mapping, and other land use regulations. Municipalities may resist state attempts to interfere with their land use policies and administration of development regulations, in which they have long-standing vested rights.

Eminent Domain

The other authority required is for property acquisition. The governor's legal documentation must therefore show that state, local, or other public agencies "responsible for implementation of the management program have available the power to acquire fee simple and less than fee simple interests in lands, waters and other property through condemnation or other means where necessary to achieve conformance with the management program."[4] As the eminent domain power is also inherent in the states, they have only to demonstrate that the power has been delegated to the agencies charged with implementing the coastal management program.

Management Techniques

The management process must also include at least one of these three techniques for controlling land and water uses:

1. State criteria and standards to guide local implementation, with local efforts subject to state administrative review and enforcement of regulations if local deficiencies are found.
2. Direct state land and water use planning and regulation.
3. State administrative review for consistency with the state management program of all plans, projects or regulations— including exceptions or variances—proposed by any state agency, local authority or private developer. The state would have the power to approve or disapprove such plans, projects, or regulations after public notice and hearings. The management program must also include a method for assuring that land and water use regulations do not unreasonably restrict or exclude land and water uses of regional benefit.[5]

Designation of Lead Agency and Governor's Approval of Management Program

Two other actions are required of the governor. One is that he "has designated a single agency to be responsible for receiving and administering grants under Section 306 for implementing an approved management program."[6] The other requirement is that "the management program must contain a certification signed by the governor . . . to the effect that he has reviewed and approved the management program and any amendments thereto."[7]

It appears from perusal of the Coastal Zone Management Act of 1972 and its rules and regulations that "adoption" by the state of a coastal management program does not necessarily involve legislative action. If, as in some states, the approach to management is to use existing laws and agencies, then the governor only has to certify that federal requirements have been met. Only if the state decides that it needs to create a new coastal zone agency and endow it with operating authority will legislative action be required. And in this case also, the governor will have to certify in the management program that the necessary actions have been taken.

These are the main features required by federal guidelines for the legal foundation of a state coastal management program. State analysis of its legal structure may be guided by these questions:

1. Are current state laws sufficient for coastal zone management under the Act?
2. Which state agency or group of agencies should have authority to implement and to administer the program?
3. Do existing state laws consider adequately property interests—the "taking issue?"
4. Should the state's coastal management program be regulatory (reactive)? Should it encourage specific uses or projects (promotional)? Should it have elements of both?
5. At what time during the program development effort should the state enact or modify pertinent laws? Are interim controls either desirable or necessary?
6. From what sources can the state finance the development and implementation of its coastal zone management programs?[8]

STATE INSTITUTION STRUCTURE FOR COASTAL ZONE MANAGEMENT

Congressional concern for program implementation is expressed in the requirement of the Coastal Zone Management Act that the management structure be devised during the program development stage and described in the management program itself. The Act asks for "a description of the organizational structure proposed to implement the management program, including the responsibilities and interrelationships of local, areawide, state, regional and interstate agencies in the management process."[9] This involves not only working out the organizational structure, but also assigning administrative responsibilities. Arrangements for interagency

planning coordination as well as participation in program development and implementation by public agencies at all levels of government and by private organizations that have interests in the coastal
zone must also be worked out.

Coordination during both the program development and implementation stages goes beyond communication of plans and program
objectives among public agencies. It includes also obtaining information inputs from private organizations to management programing and taking cognizance of their activities during plan implementation. Citizens' organizations should be involved as early as
possible in the program planning stage so that their needs and
aspirations can be considered before regulatory and development
decisions are made. Effective management of public participation
may also generate public support for the coastal management
program.

Public hearings provide a formal avenue for communication with
citizens and private organizations. Nevertheless, they are unsatis-
factory in some ways. Citizens' organizations are called on to
react to proposals and decisions already made by the public agency.
By that time the agency has a vested interest in its own proposals.
More effective citizen participation requires efforts to identify
concerned citizens' groups and provide them with the results of
technical studies and analysis so that they can make their own informed judgements about the nature of coastal problems, feasible
policy and action alternatives, and their expected costs and benefits.
Real public participation would make it possible for informed
citizen groups to make their views known before public agency
positions on the issues are hardened and decisions about policy
recommendations have already been made.

The organizational focus for coastal management is the state
agency designated by the governor to receive and administer
federal grants for implementing the management program. This
responsibility would appear to carry with it a leading role in
coordinating the activities of other participating agencies, com-
piling and controlling budget requests for coastal programs, and
evaluating accomplishments in managing coastal resources. The
state management structure would, therefore, have to contain an
"effective mechanism for continuing consultation and coordination" between the central management agency for the state and

all other public agencies and private organizations with responsibilities and interests in the coastal zone.

Nevertheless, neither the federal Act nor the rules and regulations specify a detailed institutional structure for coastal management by the states. Federal requirements are concerned more that it have particular functions and powers than that it have a specific form. The governor plays an important role in designating the central agency, approving the management program, and certifying as to the existence of the legal foundation and powers necessary to carry out the management program. It is therefore important that the lead management agency have direct access to the governor. The management structure must also have the coordinating mechanism, the power to regulate land and water uses, and the power to acquire property interests that are emphasized in the federal requirements.

The rules and regulations do indicate the criteria that will be applied by the Office of Coastal Zone Management in its review of coastal management structures proposed by the states. There must be evidence that state structures will produce and implement organized and unified programs. Even though implementation responsibilities may be shared by several state agencies, there must be a clear point of responsibility for the whole program. The state will be expected to describe the roles and responsibilities of each agency participating in the program and show how they contribute to a unified approach to coastal resources management.[10]

In a way, the Coastal Zone Management Act of 1972 and the rules and regulations promulgated under it constitute a textbook for coastal resources management for states willing to participate in the program. Like all textbooks they present principles and generalizations that must be given substantive content by accounts of actual experience of state governments. Case studies of individual state programs can provide this kind of information. This account of the general objectives and requirements of the federal law and regulations will therefore be followed by descriptions of coastal management programs that have been submitted for review to the OCZM or are in an advanced stage of preparation.

REFERENCES

[1] *Coastal Zone Management Act of 1972,* Sec. 305 (b) (4).

[2] *Ibid.,* Sec. 306 (c) (d).

[3] 15CFR 923.24 (a), (January 9, 1975).

[4] 15 CFR 923.25 (a), (January 9, 1975).

[5] *Coastal Zone Management Act of 1972*, Sec. 306 (e) (2).

[6] 15 CFR 923.23 (a), (January 9, 1975).

[7] 15 CFR 923.42 (a), (January 9, 1975).

[8] Armstrong, J., *et al. Coastal Zone Management: The Process of Program Development* (Sandwich, Massachusetts: Coastal Zone Management Institute, 1974), p. 85.

[9] *Coastal Zone Management Act of 1972*, Sec. 305 (b) (6).

[10] 15 CFR Sec. 923.22 (b), (January 9, 1975).

PART II

THE MAINE APPROACH

CHAPTER IV

COASTAL ZONE MANAGEMENT IN MAINE

INTRODUCTION

As long ago as 1967 the Advisory Council on Outdoor Recreation and Natural Resources of the State of Maine pointed out the relationship between effective resources management and institutional structure. In its report it noted that "comprehensive water planning will help us get greater returns for the dollars we spend by coordinating our efforts and setting forth broader objectives than can be achieved by the unilateral attempts of any single agency."[1] Since that time there has been some reorganization of state government by the consolidation of agencies. Nevertheless, the management structure and sources of environmental policy for the coastal zone are decentralized and fragmented. Attempts at coordination have produced a "complex interagency and intergovernmental process,"[2] which is not readily comprehended by Maine citizens and property owners; nor has it received adequate public support.

In December 1971, the state of Maine, represented by the State· Planning Office, and the New England River Basins Commission initiated a jointly funded planning partnership called the Maine Guide Plan Program. Its objectives were "to provide a preliminary plan for the wise management of water and related land resources designed to achieve broad social goals through balancing economic development and environmental conservation."[3] Two major conclusions of the study particularly relevant to coastal zone management were: (a) there is need for a formal organizational mechanism for the development and coordination of overall land and water resource policies; and (b) this mechanism should be related to the

adoption of comprehensive planning processes for land and water
resources.

The letter of transmittal of the report noted that "The reason
why state institutional arrangements are so important is the perva-
sive nature of the water and land resources issues. . . . To ensure a
continued pattern of well-being, we need to improve the coordination of all the state functions related to land and water resources."[4] To put it more strongly,

> It is the major conclusion of the Guide Plan Program that the
> fundamental water resources problem in Maine is institutional
> rather than functional. The authority for managing Maine's
> water and related land resources is fragmented among at least
> ten individual state agencies. Each has some degree of respon-
> sibility and authority to establish and enforce standards for the
> use of the resources, to undertake actions which will in one way
> or another affect the quality and quantity of these resources.
> There is no central body responsible for establishing basic
> policies for the conservation and development of Maine's water
> and related land resources or for placing those policies within
> the context of the State's overall environmental, economic and
> social goals. There is a keenly felt need for an integrated water
> and related land resource planning and management program
> which will be consistent with broad national policy objectives,
> will reflect the interests of all state agencies having water-
> related responsibilities, and will provide guidance for action
> by other levels of government and the private sector. It is
> recommended that a natural resources management policy-
> making body be created.[5]

These findings point up the significance of institutional structure and the focusing of responsibility and authority for environmental resources management. This is the broad public management
context for coastal zone resources. Maine is one of the most advanced states in awareness of environmental issues, in enacting laws
to protect and conserve its environment, and in formulating its
coastal zone management program. Its experiences so far may
prove illuminating for other states still in the process of program
and institutional development.

This review of the Maine experience can only produce an interim
report. Environmental management in its contemporary scope and

concerns is a relatively new field of responsibility for state and local governments. Legal foundation, techniques, institutional structure, and evaluation of program effectiveness are all developing rapidly. The situation in Maine will almost certainly be different by the time the reader peruses these pages.

Public hearings on the Maine coastal zone management program in preparation for formal submission to the Department of Commerce in Washington were held in May, 1975. Local government and general public opposition to the proposal was so widespread and so strongly expressed that in June, 1975 Governor James B. Longley postponed the forwarding of Maine's application for coastal management implementation grants. Early in 1976, Governor Longley issued two executive orders on advisory and policy bodies. The order of February 4, 1976 expanded the Governor's Advisory Committee on Coastal Development and Conservation to include public members and a representative of regional planning interests in addition to state agency heads, representatives of the state Senate and House of Representatives, and a vice-president of the University of Maine. The order of March 19, 1976 established a Maine Land and Water Resources Council similar in membership to the Advisory Committee, but without the public members. These organizations, which would have responsibility for reassessing the state's coastal zone and resources management programs, will be described later.

The Maine coastal management program predates the Federal Coastal Zone Management Act of 1972. In this state, coastal management is part of an effort to manage all environmental resources. During the period 1968–69, strong legislation was enacted to protect environmental values. Nevertheless, the results have not measured up to expectations. The State Planning Office has noted that "while each of these laws is commendable and the reasons for their passage were and continue to be sound, growing public dissatisfaction with them poses a threat to their continued existence and jeopardizes as well the underlying concept of resource planning."[6]

In Maine, traditional popular concepts of property rights have not been changed by new governmental concerns about the environment. Development regulation is a legitimate exercise of the state police power, but apparently many people who come in contact with Maine's land use regulation bureaucracy find it arbitrary, discriminatory, and fragmented. There is yet no public consensus on policy for land and water management or for enforcement of regulations.[7]

Three major problems of institutional structure were identified during the early years of the Maine coastal program:

1. *Coordination:* this was lacking between state agencies administering resource management programs and between state, local and federal agencies. Land use planning and regulation were fragmented by the absence of good channels for communication and the lack of comprehensive state policies. Individual land use decisions did not contribute to the attainment of long-term state purposes and were therefore confusing to the public. Insufficient funds and personnel hampered efforts to improve interagency and intergovernmental communications and program coordination.

2. *Public misunderstanding:* program emphasis on regulation neglected parallel efforts in public education and other means for conserving environmental resources, such as financial compensation to landowners for lost land value, a purposeful land acquisition program, adequate tax incentives, and technical assistance to landowners. The focus on regulation led to public misunderstanding of the need for such measures and to resentment against the constraints on private action imposed by them. Many people felt that the state was trying to get environmental conservation in the general public interest at the expense of the individual citizen.

3. *Centralization of the land use control process:* management of the regulatory system from the state capitol fostered lack of public involvement, hostility and misunderstanding. The laws and regulatory procedures were intended to cope with resource problems of statewide and regional rather than local concern, but they affected people where they were; and administration was considered too centralized and remote from the people.[8]

In response to these management problems, the developing coastal zone program is improving the regional planning structure to serve both the state and local regulatory systems. Most likely, no new environmental legislation will be required, but ways to improve the operation of existing laws and organizations are being explored.

Maine's approach to resources management started with regulation and then went on to planning, rather than the other way around. It was considered that environmental values were being eroded too rapidly to allow a leisurely period for planning. Regulatory legislation was therefore concerned with the issues that needed immediate attention. There were major environmental problems caused by large-scale development. Wetlands and the entire intertidal zone were regarded as valuable ecological resources requiring special protection. Development in the shorelands within 250 feet of mean high water was considered to have a critical influence on both land and water resources along the coast. Particular areas of scenic, historic, scientific, recreational and other environmental values also had to be identified and protected (Figure 1).

Figure 1. Port Clyde Harbor: varied demands on shorelands for residence, commercial fishing and lobstering, and related marine services. (Photo courtesy of Maine Department of Commerce and Industry.)

The four major pieces of state legislation for site location of development, wetlands protection, mandatory shoreland zoning, and register of critical areas provide the legal foundation for coastal resources management. In this approach, private initiative is allowed maximum scope; but development must take place with due regard to conserving environmental values. The regulations, therefore, provide environmental performance criteria for large-scale development, and also delimit the areas that should have limited use because of natural hazards or their unique, scarce, or fragile nature. Regulation is by a series of hopefully reasonable "thou shalt not" strictures based on the environmental characteristics of land and water areas. Within these limits private initiative and private activity are encouraged.

STATE POLICIES FOR ENVIRONMENTAL MANAGEMENT STRUCTURE

The development of an environmental management organization in Maine has produced a complex structure made up of state, regional and local components. It is a highly decentralized structure of many operating agencies guided and coordinated by a variety of policy boards and commissions. It appears to be the product of an evolutionary and *ad hoc* process rather than of deliberate organizational design. This may account in part for its fragmentation and the frustration of property owners, developers and citizens in dealing with it.

The State Role in Environmental Management

At the state level, the choice in Maine was to focus responsibility for coastal and other resources management in the office of the governor rather than in an operating line agency. Environmental management and land use regulation involves balancing diverse goals and policies. Therefore, the central agency responsible for such a program, which includes coastal management, should be responsive to executive policy and not to the interests or clientele pressures of any particular operating department. Such a department may have difficulty persuading other agencies of its coordinating role and authority. The result may be interorganizational conflict rather than cooperation. As the Maine coastal management program puts it, "the comprehensive nature of land use decisions requires considerable input from the executive level. Executive participation in the Maine coastal management program is a form of indirect control that relies more on the chief executive's authority."[9]

The State Planning Office (SPO) is directly responsible to the governor. It is responsible for coordinating the Maine coastal management program, which is the first step in the development of a statewide land use management system. SPO activities under this mandate include:

1. The development of a State Planning Office program in cooperation with the Maine Land and Water Resources Council, established by the governor, to coordinate state policy, to review regional plans, and to articulate the state's interest in such plans;

2. The development of a State Planning Office program in cooperation with the Commission on Maine's Future to incorporate statewide policy concerns into the development of regional plans, particularly such issues as energy facilities siting, fisheries development, tourism and major ports development;

3. Continuing the coordination relationship with federal agencies that has been established under the auspices of the New England River Basins Commission to assist in completing the regional land use plans;

4. The initiation within the Governor's office, in cooperation with a state interagency committee, of a capability to monitor and assess the impacts of existing and proposed uses of Maine's offshore area . . . and to assist in setting state policy for such areas;

5. The formulation, in cooperation with the Department of Conservation (Bureau of Public Lands and the Land Use Regulation Commission) of management programs and regulations for Maine's coastal islands.[10]

The state does not intend to formulate all environmental management and land use plans itself or run all the regulatory machinery. The SPO will be primarily concerned with identifying areas and activities of state concern and coordinating the formulation of comprehensive statewide environmental and development policies. These will provide the framework for working out land use policies at the regional level and controls at the local level.

The Regional Planning Commissions

Regional land use plans prepared by regional planning commissions are intended to be the principal management tools for coastal and statewide resources. They will focus state environmental policies and themselves provide guidelines for local planning and regulation. Regional planning is where diverse development and conservation goals will be reconciled. Policies of the state legislature to protect wetlands and other environmentally critical areas will help to balance contending interests and objectives.

Regional planning is expected to bring two additional benefits to the resources management process: one is to arouse public awareness and participation; the other is to bring technical resources and assistance to local decision-making. It is expected that active regional planning "could engender wide public participation by greatly increasing public accessibility to the land use decision-making process. Preparing and updating regional plans will also place the regional planning commission in an active coordinating role, capable of responding to individual requests for information and assistance."[11]

Most Maine towns do not have the money or trained personnel to prepare land use plans, particularly where state law mandates zoning in the shorelands 250 feet from mean high water. Regional planning agencies, therefore, have been given these responsibilities for helping local governments:

1. Preparing preliminary regional land use plans that incorporate local goals, regional priorities, and state interests;

2. Organizing technical planning teams, which include representatives of state and federal agencies, to offer advice to local officials and help them in preparing for development assistance;

3. Reviewing local regulatory activities for consistency with regional plans and state policies;

4. Providing technical and financial assistance to local governments for mandatory shoreland zoning, subdivision regulation, and enforcement of other codes;
5. Improving enforcement of land use regulations by providing
   legal assistance in cooperation with the Attorney General
   and District Attorney offices.

Regional planning agencies have the dual role of helping local
governments to attain their own development goals and, at the same
time, articulating state and region-wide interests and objectives. In
reconciling the full range of interests and objectives, the regional
planning agencies represent the state, and may therefore be able to
hold local units accountable for adherence to the regional plan.[12]
This was found to be a difficult mission, so the regional planning
bodies are trying to redefine their roles.

The Local Role

In the face of limited local resources for land use planning, the
Maine approach incorporates the local role as follows:

> Local planning can consist primarily of a concise statement of
> goals and objectives, and general community policy with re-
> spect to land use. The responsibility for comprehensive, com-
> plete resource and development planning should rest largely at
> the regional level. The regional plan should reflect local goals
> and objectives, and serve as a guide for assistance in making
> local regulatory efforts.[13]

As in other states, land use planning and regulation are fragmented because they are administered by local planning boards acting
from the point of view of the local interest. The Maine approach
is to try to make local efforts more effective by vesting in regional
planning commissions the responsibility for helping to prepare local
regulations in light of regional plans, and then reviewing local
enforcement.

This process is intended to produce a dialogue between local
officials and the regional planning commissions and their staffs.
Responsibility for regulatory policy is left to local officials, and
they retain the authority to adopt and amend development ordinances. Nevertheless, they have technical assistance from the

regional staffs, and ordinances are reviewed by the regional commissions for consistency with state and regional policies. When
policy problems arise, the regional commission may hold hearings
and make special recommendations on the issues.

In Maine, zoning is regarded as a regulatory tool for land use in
urban areas. Using this technique in rural areas and to implement
state policies may be counterproductive. State planning responsibility is to identify urbanizing areas that are under development
pressure and require effective zoning. For other areas, a more
flexible system of land use control based on performance standards
incorporated into the major environmental laws already described
is preferred.[14]

REFERENCES

[1] Maine State Planning Office and The New England River Basins Commission. *Management of Water and Related Land Resources in the State of
Maine: Summary Report,* Augusta, Maine (March 1975), p. 5, which
quotes from the report *Maine's Water Resources*, by the Maine Office of
the Coordinator, Comprehensive Plan, Augusta (1967).

[2] Maine State Planning Office. *Coastal Zone Management Program, Mid-
Coastal Segment* (February 18, 1972), p. 35 (mimeo).

[3] Maine State Planning Office and The New England River Basins Commission. *Management of Water and Related Land Resources in the State of
Maine: Summary Report*, Augusta, Maine (March 1975), p. l.

[4] *Ibid.*

[5] *Ibid.*, p. 8–9.

[6] Maing State Planning Office. *Coastal Zone Management Program, Mid-
Coastal Segment* (February 18, 1972), p. 2.

[7] *Ibid.*

[8] *Ibid.*, p. 3.

[9] *Ibid.*, p. 4.

[10] *Ibid.*, p. 5.

[11] *Ibid.*

[12] *Ibid.*, p. 6.

[13] *Ibid.*

[14] *Ibid.*, p. 7.

CHAPTER V

MAINE COASTAL ZONE LEGISLATION

The Maine legislative program was not enacted simply to meet federal requirements in the Coastal Zone Management Act. Legislation supporting coastal zone management applies to environmental resources management in the entire state. The Maine approach is to apply the laws and administrative structure, established to care for its resources statewide, to one of its areas defined as the coastal zone. The enactment of strong environmental legislation in Maine preceded the federal Coastal Zone Management Act of 1972. Maine has therefore adapted its legislative approach to resources management to meet federal guidelines for the coastal zone.

It is possible, however, that state laws aimed at regulating land and water use in the coastal zone will not be able to overcome a legal tradition in Maine that gives primacy to certain private rights. The report, prepared jointly by the State Planning Office and the New England River Basins Commission, describes the problem:

> The Body of Maine's water law, based on a system of riparian rights, is likely to be a hindrance in the development of programs to insure orderly future development and management of water resources. The hindrance in part relates to the involvement of the courts as a dispute-settling device since common law is court-administered, not statutory. When the law is not codified and resolution is through the judicial system, the process of solving disputes is often time-consuming, costly and may be inconsistent and contradictory.

> The question of water rights is particularly critical in light of the massive public investments in water quality improvements in recent years. It is pertinent to ask whether it is appropriate to spend large amounts of public funds for the benefit of only a few riparian owners.

> At least one alternative which should be investigated in Maine is
> the possibility of instituting a permit system in the Executive
> Branch of the State Government to allow nonriparian use of
> water under strictly defined conditions.[1]

Even allowing for this caveat, Maine environmental laws are still
powerful. A brief summary will indicate how they provide part of
the legislative foundation for the coastal zone management program.

A "Summary of Principal Environmental Legislation that Relates
to Coastal Management," prepared by the State Planning Office,
lists 43 separate legislative acts intended to conserve environmental
resources or regulate private development in accordance with environmental standards. All are applicable in coastal areas, but the
coastal management program relies on four major laws for its
authority: (a) the Site Location of Development Law, (b) the
Protection of Coastal Wetlands Act, (c) the Mandatory Shoreland
Zoning and Subdivision Controls Law, and (d) the State Register
of Critical Areas Act.

SITE LOCATION OF DEVELOPMENT
LAW 1969[2]

This law is based on the legislative determination that the location of major development projects that may substantially affect
the environment is too important a process to be left entirely to
the decisions of private developers. State scrutiny and approval of
such development locations through a permit procedure is carried
out to protect the state interest at the same time that the developer
seeks to advance his own private interest. The law is administered
by the state Department of Environmental Protection (DEP), but
the development application must be reviewed and the permit
granted by the Department's policy-making body, the Board of
Environmental Protection (BEP). The organizational structure of
these and other state units involved in coastal management will be
discussed in the next section of this book.

The projects covered by this law include all those that require a
license from the BEP under any other state laws, such as those
covering wastewater discharge and dredging, and any other development that would occupy a land or water area of more than 20 acres,
or that would build on a single parcel a structure with a ground

Figure 2. Piscataqua River boundary between Maine (on the right) and New
Hampshire: examples of major developments regulated by the Site
Location of Development Law. (Photo courtesy of Maine Department
of Commerce and Industry.)

area of more than 60,000 square feet. Such projects would include
land subdivisions covering more than 20 acres and proposals to drill
for or excavate natural resources on land or under water. Excluded
from BEP legal jurisdiction are projects to build state or state-aided
highways, borrow pits for sand or gravel regulated by the State
Highway Commission, and borrow pits of less than five acres. Excluding land subdivisions under 20 acres in area, structures with
less than 60,000 square feet of ground area, and borrow pits smaller
than 5 acres in area would seem to ignore the possible cumulative
environmental impact of two or more contiguous projects, carried
out perhaps under different auspices and at different times, but
having substantial environmental consequences nevertheless (see
Figure 2).

Project Evaluation Criteria

The Maine coastal management program does not include a
state land use plan that designates specific areas for industrial,

commercial or other uses. Under the Site Location of Development Law, the developer takes the initiative to select his own site, within the constraints of local zoning and other regulations. The Board of Environmental Protection may approve or reject the application, or it may issue a permit subject to conditions so that excessive environmental damage is avoided.

Project applications are reviewed by the Board to see if they meet the four specific criteria established by the site location law:

1. *Pollution control:* the developer has the financial capacity and technical ability to meet air and water pollution control standards, and has made adequate provision for solid waste disposal, the control of offensive odors, and the securing and maintenance of sufficient and healthful water supplies.

2. *Traffic movement:* the developer has made adequate provision for traffic movement of all types out of or into the development area.

3. *Effect on the natural environment:* the developer has made adequate provision for fitting the development harmoniously into the existing natural environment, and the development will not adversely affect existing uses, scenic character, or natural resources in the municipality or in neighboring municipalities.

4. *Soil types:* the proposed development will be built on soil types that are suitable to the nature of the undertaking.

Procedures

BEP has 30 days to act on an application. Public hearings are required when permits are denied, but approval, even with conditions, does not require a prior hearing. It has been the practice of the Board to hold hearings, however, on major projects and controversial proposals. Developers whose applications have been rejected, have 30 days to appeal to the Supreme Judicial Court of Maine. The Court's decision would be based on its consideration of whether BEP acted within the scope of its authority and on the basis of substantial evidence.[3]

The Court upheld the constitutionality of the Site Location of Development Law in a 1970 decision, *King Resources vs. E.I.C., Maine,* 270 A2d 863. In 1973 it reaffirmed the law's constitutionality in *In re Spring Valley Development by Lakesites, Inc.* In its unanimous decision, the Supreme Court ruled that BEP acted under a valid exercise of the state's police power, and that the 92-acre sub-division could not be carried out without the Board's approval.[4]

The site location law does not require municipal review or action on permit applications. Presumably the local government may comment at public hearings. Nevertheless, in practice, projects have not been approved by BEP unless they have been reviewed and approved by the local legislative body concerned.[5]

MANDATORY SHORELAND ZONING AND SUBDIVISION CONTROL ACT [6]

The act was originally passed by the state legislature in 1971 to require all organized municipalities to adopt zoning controls following state guidelines on all navigable ponds and lakes, rivers and streams, and the ocean shoreline. All land areas within 250 feet of the normal high water mark were to be zoned by July 1, 1973. These lands were also to be regulated by subdivision controls. Ponds were defined as inland water bodies with a surface area of more than 10 acres. Rivers were defined as free-flowing water bodies from their mouths to the point at which they drain a water basin of 25 square miles. An important feature of the Act was that municipal shoreland zoning and regulation of subdivisions was mandatory.

Few municipalities met the 1973 deadline, so it was extended by law for one year. The new law also gave the State Planning Office major responsibility for coordinating implementation of the Act by the BEP and the Land Use Regulation Commission. Working together, these agencies were required to prepare by December 15, 1973 zoning guidelines to help the municipalities prepare their own regulations. The Board and the Commission were directed by the law to adopt ordinances for municipalities that failed to adopt their own by the new deadline. The attorney general was also directed to start legal action against municipalities that failed to enforce their own ordinances or regulations adopted for them by the state.[7]

WETLANDS CONTROL

A Wetlands Control Act was originally passed by the Maine legis-lature in 1967.[8] It required that permits be obtained to remove, fill, dredge or otherwise alter any coastal wetland or drain or deposit

any sanitary sewage into or on any coastal wetland. Permit applications must first be reviewed and approved by the municipality
concerned and then also by the state Department of Environmental Protection. The Act also provided for judicial review by appeal
to the Superior Court within 30 days of denial of a permit.

One such appeal was taken in *Johnson vs. Wetlands Control
Board.* [9] The Court held the Act constitutional, but that denial of
the permit to fill a wetland was a taking of the property without
compensation. The Court decided that if preserving coastal wetlands was of statewide benefit, the cost should be borne by the
public.

In response to the Johnson case decision, the state legislature
passed the Protection of Coastal Wetlands Act in 1971.[10] It authorized the Department of Environmental Protection to place restrictions on the use or alteration of coastal wetlands. After notice
and allowing a 90-day period for appeal by the property owner,
the restrictions will constitute a permanent easement on the land.
If, on appeal, the Court finds the restrictions to be an unconstitutional taking of the property, then the state must either acquire it
or remove the restrictions. Under this Act, the municipality concerned will receive notice of proposed DEP restrictions, but its
approval of the restrictions is not required. Figure 3 illustrates a
typical tidal estuary and wetland.

STATE REGISTER OF CRITICAL AREAS

The Act Establishing a State Register of Critical Areas was passed
in 1974.[11] The State Planning Office was directed to establish the
Register to express official interest of the state in identifying and
conserving areas of critical environmental or historic concern. The
Act created the Critical Areas Advisory Board to advise the SPO.

The process of registration begins with the identification by the
SPO of areas considered critical. After investigation of candidate
areas and explanation of the program to the land owners concerned,
the SPO may recommend registration to the Critical Areas Advisory
Board. If there is a preliminary decision that the area qualifies for
registration, land owners are given 60 days to comment. After this
period, the Board makes a final decision about registration.

Figure 3. Coastal wetland in one of Maine's many deep tidal estuaries. (Photo courtesy of Maine State Planning Office.)

Property owners in registered critical areas are required to give the Critical Areas Advisory Board 60 days notice before undertaking any alteration of their land. During this period, the Board and State Planning Office could try to arrange with the owner ways to avoid destruction of significant environmental values. These may include cooperative agreements, easements, or public purchase of the property. The primary objective of the SPO would be to elicit the cooperation of the owners, state and local agencies, and conservation organizations to protect and conserve the critical areas.

PRINCIPAL ENVIRONMENTAL LEGISLATION THAT RELATES TO COASTAL MANAGEMENT: A SUMMARY

Land and water uses in the coastal zone, by public agencies as well as private developers, are regulated by state and local laws. Regulating powers are determined mostly by state laws, and administration and permitting authority is vested primarily in state agencies. This list is taken from "Summary of Principal Environmental Legislation that Relates to Coastal Management," prepared by the State Planning Office:

Abbreviation

LURC — Land Use Regulation Commission
DEP — Department of Environmental Protection
BEP — Board of Environmental Protection
SPO — State Planning Office
DMR — Department of Marine Resources
DIF&G — Department of Inland Fisheries and Game
DOC — Department of Conservation
MMB — Maine Mining Bureau
P&R — Bureau of Parks and Recreation, DOC
DOT — Department of Transportation
DH&W — Department of Health and Welfare
DA — Department of Agriculture

Legislation	*Administering Agency*
Mandatory Shoreland Zoning	LURC, DEP/BEP, SPO
State Register of Critical Areas	SPO
Site Location of Development	DEP/BEP
Coastal Conveyance of Petroleum	DEP/BEP
Wetlands Control	DEP/BEP
Protection of Coastal Wetlands	DEP/BEP
Waste Discharge Licenses	DEP/BEP
Permits to construct facilities in, above or under tidal waters, subtidal lands in connection with Waste Discharge Licenses	DEP/BEP
Air Emission License	DEP/BEP
Protection and Improvement of Air	DEP/BEP
Solid Waste Management	DEP/BEP
Sanitary District Enabling	DEP/BEP
Conservation & Rehabilitation of Mining Land	DEP/BEP
Minimum Lot Size & Minimum Frontage	DEP/BEP
Great Ponds Classification	DEP/BEP
Great Ponds Dredging, Causeway and Marina Permits	DEP/BEP
Leasing of Marine Areas for Aquaculture	DMR
Conservation of Renewable Resources	DMR

Records for Coastal Activities	DMR
Watercraft Registration & Safety	DIF&G
Land Use Regulation for Wildlands	LURC (DOC)
Mining on State-Owned Lands	MMB (DOC)
Oil & Gas Conservation Act	MMB (DOC)
Coastal Island Registry	DOC
Water Safety Aids to Navigation, Boating Facilities	P&R (DOC)
Keep Maine Scenic	P&R (DOC)
Maine Transportation Act	DOT
Outdoor Advertising	DOT
State Plumbing Code	DH&W
Wildlife Sanctuaries	DIF&G
Alteration of Streams	DIF&G
Pesticides Control Board	DA
Soil & Water Conservation Commission	DA
Subdivision Law	Municipal
Municipal Powers	Municipal
Coastal Island Trusts	Municipal
Conservation Easements	Municipal
Farm and Open Space Law	State Tax Assessor
Tree Growth Tax Law	State Tax Assessor

The state takes primary responsibility for the critical areas program through the Critical Areas Advisory Board assisted by the State Planning Office. Large-scale development permits under the Site Location Law, and permits for dredging, waste disposal, petroleum transportation and other activities noted on the list are issued by the Board of Environmental Protection, with administration and technical assistance provided by the Department of Environmental Protection. Wetlands are regulated by state law, but permits for alterations of wetlands are issued by local governments, with the concurrence of BEP. Local governments are responsible for devising and enforcing zoning ordinances and subdivision regulations. These regulations are mandated by state law for the shorelands within 250 feet of the mean high water line. State supervision and technical assistance to municipalities is coordinated by the State Planning Office. Projects by government agencies and private developers may be affected by several of these regulations, and they must be able to find their way through the complex system of laws and procedures.

REFERENCES

[1] Maine State Planning Office and New England River Basins Commission. *Management of Water and Related Land Resources in the State of Maine,* Augusta, Maine (March, 1975), pp. 9, 10.

[2] Site Location of Development Law, *Title 38 Maine Revised Status Annotated (MRSA),* Sec. 481-488 as enacted by P. L. 1969, c.57 and amended by P. L. (1971), c.256, c.476, 613, and P.L. (1973), c.423, 625.

[3] Maine State Planning Office. "Preliminary Application for Program Approval," *Coastal Zone Management Program, Mid-Coastal Segment,* Augusta, Maine (February 18, 1975), pp. 28-31.

[4] "Report of Decisions," Docket No. 885, *Law Court Docket* No. 1341 (February 9, 1973).

[5] Maine State Planning Office. *Summary of Principal Environmental Legislation that Relates to Coastal Management,* Augusta, Maine (undated), p. 6.

[6] Mandatory Shoreland Zoning and Subdivision Control Act, 12 MRSA 4811-4814, P. L. (1971), c.535; P. L. (1973), c.424.

[7] State of Maine. *Coastal Zone Management Program, Mid-Coastal Segment* (February 18, 1975), pp. 25-27.

[8] *Wetlands Control Act,* 12 MRSA 1701-4709; P. L. (1967), c.348; (1969), c.379; c.336 and c.618; (1973), c.256.

[9] ME 250 A. 2d 825 (1969).

[10] Protection of Coastal Wetlands Act, 12 MRSA 4751-4758, P. L. (1971), c.541, c.618; (1973), c.537.

[11] State Register of Critical Areas Act, MRSA 3310-3314, P. L. (1974), c.312.

CHAPTER VI

ORGANIZATIONAL COMPONENTS OF THE MANAGEMENT STRUCTURE

THE GOVERNOR AND STATE AGENCIES

A new governmental organization has not been established in Maine to manage its coastal zone. Instead, existing organizations have been assigned responsibility for the program. Maine state government is intentionally decentralized. There are many sources from which policy initiatives may arise, and authority is diffused.

The Governor and Executive Department

The governor is the only Maine official who has a statewide constituency, for he gains office by vote of all eligible voters. The Maine coastal management program notes that, "through his appointments to his cabinet, submission of the state budget to the legislature, authority to make executive orders, and the publicity attendant upon his position, he is in a unique position to shape policy within the framework of the law and coordinate its execution."[1]

Although the governor is the head of the executive branch, his authority is limited by institutional arrangements peculiar to Maine. He does not appoint the secretary of state, the state treasurer, or the attorney general; they are elected biennially by the state legislature. Nevertheless, the attorney general can play an important role in coastal management. He is the governor's counsel and is responsible for the enforcement of many statutes relating to land use management. He also advises the legislature on the

drafting of bills and the constitutionality of laws. With his cooperation, assistant district attorneys, using coastal zone management
funds, provide part-time legal assistance to the towns in the enforcement and administration of shoreland zoning ordinances and subdivision regulations. The attorney general's office is also concerned
with finding ways to improve public access to the shore. (Figure 4.)

Figure 4. Rocky shore and beach near East Boothbay: one of the few places
in this region where, by permission of the property owner, the public
has access to the shore.

The governor appoints all department heads and members of
many boards, commissions, and agencies involved in coastal management. Yet this important power is limited by the requirement that
appointments must be with the advice and consent of the Executive
Council, a vestige of colonial government. It consists of seven
members and is elected biennially by the legislature "to advise the

Governor in the executive part of government." Members represent special executive council districts, which do not have equal population. They are nominated by legislators from the various districts and are elected by the legislative majority. The executive council has a one-party political composition that is often in opposition to the governor's party. In this situation the governor is often frustrated in making appointments. Many attempts have been made to abolish the Council and transfer confirmation of appointments to the legislature, but without success.[2]

The State Planning Office and the Office of Energy Resources are located in the executive department. Their directors are appointed by the governor and Executive Council. They are both planning agencies and advise the governor, the legislature, and other governmental agencies on development policy. An interagency Committee on the Outer Continental Shelf is also to be established in the governor's office.[3] By executive order, the governor has established the Governor's Advisory Committee on Coastal Development and Conservation for management coordination and clarification of state policy with respect to priority of uses for the Maine coastal zone.

The State Planning Office

Established in 1969, it is directly responsible to the governor. Its statutory responsibilities include giving planning assistance and advice to the governor, legislature, state agencies, and to regional and local planning bodies. The SPO also provides staff services for the Commission on Maine's Future and the Governor's Advisory Committee on Coastal Development and Conservation. It manages the federally mandated Office of Management and Budget Circular A-95 notification and review program, a device for coordinating public works and development proposals by state and local governments. The SPO coordinating responsibility also includes bringing together legislative, agency, and political policy determinations into a State Policies Plan, which includes a tentative state land use policy.

SPO has the responsibility for acting as the state agent for disbursing federal planning funds, and it also maintains budgetary control over participants in the implementation of the coastal zone management program. Of particular importance for the coastal program, the State Planning Office has been designated by the governor as the single state agency responsible for receiving and administering federal grants under Sec. 306 of the Coastal Zone Management Act and for coordinating the implementation of a federally approved management program.

The State Planning Office provides advice to many other units in the state government but is itself advised by two statutory councils. One is the State Planning Council, which advises both the governor and SPO on planning policy. It may have up to 15 members including the Speaker of the House, the President of the Senate, representatives from the public and from local and regional planning, bodies and members drawn from the fields of health, education, natural resources, and commerce and industry.

The other advisory body is the Critical Areas Advisory Board. SPO is responsible for keeping the State Register of Critical Areas, which includes areas of environmental concern to coastal management. The register is a means for identifying critical areas and is advisory only; there is no authority for use regulation under this procedure. The board consists of 11 appointed members, including the director of SPO. The board may recommend acquisition or management, by agreement with the owner of a designated critical area, by an appropriate state, local, or private organization.[4]

Within its organizational structure, SPO has a Resource Planning Division. It has the specific function of administering SPO responsibilities for developing the coastal zone management program, the coastal resources inventory and atlas and related studies, and administering federal coastal zone grants. The structure of the SPO and the location of the Resource Planning Division within it are shown in Figure 5.

The Commission on Maine's Future

This body contains 40 members; 27, including the chairman, are apportioned among the planning and development districts of the state. The remaining members are legislators appointed by the leaders of both houses in proportion to party affiliation. The

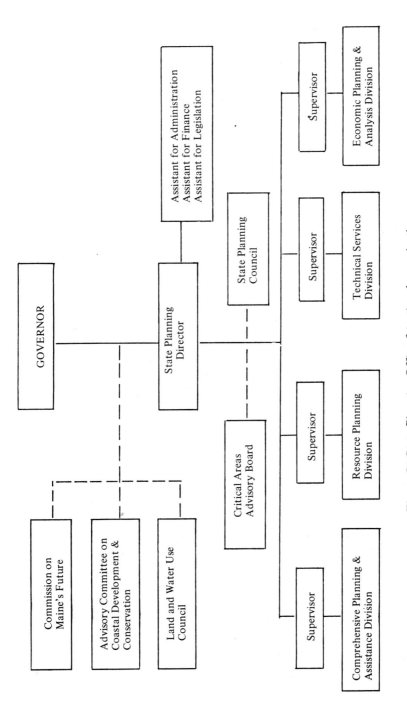

Figure 5. State Planning Office functional organization.

director of the SPO is a permanent member. The mission of the
Commission for Maine's Future is to prepare a growth and development policy for the state with proposals for implementation programs. Its final report is due in June, 1977. The SPO will coordinate state agency inputs with the results of conferences and public
hearings.

The Governor's Committees

Alec Giffen, who is in charge of the Resources Planning Division
of SPO, pointed out in an August, 1975 interview that there is no
central focus of state policy-making for the coastal zone and no
central point for input of local government and public participation
in policy-making. The State Planning Office is a technical unit and
does not make policy. There is an advisory State Planning Council,
but it meets infrequently and has not been involved in the development of the coastal zone management program. Giffen, therefore,
favored the establishment of a statewide "board of directors" to be
the visible focus of responsibility for policy-making and for the
consequences of the program.

Perhaps this idea eventually reached the governor from the
State Planning Office. In any case, Governor Longley established
by executive orders two new bodies to focus environmental policy-
making for the state. One was to be particularly concerned about
coastal zone management. The other was to examine land and
water resources policy for the whole state.

By executive order Number 10, dated February 4, 1976, the
governor established the Governor's Advisory Committee on
Coastal Development and Conservation. The executive order declared that, "a forum within which state, local and private interests
can participate is desirable," and the Advisory Committee was
therefore composed of the following members:

> Commissioner of the Department of Conservation
> Commissioner of the Department of Environmental Protection
> Commissioner of the Department of Marine Resources
> Director of the State Planning Office
> Director of the State Development Office
> Director of the Office of Energy Resources

Attorney general
A member of the Senate
A member of the House of Representatives
Six residents at large, to be appointed by the governor, at least
four of whom shall reside in towns within the coastal area
Vice-president for Research and Public Service of the University
of Maine
One representative of regional planning interests within the
coastal area to be appointed by the governor from nominees
submitted by the coastal regional planning commissions.

This executive order charged the Governor's Advisory Committee on Coastal Development and Conservation with this responsibility, among others:

The Committee's overall responsibility shall be to advise the
governor and state agencies on issues of coastal planning and use,
including development and conservation policies and any work
performed pursuant to the Federal Coastal Zone Management
Act of 1972. A principal function of the Committee shall be
to coordinate an effective program of community and individual citizen participation in coastal planning activities.

The State Planning Office suggested that the Advisory Committee might organize itself for carrying out these responsibilities by forming subcommittees to deal with each of the highest priority tasks:

1. Management Program (306) Subcommittee: to develop a
   broadly supported coastal management program that would
   qualify for administrative grants under Section 306 of the
   Coastal Zone Management Act.
2. Outer Continental Shelf (OCS) Subcommittee: to monitor
   OCS activities and plan to deal with them and their impacts
   on the Maine coast.
3. Coastal Development Subcommittee: to formulate a
   coastal economic development policy and strategy.
4. Coastal Conservation Subcommittee: to identify areas of
   the Maine coast requiring high priority for conservation
   and formulate a conservation policy and strategy.
5. Coastal Research Subcommittee: to develop research
   priorities that would meet the information requirements for
   planning and resources management.

6. Integrated Coastal Policy Development Subcommittee: to analyze the legal, institutional and organizational structure and procedures for formulating an integrated coastal policy for the state.[5]

The other body created by the governor was the Maine Land and Water Resources Council. It was established by executive order Number 12, March 19, 1976. This was composed entirely of public officials, for its purpose was to coordinate the activities and programs of state organizations with the responsibilities for planning and managing land and water resources. Its membership was different from the Governor's Advisory Committee on Coastal Development and Conservation in that it had no public members, but had, in addition to the officials on the Advisory Committee, the Commissioners of Agriculture and Inland Fisheries and Wildlife. The governor's executive order stated the purpose of the Council:

> The fundamental task of the Council shall be to advise the governor, legislature and state agencies in the development of a comprehensive, integrated land and water resources planning and management program for the State of Maine to achieve broad social and economic goals. Any state, federal, regional, local and private agency is invited to interact with the Council in fulfilling this mission.

Particular responsibilities of the Council would be to improve the resources information base and apply it to planning and management programs, to evaluate Maine's land use regulatory system, and assume leadership in the development of a comprehensive land use program for the state.

State Line Departments

The operating agencies represented on the Governor's Advisory Committee and Resources Council all have some role in coastal zone program development and implementation. Some of these line departments have their own policy-making bodies that are important components of the coastal development permitting system.

Department of Environmental Protection

Environmental concerns in Maine are divided between two departments. One is concerned with protecting air, land, and water from contamination; the other with conserving the state's natural resources. DEP is responsible for containing pollution and regulating its sources. The Department's primary function is to administer and enforce pollution control regulations, and provide technical assistance to the Board of Environmental Protection. This is the autonomous component of the Department that designs the regulations and issues permits under them. The Commissioner of the Department is chairman of BEP, and its statutory composition provides for two representatives each from industry, conservation interests, municipalities, the general public, and air pollution control technology. Members serve for three years.

Water and air pollution control regulations are adopted by the state legislature on the recommendation of BEP. Water quality regulations include a classification of state waters according to use and quality standards. BEP is responsible for licensing the discharge of pollutants into state waters and conveyance and transfer of oil along the coast. Air pollution regulations define five air regions throughout the state and five ambient air standards and permitted emission concentrations in each one. Licensing of emissions into the air is also a function of the Board. Licensing of land use is carried out by BEP under the Site Location of Development Law. It also shares with the State Planning Office and the Land Use Regulation Commission (Department of Conservation) supervision of mandatory municipal shoreland zoning.

Department of Conservation (DOC)

The mission of the Department is "to preserve, protect, and enhance the land resource of the state . . . and to insure that coordinated planning for the future allocation of lands for recreational, forest production, mining, and other public and private uses is effectively accomplished; and to provide for the effective management of public lands in the state."[6] The operating divisions of

DOC are the Land Use Regulation Commission, Bureau of Forestry, Bureau of Parks and Recreation, Bureau of Public Lands, and Bureau of Geology.

The Land Use Regulation Commission (LURC) is an organization unique to Maine, which has about half of its land in "unorganized territory." Much of it is forest wilderness, prime agricultural land, and some coastal islands. The Commissioner of Conservation is *ex officio* chairman of LURC, and other members are appointed to represent industrial, fisheries, wildlife, forestry, and conservation interests as well as the public. Within its area of jurisdiction, LURC is responsible for comprehensive planning, with the authority to establish the boundaries of land use districts and set standards and issue permits for development.

Other State Agencies

As state agencies have statewide interests and responsibilities, their activities inevitably have some impact on the coastal zone. All agencies that have membership in the Governor's Advisory Committee and Resources Council and several noncabinet agencies have responsibilities that particularly affect coastal lands and waters. These are:

1. Department of Inland Fisheries and Game
2. Department of Marine Resources
3. Department of Agriculture
4. Department of Transportation
5. Department of Health and Welfare—Division of Health Engineering
6. Department of Educational and Cultural Services—Maine Historic Preservation Commission
7. Department of Commerce and Industry
8. Public Utilities Commission
9. Maine Port Authority
10. Office of Energy Resources
11. Maine Housing Authority

REGIONAL PLANNING AND THE
COASTAL ZONE

By executive order, the governor has established regional planning and development districts conforming to the major water
basins of the state. Within these districts regional planning commissions have been established. The function of these commissions
is:

> ... to promote cooperative efforts towards regional develop-
> ment and maintain a comprehensive regional plan, coordinate
> with state and federal planning and development programs,
> and to provide planning assistance and advisory services to
> municipalities. ...[7]

The regional planning commissions mediate between state and local
governments and offer state and federal financial and technical
assistance to local governments. Chief municipal officials appoint
representatives, at least one of whom must be a municipal officer,
to the regional commissions. The number of representatives from
each jurisdiction is determined according to population.

Regional planning commissions are authorized by a governor's
executive order to review and comment on federal or federally
funded projects, large-scale state and local projects, and state projects affecting more than one community. When projects affect
"unorganized areas" of the state, the Land Use Regulation Commission participates in the reviews. The Maine coastal zone management program describes the regional planning commissions this
way:

> The relationship between an RPC and its member communities
> and other levels of government is strictly advisory. It recom-
> mends, coordinates planning, and on invitation assists in solving
> local planning problems. The amount of planning assistance it
> can render depends entirely upon the size of its staff. ... Most
> of the RPC's programs have a significant impact on land use.
> Chief tools are planning services, education of policy makers
> and the public, and coordination.[8]

PLANNING AND DEVELOPMENT
REGULATION AT THE LOCAL LEVEL

As in other states, land use planning and regulation in Maine has been a local responsibility. A 1970 home rule amendment to the state constitution eliminates the need for enabling legislation by the state. Municipalities now have the authority to set the composition and terms of their planning boards. State legislation strengthened local planning further by defining the necessary components of a comprehensive plan. It also required that municipalities, counties, and other local districts must be *governed* by the zoning ordinance. Local ordinances, however, are only advisory to the state, which is not required to adhere to them in planning state activities.

Of particular importance to land use planning and regulation in Maine is the strengthened role of the state in mandating or supervising local activities, in spite of greater home rule. Under the Mandatory Shoreland Zoning Act of 1974, municipalities are required to zone their shorelands 250 feet from mean high water in accordance with state guidelines. Communities that fail to do so are zoned by the Land Use Regulation Commission and the Board of Environmental Protection, with coordination by the State Planning Office. Local planning boards must also observe other state laws that mandate action. Subdivision proposals must be reviewed according to the criteria established in the Municipal Regulation of Land Subdivision Law.[9]

These criteria cover effects on water and air pollution, water supply, soil erosion, traffic, sewage disposal, solid waste disposal, conformance to the local zoning ordinance, and the financial and technical capability of the subdivider to meet environmental standards. Where there are no planning boards, some other agency or officer is designated to review subdivision proposals. Municipalities that fail to establish planning agencies find the state intervening to perform land regulation functions itself. This threat to local autonomy has encouraged local governments to establish planning boards. The 1975 coastal zone management program notes that 401 out of 440 municipalities now have them.[10]

Enforcement of local land use regulations and certain state codes is the responsibility of local code enforcement officers, who have power to issue permits for the regulated development activities.

Local zoning boards of appeal may grant exceptions, conditional use permits, and variances from local zoning ordinances. Appeals boards are governed by state standards as to the range of their discretion, which are set forth in their enabling statute.[11]

Environmental considerations in local planning are promoted by conservation commissions that may be established by municipalities. Inventories of open space, woodlands, and wetlands to identify scenic, historic, wildlife, and recreational values are the basis for recommending the best use of the community's natural resources. Conservation commissions may also act as agents for municipalities in acquiring land and conservation easements.[12]

PUBLIC PARTICIPATION

The Maine tradition of local self-determination and respect for property rights makes public participation in coastal planning and management of particular importance. Innovative state legislation for environmental protection has brought expected consequences of problems and expense of implementation and enforcement. Local officials and citizens must, therefore, reach their own assessment of how they will carry out their responsibilities. The management program notes that:

> The need for education is acute; particularly needed are advice and assistance to local planning boards and enforcement officers who must, in the final analysis, be the persons responsible for successful accomplishment of the purposes of the Shoreland Zoning Law. One of the major 'targets' of the public participation program has been, therefore, the local planners, conservation commissioners, and others with a direct responsibility for or interest in the laws which affect land and water uses in the coastal zone.[13]

The primary vehicle for this education process is contractual agreement between the State Planning Office and regional planning commissions by which local input into the Maine Coastal Plan may be generated. Public participation efforts have, therefore, been tied into the activities of the regional planning commissions. Resource inventories and analyses are offered as the rational information basis for considering local conservation and development issues

and for devising policies to deal with them. These policies are
intended to provide a reasonable context for administering local
land use regulations and give local officials some meaningful measure of control in setting the direction for their own future development. With help from the State Planning Office the regional
planning commissions will assist municipal governments to evaluate
their own land use policies and evaluate their potential for achieving
local goals.[14]

This effort is aimed at two-way communication. Local input is
desired in the formulation of regional and state coastal policies
and programs. Important contributions to them can be made by
poeple who actually live in the coastal communities. Therefore,
the regional planning commissions held series of regional meetings
to provide a forum for discussion of coastal management issues.
These are intended to contribute to the education of state officials
by the local people as well as vice versa.

In addition to the institutionalized device of regional meetings,
the state has developed a variety of public information activities
to help give the people a broader perspective on the environmental
values of the Maine coast and how the state proposes to conserve
and protect them through the coastal zone management program.
Organized environmental interest groups have been identified and
contacted. Articles and news releases about the program and
notices of public meetings have appeared in the newsletter of the
Natural Resources Council of Maine and a publication that reaches
commercial fishermen. A film has been prepared to help focus the
discussion at regional and other public meetings. A variety of
booklets and pamphlets have also been prepared to disseminate
information about the coastal program and environmental legislation. To receive as well as give information, the State Planning
Office took a public opinion poll to find out the attitudes of
coastal people toward policies for the area.[15]

A significant institutional device for public participation was the
establishment of coastal advisory committees in each region. Their
responsibility was to review and comment on the coastal zone program. They were not simply to be presented with policy decisions
already made at the state level, however. Hopefully they would
also suggest alternative policies on major issues of coastal management. Among the channels for communicating coastal advisory

committee ideas to the state would be their advisory input into the decisions made by the Commission on Maine's Future.

The State Planning Office summarized the objectives of its public participation effort this way:

> ... we are philosophically committed to implementing the Maine Coastal Plan through the existing management structure of laws and institutions with as few amendments as possible. Most of the regional planning commissions are working diligently to educate the public in this system, to make it a framework for policy considerations, and to make it administratively effective. Our role in part is to support them in this effort.[16]

FAILURE OF INITIAL EFFORTS FOR PUBLIC PARTICIPATION

The institutional structure and programmatic activities to induce public participation described above were not successful. Maine residents in coastal towns felt they were being propagandized to accept coastal zone management and that the state wanted to impose decisions on communities that had a long history of self-determination. They accused the state of expecting them to rubber-stamp decisions made by the planners in Augusta rather than inviting them to participate in decision-making.

The Maine coastal zone planners were counting on the regional planning commissions as the medium for local participation. The system apparently did not work, for as one investigator put it:

> State planners . . . counted on four midcoast regional planning commissions to spark local people with enthusiasm for the program without asking for local advice first.
>
> Local sentiment toward regional planning is none too enthusiastic, since the regional commissions are viewed as an extraneous level of government.[17]

It was not enough for the state to have a strong arsenal of environmental protection laws and a strong state planning program. Effective coastal management required understanding and acceptance of the program by the people who were directly affected by it; but few of them had heard of coastal zone management and most were suspicious of State Planning Office's underestimation of the importance of citizen understanding and support:

> Last winter, as a planner with the Southern Midcoast Regional Planning Commission, [Francie Vinal] helped set up a southern midcoast area citizens group at the request of the State Planning Office, but without being told the group's purpose. That purpose, apparently, was to rubber-stamp the state's coastal management program for the southern midcoast region, not to help formulate it. The group first met last January, and, according to Vinal, 'two months after it was set up, with irregular attendance and people on it who wanted to stop the program,' the group was asked to approve the application for federal management money. In other words, an unprepared and sometimes hostile group of local people who had not yet even seen a copy of the federal Coastal Zone Management Law were being asked to endorse a complex state program.[18]

There were plenty of local leaders who opposed the program to focus citizen reaction against it in the citizens' groups, in local newspapers, and in letters to the governor and federal officials. Federal hearings in May, 1975 gave local opponents another opportunity to make their feelings known. Even some who favored coastal management and land planning in principle opposed the state program. In response to this vocal opposition, in June, 1975, Governor James B. Longley withdrew Maine's application to the federal Office of Coastal Zone Management for management funds. Coastal management in Maine is not dead, however; the State Planning Office is revising its plans and strategy for public participation.[19] SPO has started its own newsletter and will expand its use of the news media.

In its Coastal Planning Newsletter of December 1, 1975, the State Planning Office listed these specific public objections to the coastal zone program:

1. It was felt that there was insufficient public participation in the development of the program.
2. The previous program was vague and ambiguous.
3. Segmented approval would set precedents without allowing full participation by residents in other areas of the coast.
4. The program was being imposed on localities by the state.

5. Too much emphasis was placed on the regional planning commissions.
6. New regulatory laws would be needed to implement the coastal zone management program.
7. Resource information was not collected in enough detail or on a scale suitable for town planning.
8. The number of public employees would have to be increased, creating a burden that would have to be assumed by the state eventually.
9. The coastal planning effort was not legitimate in that it was not endorsed by the governmental units involved.
10. The program would result in a worsening of the land use regulatory system already perceived as an onerous burden.
11. There was not enough time allowed for public participation in developing the program.
12. The approval of the application for program administration would have increased federal intervention in local land use decisions.
13. The program was oriented toward planning for conservation.

These objections were being carefully considered by the State Planning Office, and further public involvement was being sought in developing ways to avoid these problems.[20] There is evidence that public sentiment is changing in favor of governmental action to acquire and conserve significant scenic and other environmental resources for public benefit. Perhaps the controversy aroused by the coastal management program had the long-term positive effect of heightening public awareness of the threat to the manificent natural heritage of the state from unrestrained development.[21]

REFERENCES

[1] Maine State Planning Office. "Preliminary Application for Program Approval," *Coastal Zone Management Program, Mid-Coastal Segment*, Augusta (February 18, 1975), p. 35.

[2] *Ibid.*, p. 37.

[3] *Ibid.*, p. 39.

[4] *Ibid.*, p. 45.

[5] State Planning Office. "The Role of the Governor's Committee on Coastal Development and Conservation" (March 18, 1976) (Mimeo).

[6] 12 MRSA Sec. 5100 *et seq.*

[7] 30 MRSA Sec. 4511.

[8] Maine State Planning Office. *Coastal Zone Management Program, Mid-Coastal Segment,* Augusta (February 18, 1975), p. 35.

[9] Municipal Regulation of Land Subdivision Law, 30 MRSA 4956 as amended by P.L. (1971) c.454; (1973) c.465.

[10] Maine State Planning Office. *Coastal Zone Management Program, Mid-Coastal Segment*, Augusta (February 18, 1975), p. 40.

[11] 30 MRSA 2411.

[12] 30 MRSA 3851.

[13] Maine State Planning Office. *Coastal Zone Management Program, Mid-Coastal Segment,* Augusta (February 18, 1975), p. 63.

[14] Maine State Planning Office. *An Introduction to the Maine Coastal Plan* (November 20, 1974), pp. 42–43.

[15] University of Maine at Orono, Social Science Research Institute. *Citizen Evaluation of Public Policy in the Coastal Zone* (May 1, 1975).

[16] Maine State Planning Office. *An Introduction to the Maine Coastal Plan* (November 20, 1974), p. 42.

[17] Lewis, S. "Coastal Plan Runs Aground," *Planning,* 41:13 (November, 1975).

[18] *Ibid.*, p. 14.

[19] *Ibid.*, pp. 15–17.

[20] State Planning Office. *Coastal Planning Newsletter* (December 1, 1975), pp. 6–7.

[21] Interview with Rob Elder, Resources Planning Division, SPO, Augusta (July 17, 1976).

CHAPTER VII

THE MAINE COASTAL ZONE MANAGEMENT PROGRAM

The Maine approach to managing its coastal zone relies generally on state policies for environmental resources management. Its environmental legislation is applied state-wide, and it uses existing institutions for dealing with conservation and development in the coastal zone as well as in the rest of the state. The management program relies on a detailed inventory of coastal resources for basic information about area development capability, identification of areas of critical concern, priorities for development, location of uses of regional benefit and national interest, and regulation of land and water uses.

The management program has not simply expanded the traditional techniques and procedures of urban land use planning to cover the whole coastal territory. Its lands and waters have not been cut up into zones with fixed boundaries in which designated uses are segregated from one another. Instead, the coastal zone has been carefully surveyed to determine its capability for continued urbanization and development and to identify areas that should be restricted to limited use or conserved in their natural state. Criteria and standards have been formulated by which to assess the environmental impact of development to judge whether it is appropriate for the particular sites chosen by the developers. State institutions apply this regulatory procedure state-wide.

Additional development parameters are specified by state-enforced regulations concerning the shores of coastal waters and inland bodies of fresh water. A state register of critical areas provides the basis for negotiation with landowners in these areas for the conservation of their environmental values.

Resources management and development regulation at the state level relies on information about the nature of these resources and on standards and criteria for evaluating private development initiatives. This system is applied state-wide, but the management program also has a more detailed shorelands component. Shoreland is defined as the area within 250 feet of the mean high water mark of tidal waters and certain freshwater ponds and streams. Here, in addition to state-enforced regulations, local governments have responsibility for detailed determination of development parameters through zoning and subdivision regulations. Here also, state guidelines provide an informational and procedural framework for local rule-making and enforcement. The state–local partnership is facilitated through regional planning organizations that provide technical assistance to local governments and identify regional environmental concerns and development objectives. Coastal zone management in Maine is not intended to be a purely bureaucratic enterprise. The policy framework and objectives have been determined by the political process that culminates in the state house. Equally important, but more difficult to elicit and comprehend, is the direct input of Maine citizens into management decision-making.

The coastal planning group in the Maine State Planning Office described its coastal management program this way:

> The Maine coastal plan is not so much a single document, but a process wherein: (a) data is gathered and analyzed, (b) the facts made known to the citizen, (c) a decision is made as to the desirable future of the coast, and (d) the logical steps to proceed towards achieving that future are outlined.[1]

INVENTORIES AND INFORMATION BASE

The Natural Resources Inventory

There are two major components of the Maine coastal zone management program data base. They are inventories of natural and socioeconomic resources. The natural resources inventory provides information about economically exploitable resources as well as those that must be conserved and protected. Without such information it is not possible either to make accurate assessments of the environmental impact of various kinds of physical development or to formulate programs for encouraging economic development or improve job opportunities and income for the resident population. The natural resources inventory of the Maine coastal zone includes the following components:[2]

Geological resources
Slopes
Hydrology
    Drainage and watersheds
    Groundwater
    Water quality classification
    Coastal lakes
Land use cover types
Living resources
    Wildlife habitats
    Marine environments
    Marine resources
Scenic resources
Recreational resources

Some of this information had already been accumulated by various state agencies, but much of it must be collected by new field surveys. The Bureau of Geology collects and maps much of the physiographic information with the cooperation of the University of Maine Department of Geological Sciences. The Soil Conservation Service provides soil maps. Water quality studies and classification involve the Department of Environmental Protection, and biological studies are produced by the Department of Marine Resources and the Department of Inland Fisheries and Game. The Bureau of Parks and Recreation and the University of Maine's Environmental Studies Center have also contributed to this inventory. Figures 6 and 7 illustrate examples of Maine's magnificent scenic and recreational resources.

Coordinating the entire natural resources inventory effort is the Maine State Planning Office. Once the inventory maps have been completed they will be published, together with other descriptive information, in a Coastal Resource Atlas. As the atlas is intended to serve the needs of citizens as well as professional contributors

Figure 6. Rocky shore at Pemaquid sight

Figure 7. Coastal forest and islands. (Photo courtesy of State Planning Office.)

to resources management decision-making, it will be designed to be readily understandable by laymen.

The Socioeconomic Inventory

Information about the social and economic factors affecting the coastal zone is more difficult to obtain and analyze than information about natural resources. Uncertainty about future events, which may have the impact of the unanticipated energy crisis, makes forecasting social change difficult. Nevertheless, the State Planning Office has assembled information to prepare social and economic profiles of communities in the coastal zone and forecasts for the direction of change. This information may be helpful in determining trade-offs between economic development and resources conservation. It will also be useful to regional and local planning agencies in deciding land use planning issues. The socio-economic inventory has the following components:

1. *Population:* relevant management program information on age profiles; town population growth rates, and how they are influenced by births, deaths, and migration; the direction of population movement within the state; and peak seasonal population.

2. *Taxation:* real property tax data about local and other governmental financial resources and the effect of development on the tax base.

3. *Land use:* roads and other transportation facilities, water supply and sewerage systems, public service facilities, and land in private use for residence, commerce, and industry.

4. *Economics:* data to show trends in taxable sales, value of manufactured products, wages, bank deposits and loans, occupations, agriculture, and revenues and expenditures of county governments.

5. *Housing:* inventory of the housing stock and its condition, housing needs, and housing construction.

6. *Transportation:* Information about the existing land and water transportation systems as well as their capacity to meet present and future demands.

7. *Education:* survey of levels of educational attainment of residents in the coastal zone and attendance at various kinds of schools.

8. *Recreation:* information about the economic impact of
tourists, trends in park attendance, and the location of various kinds of facilities.

Other social and economic information is also being collected,
including poverty and health indices, timber supply and demand,
mineral production, and fisheries supply and demand. The complete inventories of natural and socioeconomic resources provide
the basic data for regional and local planning as well as for developing the coastal zone management program. Their management
application focuses on the use and development capability of lands
and waters. There is no attempt to designate specific uses for various land areas, but rather to identify suitable general uses.

Inventory data are assembled and synthesized to produce the
following maps of significance for the program:

1. *Areas of particular state concern:* environmental hazards; ecological fragility; important habitats, scenic areas, and locations
of development pressure. Figures 8 and 9 illustrate development pressure on Maine shorelands and beaches.

Figure 8. Boothbay Harbor: fishing and fish processing facilities compete for
shore sites with marinas, resort hotels, transportation, residences, and
other uses in urban areas. (Photo courtesy of Maine Department of
Commerce and Industry.)

Figure 9. Beach at Wells: crowded vacation homes have obliterated dunes and restricted public access to the beach. (Photo courtesy of Maine Department of Commerce and Industry.)

2. *Suitability of land and water areas for selected activities of major state concern:* designation of sites for selected kinds of large-scale development; suitability of surface waters for waste discharge caused by development; and priorities for various uses.

3. *Preliminary regional land use plans:* designation of areas for broad categories of land use: land use class I—moderate- to high-intensity development; class II—low-intensity developments; class III—agriculture and resource management; class IV—areas with significant public values.

These components of the Maine coastal zone management program will be described in greater detail in the following sections.

DEFINITION OF THE COASTAL ZONE BOUNDARY

The Maine coastal zone is defined in terms of four subzones, each assigned to specific government jurisdictions to be managed according to the provisions of particular state laws.[3]

Upland Developed and Undeveloped Areas

For planning purposes the widest band of upland territory is marked by the coastal watershed boundary. For management purposes, however, the jurisdictional boundary of the first tier of towns on tidewater delimits the developed uplands. High-impact development, which comprises projects with buildings over 60,000 square feet of ground area or covering more than 20 acres, must receive state permits according to procedures prescribed by the Site Location of Development Law for this entire subzone.

Shorelands

This is the band of upland area 250 feet from mean high water. Here, local governments regulate all land uses as required by the Mandatory Shoreland Zoning Act of 1971. Local zoning is supplemented by state review and approval. The state also issues permits here under the Site Location of Development Law, as noted above.

Intertidal Area

The entire area within the reach of tidal influence is regulated under the Wetlands Control and Protection Act of 1972. Permit applications are submitted to the municipality concerned for initial comment and reviewed by the state, and then permits are issued by local governments.

Offshore Area

The federal Coastal Zone Management Act has established the seaward boundary of the Maine coastal zone as the outer limit of the U.S. territorial sea, which is three nautical miles from shore. The governor's cabinet committees on offshore policy coordinate management controls and policies in this area. They are composed of the commissioners of the principal agencies that have statutory responsibilities in the offshore subzone.

Areas of critical environmental concern are also identified as part of coastal zone boundary determination. This process will be described in a later section on the management program. Federal lands have also been mapped and are excluded from the state definition of the coastal zone.

DETERMINATION OF PERMISSIBLE LAND AND WATER USES

The Maine coastal resource inventory provides the information base for determining permissible land and water uses that "have a direct and significant impact on coastal waters." The management program does not specifically permit or exclude particular uses from the coastal zone. Instead it provides performance standards and an analysis of land capability and suitability based on the resource inventory as guidelines for local zoning of the shorelands and for state action under the Site Location of Development and Protection of Coastal Wetlands Acts.[4]

Land uses considered to have direct and significant impact on the environment have been generalized into three categories for the purpose of formulating development standards and assessing the suitability of coastal lands for each of these classes of land use. They are: (a) large buildings with over 60,000 square feet of ground areas; (b) large subdivisions over 20 acres in area that rely on individual septic systems for sewage disposal; and (c) large subdivisions served by sewage collection systems.

Lands in the coastal zone have been mapped and designated as (a) suitable, (b) of intermediate suitability, or (c) unsuitable for each of these major categories of land use. Analysis of the carrying capacity of coastal lands was based on information about their natural features and characteristics as determined in the preparation of the coastal inventory. Particular determining features were:

1. Soils and surface geology with poor drainage, instability, or other conditions that make sites unsuitable for construction and maintenance of large buildings.

2. Bedrock geology that is water-bearing, unstable, or otherwise unsuitable to support foundations for large buildings.

3. Areas of particular concern, such as those having scientific, historic, or scenic value or flood plains, wetlands, beach and

dune systems, shoreland areas vulnerable to erosion, wildlife habitats, or other environmentally or ecologically sensitive areas.

4. Capacity of surface and subsurface waters to assimilate polluting discharges that current technology cannot avoid, which may result from development.

In supervising local zoning in the shorelands subzone and in reviewing all applications for permits for the three classes of land use in the uplands subzones that have direct and significant impact on the environment, the Board of Environmental Protection will apply these performance standards:

1. *Pollution control:* the developer has the financial capacity and technical ability to meet air and water pollution control standards, and has made adequate provision for solid waste disposal, the control of offensive odors, and the securing and maintenance of sufficient and healthful water supplies.

2. *Traffic movement:* the developer has made adequate provision for traffic movement of all types out of or into the development area.

3. *Effect on the natural environment:* the developer has made adequate provision for fitting the development harmoniously into the existing natural environment, and the development will not adversely affect existing uses, scenic character, or natural resources in the municipality or in neighboring municipalities.

4. *Soil types:* the proposed development will be built on soil types that are suitable to the nature of the undertaking.[5]

DESIGNATION OF AREAS OF PARTICULAR ENVIRONMENTAL CONCERN

Areas of particular state concern are identified on the basis of the coastal resources inventory and analysis. State concern with resource use in these areas is to assure it is consistent with the public interest. The 'public' interest is difficult to define because there are different 'publics' involved: property owners, entrepreneurs, and the general public, for example. It is out of the identification and reconciliation of these conflicting interests that the state interest may be identified. Areas of particular state concern are identified on the basis of these characteristics:[6]

1. *Natural hazards:* tidal and freshwater flood plains, land subject to erosion or subsidence, other areas that may be dangerous to life or property.

2. *Significant natural, scientific, historic, cultural, or archeological resources.*

3. *Areas under intense development pressure that significantly affects the general public:* examples are the shorelands and the borders of federal and state highways.

4. *Valuable natural resources:* these are of actual or potential economic significance to the region; they include mineral deposits, agricultural areas, sites suitable for agriculture.

5. *Ecologically sensitive areas:* fresh- and saltwater wetlands, beach and dune systems, and other areas vital to the functioning of natural systems, and which are vulnerable to destruction by development.

6. *Recreational resources:* of concern because recreation demands are increasing in the coastal zone and most land with recreation potential is in private ownership.

7. *Scenic areas:* scenic views are among the most important values and resources of the Maine coast.

8. *Routes for public access:* public rights to use coastal areas may be nullified by private ownership of the bordering lands. Public access ways are not readily available along the Maine coast.

9. *Biological habitats:* terrestrial and aquatic areas that support significant populations of species valuable for commerce or sport, or which are rare and endangered.

The legal basis for improving the management of these areas of particular state concern is found in the Critical Areas Registry Act.

DETERMINING PRIORITY OF USES

The Maine coastal zone management program does not assign priorities for specific uses in particular areas. Instead, state guidelines have been defined for high and low priority uses in various categories of areas of particular concern either for development or for conservation and protection. The ordering of priorities is based on continuing analysis of state and local development needs as well as their potential effect on area resources. A rigid ordering of priorities is precluded by the variability of characteristics and impacts of potential uses and by the changing natural and socio-political environment.[7]

> The important step in meeting the intent of this section [of the Coastal Zone Management Act] is the establishment of a viable process and a mechanism to prepare and revise priorities on a continuous creative basis. Also in keeping with this approach and philosophy, permissible land and water uses have been defined and are managed on a performance basis, not on the basis of the characteristics of specific potential uses.[8]

General priorities for uses of the coastal zone are contained in the acts of the state legislature that provide the legal foundation for the coastal zone management program. The most important laws have already been mentioned: (a) Site Location of Development Act, (b) Mandatory Shoreland Zoning Act, (c) Protection of Coastal Wetlands Act, and (d) State Register of Critical Areas Act. The Act Relating to the Coastal Conveyance of Petroleum also contains a definition of what are considered the "highest and best uses" of the Maine Coast.

> The legislature finds and declares that the highest and best uses of the seacoast of the state are as a source of public and private recreation and solace from the pressures of an industrialized society, and as a source of public use and private commerce in fishing, lobstering and gathering other marine life used and useful in food production and other commercial activities.[9]

Two other organizations have also been established to refine and clarify coastal zone priorities. One is the governor's cabinet Committee on Land Use, which among other duties will "review, revise, and update priorities and policies for land use in the coastal zone."[10] The other is the Commission on Maine's Future, which provides the process and mechanism for considering goals and objectives, policies and priorities for the state as a whole.

Within the general requirements for ordering priorities, the Coastal Zone Management Act specifies particular kinds of use to which high priorities must be given and for which areas must be designated. These are: (a) consideration of the national interest involved in the siting of facilities necessary to meet requirements other than local in nature, (b) areas for preservation and restoration, and (c) uses of regional benefit.

Facilities in the National Interest

Using information from the federally sponsored New England River Basins Commission, the state identified such uses in its publication *Regional and National Demands on the Maine Coastal Zone*. Energy production is the dominant federal interest and national concern in Maine. Policy guidance has been provided by the governor's Task Force on Energy, Heavy Industry, and the Maine Coast. Its 1972 report recommended that future heavy industries should locate in only two regions—Portland-Casco Bay and Machias Bay. Petroleum-related industries, however, should be confined to the Portland-Casco Bay region.

Areas for Preservation and Restoration

Under the auspices of the Nature Conservancy and the Smithsonian Institute, the Maine State Planning Office analyzed unique and important areas for preservation along the coast. Thirty-two conservation zones were designated as critical areas needing immediate consideration. Priorities were established between zones and also within each zone so the steps could be taken to protect the most vulnerable or valuable areas. The Department of Conservation has undertaken a pilot project in Merrymeeting Bay and Petit Manan to test out the principles in the state conservation priorities plan.

Uses of Regional Benefit

Developments that would have regional impact must have state permits issued according to the provisions of the Site Location of Development Act. Local governments are given the opportunity to support or oppose such proposals, but final decisions are made by the state Board of Environmental Protection. Nevertheless criteria for such "regional impact" projects are concerned primarily with their possible harmful effects on the environment. Consideration of their potential regional *benefit* is not included in the evaluation procedures required by state law. This appears to be a deficiency in the Maine management program as far as conforming to federal guidelines is concerned.

LEGAL STATUS OF THE MAINE COASTAL ZONE MANAGEMENT PROGRAM

Major state environmental legislation regulating large-scale development, wetlands, shorelands, and critical areas provides the basic legal foundation for coastal management. State and local agencies have both police and eminent domain powers to implement the program when regulation and property acquisition are required. Additional formal actions by state institutional participants in coastal management are as follows:

1. Establishment by executive order of the governor's Advisory Committee on Coastal Development and Conservation and the Land and Water Resources Council to coordinate state land use policy and take appropriate measures to incorporate the natural resources inventory and analysis for the coastal zone.

2. Adoption of policy statements incorporating the coastal zone natural and resource policy analyses as a basis for regulatory decisions made by the following organizations:
   a) Bureau of Environmental Protection
   b) Shoreland Zoning Policy Task Force
   c) Land Use Regulation Commission
   d) Critical Areas Registry Board

3. Adoption of policy statements by the mid-coast regional planning commissions supporting the state coastal zone management program and expanding their land use management service and coordination role with respect to local government.[11]

Program Revision

The governor's Advisory Committee on Coastal Development
and Conservation was assigned the tasks of determining the future
direction of Maine's coastal planning program, priorities for research, and an integrated coastal and marine policy. In relation to
the problem of revising the coastal management program, the
Advisory Committee had the job of suggesting a new direction
that would satisfy the federal requirements and also have popular
support in Maine. This involved formulating complementary strategies for coastal economic development and coastal resources conservation. Developing recommendations on policies for oil and
gas resources on the outer continental shelf would be an additional
task.[12]

REFERENCES

[1] State Planning Office. *An Introduction to the Maine Coastal Plan,* Augusta
(November 20, 1974), p. 3.

[2] *Ibid.,* pp. 8-25.

[3] Maine State Planning Office. *Coastal Management Program, Mid-Coastal
Segment: Preliminary Application for Program Approval* (February 18,
1975), pp. 9-10.

[4] *Ibid.,* pp. 10-14.

[5] *Ibid.,* p. 14.

[6] *Ibid.,* pp. 14-17.

[7] *Ibid.,* pp. 17-18.

[8] *Ibid.,* p. 18.

[9] *Ibid.,* p. 18.

[10] *Ibid.,* p. 19.

[11] *Ibid.,* p. 19.

[12] State Planning Office. "The Role of the Governor's Committee on Coastal
Development and Conservation" (March 19, 1976) (mimeo).

PART III

COASTAL RESOURCES MANAGEMENT
IN RHODE ISLAND

CHAPTER VIII

COASTAL MANAGEMENT PROGRAMS
IN RHODE ISLAND

Many coastal states have extensive shorelines, and that is where most of their population, commerce, industry, and urban centers are located. Consequently, there is very little that any state agency does that does not either take place in or affect the coastal zone, however that area may be defined. Tracing out every last state organization's role in the coastal zone would inevitably involve almost the whole state structure; and many of the units would be found to have overlapping functions and jurisdictions. The state institutional structure for coastal resources management in Rhode Island is concerned, therefore, with identifying out of the whole complex structure of state government those agencies and organizations that have major responsibility for performing the function described in federal and state laws as coastal resources management.

RESOURCES MANAGEMENT

In March, 1970 the governor's Technical Committee on Narragansett Bay and the Coastal Zone published a report that described the Rhode Island coastal zone and its problems and recommended an action program to the governor.[1] Several categories of problems were noted; environmental pollution, resources management, regulation of marine-oriented and related development, competing uses, and the multiplicity of uncoordinated governmental jurisdictions. These are the problems that must be analyzed in detail and dealt with by the state coastal zone management program.

Environmental Pollution

Municipal and industrial wastes were the major source of water pollution. The state had adopted water quality standards, classification of water bodies, and a water pollution law; and federal and state financial aids were available for the construction of municipal sewage treatment plants. As a consequence of these activities, only one percent of municipal sewage was untreated. Nevertheless, industrial pollution was worsening. Agriculture was also a serious source of water pollution. From 1945–1969 the number of commercial farms had declined from 3600 to 800. There had also been a drastic decline in farm production. Despite the reduced area devoted to agriculture, surface runoff from farmland caused pollution by fertilizers, pesticides, and other chemicals.

Industrial cooling significantly raised the temperature of adjacent water bodies, reducing the amount of dissolved oxygen and degrading the habitat for fish. The considerable traffic of shipping, military vessels, and pleasure boats in Narragansett Bay were major sources of sanitary wastes. Oil spills were also a serious cause of pollution in the Bay. Floating debris, while not vitally affecting water quality, was hazardous and unsightly.

The Rhode Island coastal zone also suffered from air pollution. It came mostly from industrial areas in the Providence region. Local refuse dumps and the transportation network contributed to the air pollution. The governor's committee reported that the state's air pollution laws had been judged ineffective.

Natural Resources

In only a few decades fish and shellfish had seriously declined as important contributions to the Rhode Island economy. The sport and commercial finfish catch was reported declining, which affected tourism and the economy of fishing communities. Fifteen million pounds of oysters had been harvested in 1910; by 1960 there were none. The scallop fishery, which had produced two million pounds in 1940, had also ceased by 1960. The lobster yield, which had been two million pounds in 1921, was reduced to 200,000–300,000 pounds by the 1960s. Quahog clam production had been cut in half between 1955 and 1961. Water pollution and overfishing were identified as the major causes of these resource problems.

Minerals were also an important coastal resource. Gravel mining was already a developing industry, but it was completely unregulated. Sand and gravel were extracted from state lands under water by private operators without regard to conservation of this resource or ecological problems caused by disturbance of the bottom. Oil was a potential resource in the outer continental shelf, and drilling might be inevitable. Unregulated mineral extraction could lead to depletion of the resources, water pollution, adverse ecological effects, and less potential state revenue from fees and licensing.

There were also resource problems on the land bordering coastal waters. Although the state granted permits for dredging, filling, and the construction of piers and bulkheads, there was no state policy on such alterations of the shoreline. The laws governing wetlands and intertidal salt marshes were confusing and difficult to enforce. Abandoned wrecks and docks were eyesores, hazardous, and waste of shorefront land. They could be removed by the state only if they were hazards to navigation, and the state had no legal means to require the owners to remove them at their own expense.

The shore and coastal waters are themselves major resources, but they were not given optimal use. Public access to the shore was limited because most of it had been preempted by private owners and governmental uses. Shore facilities in the form of boat launching ramps, piers for unloading fishing boats, and bulkheads and shore protection works were inadequate. Harbors and channels had problems of silting and traffic control. Narragansett Bay attracted numerous pleasure craft, which were inadequately controlled or protected (Figure 10).

The Rhode Island coastal zone is the focus of communal and productive activities, so it is inevitable that there are conflicting demands for use of its lands and waters. Recreational boating and commercial shipping are in conflict because small boats encroach on the shipping lanes, and large ships produce strong wakes and pollution. Recreational and commercial fishing compete for the shorefront. Recreational use requires parking, motels, marinas,

Figure 10. Popularity of boating and waterfront sites for residences puts
heavy demands on shoreline and waterways. (Photo courtesy of
University of Rhode Island.)

and fishing sites. Pier and processing facilities for commercial fishing are often crowded out. Different kinds of recreation are
themselves in conflict. Swimmers and surfers should not use the
same beach; swimmers are disturbed by water vehicles, especially
when they tow water skiers; and beach buggies disturb sun bathers
and picnickers on the sand. Commercial shipping is hampered by
pipelines that have been laid across Narragansett Bay. Competition for land along the shore brings conflict between military and
civilian use, development and reservation of open space, residence
and commerce. The last of these conflicts is caused partly by
overzoning for low-density residential use. Resolving these many
conflicts of interest in the coastal zone is one of the most sensitive
tasks of resources management.

INTERGOVERNMENTAL RELATIONS

Competition for use of the physical resources of Narragansett Bay and the coastal zone brings conflict over jurisdiction between municipalities, between municipalities and the state, and between state agencies. Federal agencies are also involved. Military and coast guard installations require large shorefront and land areas. Other federal agencies are concerned with commerce, navigation, and natural resources. They not only own extensive properties, but they also operate various programs and regulate private sector activities.

Rhode Island State Agencies

The state had considerable direct authority under its police power for regulating activity in the coastal zone, but it had apparently neglected its central management role.

> The state of Rhode Island should serve as a central link among
> all kinds of coastal participation within its territorial boundaries.
> However, the fragmentation and diffusion of the state's programs
> seriously hinder the effectiveness of any federal-state relationship
> and simultaneously create an inherently weak and strained inter-
> nal structure.[2]

Department of Natural Resources

This department is most intimately involved with coastal resources management. It houses the staff of the Coastal Resources
Management Council, and its operating programs directly affect
the coastal zone. It has these divisions:

1. *Parks and Recreation:* operation and maintenance of state
   parks and recreation areas, most of which are in the coastal
   zone.
2. *Conservation:* management of 30,000 acres of state natural
   areas, including marshes and wetlands; fish and game management; delineation of intertidal salt marshes for state regulation.
3. *Enforcement:* boating safety and security; enforcement of
   pollution laws for the Department of Health and prevention
   of shellfishing; patrol officers have power of arrest.

4. *Planning and Development:* land acquisition and engineering; assembles state and federal financial aids to help communities acquire land for open space preservation, recreation, and conservation; design and engineering for all other DNR divisions; evaluates all proposals for projects, facilities, construction, and improvements in the estuarine environment.

5. *Coastal Resources:* formerly Division of Harbors and Rivers; renamed after designation as staff for the state Coastal Resources Management Council; administers procedures for regulation of coastal waters and major facilities on land that affect the coastal waters.

Department of Health

This is the state air and water pollution control agency. The department promulgates pollution control rules and regulations, decides on permits for sewage treatment facilities, and reviews all applications to the federal Environmental Protection Agency for permits to discharge wastes into navigable waters under the Water Pollution Control Act. This department also classifies water bodies in the state according to their various uses.

Department of Transportation.

Roads and bridges are significant physical features in the Rhode Island coastal zone. Interstate highways penetrate the urban areas, and major bridges connect islands to provide roadways across Narragansett Bay. The Department of Transportation is responsible for the location, construction, and maintenance of the highway component of the state transportation system.

Department of Community Affairs

This organization offers technical and financial aids to communities for planning, zoning, environmental development, and conservation. Local governments have considerable influence over land use and development in the coastal zone. This department is in a position to act as a communication link between state and local governments in the formation and implementation of coastal resources management policy.

Department of Economic Development

The department is concerned with the development of business, industry, and tourism. Its objectives may sometimes conflict with those of other organizations concerned with environmental protection and conservation. State policies and programs must therefore try to ensure that economic development takes place without unduly destroying environmental values.

Statewide Planning Program

This is a component of the Department of Administration. It is responsible for preparing the state guide plan for land use, transportation, and other aspects of development. It is the lead agency for managing the program development stage of the state's federally aided coastal zone management program.

Local Governments and the Coastal Zone

State legislation delegates substantial powers to local governments by which they may control development in the marine environment. However, these are enabling laws; they do not require local assumption of regulatory responsibilities.

> This arrangement, which has given very broad powers to local
> areas, produces an uncertain arrangement whereby communities
> are in a position to assume as much or as little responsibility as
> they desire. In reality, each political subdivision determines on
> the basis of its needs and resources the role it will assume in
> such marine activities as coastal recreation, pollution control
> and waste disposal, navigation, and economic development.[3]

Zoning is traditionally the most powerful tool for local land use regulation. It is often undermined, however, by pressure from developers and by government objectives for increasing property tax revenue. Nevertheless, land use control is a state constitutional power, and critics of local zoning practices advocate stronger state review and supervision. The objective of a stronger state role is to bring statewide concerns to bear on zoning decisions that might otherwise be made solely on the basis of local values and interests.

Local governments also have direct responsibility for certain kinds of infrastructure development and operation. Coastal municipalities may have local beaches and other recreation facilities in the coastal zone. Waste disposal and water pollution control are also local responsibilities, although the state helps out with the one and supervises the other. The state has created a solid waste management corporation to prepare a statewide plan for solid waste disposal, construct and operate disposal facilities, and by means of these facilities provide disposal services to municipalities under conditions specified in the law. With regard to water pollution control, municipalities must obtain Department of Health approval for construction or alteration of sewage treatment facilities.

Need for a Coastal Resources Management Structure

Having investigated in some depth the problems of coastal resource management and intergovernmental relations that have been only briefly noted here, the governor's Technical Committee on Narragansett Bay and the Coastal Zone focused its recommendations on what appeared to be the single most important factor for dealing with these problems, namely an institutional structure to develop management policies and coordinate government efforts to implement them.

> The Technical Committee found, through all groups appearing before it, a general recognition of the need for an overriding body to provide the direction and leadership for the development and utilization of Rhode Island's vital coastal zone, a management body that could determine basic policy guides, that could develop and maintain a workable coastal zone plan, that could implement this plan, that could coordinate the efforts of all governing agencies and groups in this endeavor, and that could carry out necessary study and investigational work to solve conflicts and other coastal problems.[4]

The governor, the legislature, the Technical Committee, and the statewide planning program took up this challenge and in little more than a year had drafted and enacted legislation to create an institutional structure for coastal resources management.

REFERENCES

[1] Rhode Island Governor's Technical Committee on Narragansett Bay and the Coastal Zone. *Report of the Governor's Committee on the Coastal Zone,* Providence (March, 1970).

[2] *Ibid.,* p. 36.

[3] *Ibid.,* p. 49.

[4] *Ibid.,* p. 101.

CHAPTER IX

RHODE ISLAND COASTAL RESOURCES
MANAGEMENT STRUCTURE

Primary components of the coastal management structure are the governor and the State Assembly. Together they must decide whether the state will assume responsibility for coastal resources management in the first place. Then they must enact the laws establishing the management structure and assigning specific powers and responsibilities to it. The courts are also involved, but their role becomes evident only after the coastal resources management program has been established. They are concerned primarily about the constitutionality of the program and the adjudication of disputes that arise because of it.

Four state organizations have been designated by law or executive order to constitute Rhode Island's coastal zone management team. They are: (a) the Coastal Resources Management Council, (b) the Division of Coastal Resources, Department of Natural Resources, (c) the Coastal Resources Center, University of Rhode Island, and (d) the Statewide Planning Program, Department of Administration. Each of these organizations will be described in the sections that follow. It may be pointed out here that the Statewide Planning Program is the designated lead agency to administer federal grant funds during the program development stage. These activities fall under Section 305 of the federal Coastal Zone Management Act. Administration of a federally approved program, under Section 306 of the Act, is expected to be the responsibility of the Coastal Resources Management Council. (Figure 11).

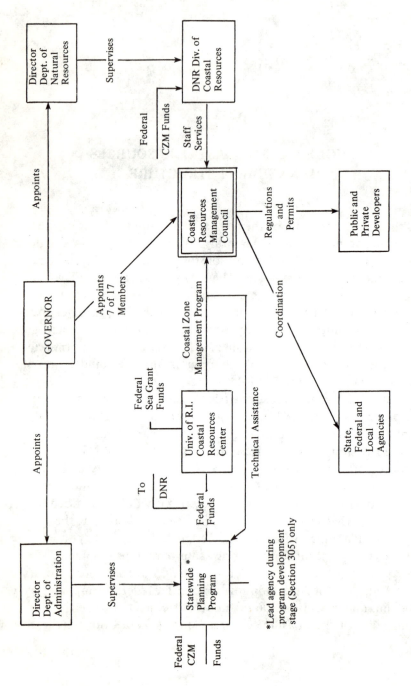

Figure 11. Rhode Island Coastal Zone Management Structure

THE GOVERNOR

The governor has a special role under the federal Coastal Zone Management Act. He must initiate the preapplication procedure to obtain program development grants from the Department of Commerce through its responsible agencies, NOAA and the Office of Coastal Zone Management. In the preapplication, the governor designates the state agency that will apply for and administer the grant.[1] The formal application itself must later also be submitted by the governor.[2] When the management program is completed, it is submitted to the Secretary of Commerce for approval. The application for administrative grants to implement the program ". . . must contain a certification signed by the governor of the coastal state to the effect that he had reviewed and approved the management program."[3]

In Rhode Island, the governor played an important role in coastal resources management several years before the federal program was enacted in 1972. As far back as January, 1969, Governor Frank Licht received a report from the Natural Resources Group, a private citizen's organization, which pointed out that in spite of the importance of the coastal zone for Rhode Island there was no governmental mechanism for managing it.

> Narragansett Bay is Rhode Island's greatest natural resource substantially supporting industrial, commercial, military, recreational and domestic activities; yet there exist no satisfactory means of guiding or directing its use and development for the best overall interests of the state and its people.[4]

The First Governor's Committee on the Coastal Zone

In its report, the Natural Resources Group asked Governor Licht to sponsor legislation to establish an administrative mechanism for the coastal zone. In response to this proposal he appointed the Governor's Technical Committee on Narragansett Bay and the Coastal Zone in March, 1969. It consisted of representatives of the governor's office, various state agencies and the University of Rhode Island. The Committee set out to examine the state's coastal zone and then focused on ". . . creation of a mechanism within state government which can formulate policies for the coastal zone, prepare plans based on these policies, and coordinate public and private actions toward the achievement of the objectives set by these plans."[5]

The Committee's primary objective was to insure

> ... that the state has the ability to guide the development and use of coastal lands and waters, and to work effectively with the many federal, regional, state, local, and private interests which are concerned with the preservation, utilization, and regulation of the coastal zone.[6]

The Governor's Committee noted that although there was a great deal of government in the Rhode Island coastal zone, there did not seem to be much effective management. There were a great variety of federal, regional, state and local governments with concerns and powers in coastal affairs, but there was no focus of responsibility.

> With so much interest, one would imagine that the problems of the Rhode Island coastal area are being carefully attended to. However, much criticism has been directed at this diffusion of government jurisdiction, as it is felt that it greatly hinders meaningful and effective management. The critics contend that at each level of government, responsibility is indiscriminately and haphazardly assigned to an agency, resulting in a serious lack of coordination between these agencies and also between the different levels of government.[7]

One year after it was established the Governor's Committee submitted its report. It was convinced of the need to establish some kind of coastal zone council to take on responsibility for planning, coordination, resource management, and regulation. Two basic alternatives were considered. One was to establish the council as a new independent agency; the other was to locate it in an existing state agency. The pros and cons of each alternative were identified as follows:

A Separate Agency

Advantages. An independent council would give coastal affairs greater visibility. It would be more likely to arouse support from the public and the federal government, and thereby enable it to attract favorable financial resources. Independence would also give the agency more freedom to formulate policies, administer regulations, and maintain relationships with other state agencies.

Disadvantages. A separate agency would add to the proliferation of state organizations and further complicate the government structure. A council might not be effective in performing administrative and line functions. In the course of time even an independent council might become less visible and more removed from direct responsibility to the governor. A new agency also provides opportunities for empire building.

A New Division Within the Department of Natural Resources

Advantages. This arrangement would minimize organizational and administrative problems. It would take advantage of the knowledge and expertise available in the existing agency and facilitate coordination of coastal management with other functions of the agency. It would also maintain the principle of strong executive leadership and clear lines of authority and responsibility.

Disadvantages. The new council would have an ambiguous position in relation to the director of the Department of Natural Resources and to its staff, which would be one of the divisions in the Department. Identified with one agency, the council might have difficulty in coordinating coastal zone affairs with other state agencies.

Proposal for a New Coastal Zone Council

The March, 1970 report makes no mention of the basis for its choice of a council as the mechanism to administer the coastal zone. Why would a multi-member council be more appropriate for receiving development applications and issuing permits than a responsible administrator? How could part-time, unpaid public and *ex officio* council members devote the time required to consider many individual permit applications and study the multifarious problems of coastal resources management? If the council were to be independent, but its staff organized as a division of the Department of Natural Resources, would the staff find itself trying to serve two masters; and could the council find itself unable to exert direct control over its staff?

Having decided on a council as the appropriate management mechanism, the Governor's Committee on the coastal zone made the following recommendations, among others:

1. The Rhode Island legislature should establish a Coastal Zone Council as the principal management mechanism for the coastal zone. Members should be appointed by the governor. The staff for the council and its director should be located in the Department of Natural Resources for administration, but they should be under the direction and control of the council.

2. The University of Rhode Island should be designated as the state coastal zone laboratory. It should have principal research responsibility for surveys and technical studies on which the council could base policy and management decisions.

3. The coastal zone council should prepare a coastal zone plan.

4. The council should clarify the legal jurisdiction of the state and its political subdivisions in coastal lands, waters, and submerged lands.

5. The council should review existing statutes relating to the coastal zone and recommmend necessary changes for proper management.

6. The council should review all current programs and projects in the coastal zone and make recommendations concerning their future direction.

7. The council should develop and maintain an inventory of shoreline and estuarine resources.[8]

A coastal zone management bill was submitted to the state legislature with provisions based on these recommendations. The bill was introduced at the 1970 session of the General Assembly, but did not pass. This failure was attributed to the late date of introduction of the bill, so that some legislators were not well informed. There were also objections to some provisions of the bill that aroused fear of encroachment on local powers, such as zoning, and also fear of the loss of personal liberty resulting from extension of governmental authority. Some coastal municipalities preferred not to plan for or control development within their boundaries, and they did not want to be forced to do so.[9]

These objections by property owners and municipalities were primarily in response to the provisions of the bill that would give the state authority over a zone 200 feet inland from or 20 above the mean high water line, whichever covered a larger land area. This is the approach to defining the coastal zone boundary in Maine and Washington, and it would also appear to conform to the requirements of the federal Coastal Zone Management Act that would be passed in 1972. In response to these objections, Rhode Island lawmakers adopted a unique approach to defining the coastal zone that did not include a specified landward boundary. This definition of the coastal zone will be described in a later section on the Coastal Resources Management Council.

Although this bill did not pass, public interest in the coastal zone was heightened by current events. A proposal had been advanced to build an oil refinery on upper Narragansett Bay with a production capacity of 65,000 barrels per day; and other proposals had been made for facilities to store liquified natural gas at two sites on the Bay. The Narragansett Electric Company announced plans for a nuclear power plant. Other development proposals involved dredging or filling of wetlands and other significant changes in the coastal environment. Without a law such as the one proposed by the Governor's Committee, the state had no effective authority to protect the public interest in the coastal zone. Decision on these proposals was the sole responsibility of the municipalities concerned. There was no legal requirement that they consult other affected communities.[10]

The Second Governor's Committee
on the Coastal Zone

The governor's response to the setback of the bill in the legislature was to expand his Technical Committee on Narragansett Bay and the Coastal Zone to 75 members.[11] It now had representatives from every municipality in Rhode Island, the General Assembly, state agencies, and interested private organizations. It reviewed and updated the technical studies of the earlier group and concentrated on refining the management mechanism proposed in the March, 1970 report. Two approaches to devising a management

structure were proposed. One was by Daniel W. Varin, Chief of
the Statewide Planning Program, who had worked closely with the
first Governor's Committee. The other was by Glenn Kumekawa,
a committee member from Warwick, who was then also that city's
Director of City Planning.[12]

Daniel Varin's approach was based on the work of the first
Governor's Committee on the Coastal Zone. Its objective was to
overcome the objections that had been raised to the previous year's
coastal zone bill. The major objections were that the proposed
coastal zone council might encroach on local powers, especially
zoning, and that the council would be able to use public funds to
acquire coastal lands. Varin's suggested compromise was that the
coastal resources council should have broad powers over the water
areas of the coastal zone, but limited powers over the land areas.
Under this proposal, the regulated water areas would extend from
the mean high water line to the seaward limit of state jurisdiction.
Instead of granting the coastal zone council authority over a geographically defined land area, Varin suggested that the council
should be concerned only with specified public and private activities on the landward side of the shore. It would only review applications and issue permits for the design, construction, and operation of major installations, such as power plants, manufacturing,
petroleum and chemical plants, sewage treatment, and other
activities that would discharge stated amounts of effluents or
otherwise affect the coastal environment. Varin also proposed that
the council would adopt standards according to which its permitting and regulatory authority would be exercised.

The alternative approach suggested by Glenn Kumekawa started
with a substantive analysis of coastal resources management. Once
management problems and functions were identified, an organization could be devised and given the roles and powers appropriate
for effective performance. Kumekawa's method was to use a
matrix with coastal problems listed in one dimension and the various means to deal with them in the other dimension. The role
models he suggested were: (a) constrainer of private and public
action, (b) developer/promoter of necessary or desirable projects,
(c) moderator/arbitrator/interdictor in disputes, (d) resources
manager, and (e) policy formulator.

The expanded Governor's Committee found that the matrix analysis would require more time and resources than were available. Varin's suggestions were therefore incorporated into a second bill, which was sent to the General Assembly in 1971. This Committee's report was sent to the governor in March of that year, almost exactly one year after the first Committee's report. The bill appears to have been motivated by a "thou shalt not" approach to resources management. Land and water development capability analysis is fundamental to this approach, and it leads to the identification of uses and activities that designated areas should not be put to. The burden of proof would then be on the developers, public or private, to show that their proposals would not exceed the development capability of the area or degrade the environment beyond defined limits.

The second bill was found acceptable by the General Assembly. It passed the Act to create the Rhode Island Coastal Resources Management Council on July 14, 1971. This was in the year before Congress passed the federal Coastal Zone Management Act. The Governor's Technical Committee on Narragansett Bay and the Coastal Zone passed out of existence. The governor continues to influence coastal affairs, however, by his appointments to the Coastal Resources Management Council and by his review and approval of submissions to Washington that give Rhode Island a place in the federal program.

THE GENERAL ASSEMBLY

Rhode Island's concern for its coastal zone before the federal program was established has already been noted. The state legislature played a crucial role in environmental affairs by providing the legal foundation for action by state agencies. In 1965 it had already approved legislation to protect tidal wetlands. In 1971 this protection was extended to freshwater wetlands. Rhode Island wetlands law is confusing, however, because the General Assembly passed two different laws in 1965. One is called the Coastal Wetlands Act, the other is the Intertidal Salt Marsh Act.

Tidal Wetlands

The state constitutional basis for the Coastal Wetlands Act is the guarantee of free right of fishery to the people of Rhode Island.[13] Degradation of tidal wetlands would impair this right because they are spawning and nursery areas for the important fishery species. Tidal wetlands also have esthetic value and are important as reservoirs to store flood waters. The Act defines a coastal wetland as any salt marsh bordering on tidal waters, including the 50-yard border of contiguous upland. The salt marsh itself is identified by the presence of particular plant species[14] (Figure 12).

Figure 12. Patience Island (upper left) and the northern end of Prudence Island have beaches, wetlands, and woodlands that support natural ecological systems on one of the few remaining large blocks of undeveloped land in Narragansett Bay. (Photo courtesy of the University of Rhode Island.)

The Coastal Wetlands Act was intended to regulate wetland uses by a kind of state zoning under the police power. The Department of Natural Resources was authorized to promulgate written orders designating protected salt marshes and permitted uses in them. Such orders were to take precedence over local zoning and other regulations. The police power of the Act is weakened, however, by the provision that an owner of property in the wetland may claim compensation in the Superior Court for financial damages caused by the order restricting the use of his land.

Because of this provision, the law has never been implemented. Damage awards were to be paid from state funds appropriated for this purpose or from the Recreation and Conservation Land Acquisition and Development Fund. No appropriations have ever been made for this purpose, however, and the Recreation and Conservation Fund is considered inadequate even for its primary purposes. In this connection it is interesting that in Massachusetts more than 23,000 acres of wetlands have been protected since 1965 under a similar law. The Massachusetts law, however, allows the state to modify or withdraw an order if it cannot pay damages set by a state court. The conservation agency in Massachusetts has not hesitated, therefore, to issue orders restricting the use of wetlands, apparently without much challenge from property owners.

The other Rhode Island wetlands law, the Intertidal Salt Marsh Act, was also enacted in 1965, and it was amended in 1967 and 1969.[15] Its criteria for defining a salt marsh include the presence of both designated plant species and salt marsh peat. This Act is also based on the constitutional guarantee of free right of fishery. Under the Act a permit is required from the Department of Natural Resources for dumping mud, dirt, or rubbish in a salt marsh or for disturbing the ecology of the marsh by dumping, filling, or excavating. Violators of the law are subject to penalties and may be required to restore the marsh to its original condition.

Because compensation to property owners is not required, this law has been used successfully to regulate uses in and avoid alteration of salt marshes. However, it lacks the 50-yard upland buffer around salt marshes that is provided in the Coastal Wetlands Act, so development has taken place right to the edge of some marshes.

Since 1971, when the Coastal Resources Management Council was established, that agency took over administration of the Intertidal Salt Marsh Act from the Department of Natural Resources. DNR, however, still administers the freshwater wetlands legislation.

Freshwater Wetlands

The General Assembly also enacted a freshwater wetlands protection program before the federal Coastal Zone Management Act of 1972. The Freshwater Wetlands Act was passed in 1971 and amended in 1974. Under the police power it protects freshwater wetlands by prohibiting their alteration without permits from the state Department of Natural Resources and the local government having jurisdiction. In practice, the state acts only after local approval has been granted.

A property owner denied a permit may petition the Superior Court to be compensated for the fair market value of the land as wetland. The Court would award compensation if it determines that ". . . the proposed alteration would not essentially change the natural character of the land, would not be unsuited to the land in the natural state, and would not injure the rights of others."[16] Such a circumstance would in effect be denial of a permit for an activity that was not in conflict with the objectives of the act and probably should have been approved.

Coastal Resources Management Council

The events leading up to the 1971 Act creating the Coastal Resources Management Council have already been recounted. The provisions of the law regarding membership in the Council and its responsibilities and powers will be described in the following section. What may be noted here is that by the time the federal coastal zone management program was enacted the Rhode Island legislature had already established a foundation of laws and institutions for coastal resources management.

THE COASTAL RESOURCES
MANAGEMENT COUNCIL

The Rhode Island Coastal Resources Management Council was established by an act of the General Assembly on July 14, 1971.[17] The legislative findings incorporated into the Act note that Rhode Island's coastal resources are important for the economic and social well-being of the state, and therefore

> . . . it shall be the policy of this state to preserve, protect, develop, and where possible, restore the coastal resources of the state . . . through comprehensive and coordinated long-range planning and management . . . and that preservation and restoration of ecological systems shall be the primary guiding principle. . . . [These] policies can best be achieved through the creation of a coastal resources management council as the principal mechanism for management of the state's coastal resources.[18]

Membership

The Council's 17 members are appointed by a complicated process intended to assure representation by a wide variety of interests. They are designated as follows:

1. *By the governor:* 7 members. Four are local officials, three of whom must represent coastal municipalities; three are public members, all representing coastal municipalities.
2. *By the lieutenant governor:* 2 senators who represent coastal municipalities.
3. *By the speaker of the House:* 6 members. Two are members of the House, at least one representing a coastal municipality. Four are public members, two of whom serve three-year terms and must be from coastal municipalities; the other two serve two-year terms and may be from any municipality.
4. *Ex officio:* the directors of the state Department of Health and the Department of Natural Resources.

It has already been noted that a bill introduced into the legislature the previous year failed to pass, among other reasons, because some legislators feared that the Council would infringe on the rights and powers of local governments. This objection was apparently at least partially overcome by placing four local officials on the Council, and requiring that at least 8 of the remaining 11 appointed members represent coastal municipalities.

The governor designates the Council chairman and vice-chairman from the appointed members. The Council elects its own secretary from either its own membership or from its staff. Council members are compensated $50.00 per meeting and are reimbursed for expenses.

The significance of the method of selecting Council members will become apparent from a description of Council responsibilities and powers. Any private or public proposal for operations or physical changes affecting the seaward side of the coastal zone must be approved by the Council. It also regulates major development on the landward side. Its regulations have the force of law and it has the last word on their administration, except for appeal to the courts. The question might therefore be raised about the appropriateness of entrusting this function to a part-time council whose members have other important public and private occupations and responsibilities.

Experience during the first two or three years of the Council's operations indicates that it works quite well. It had problems that might be expected with a new organization that had unprecedented responsibilities and untested dependence on other agencies for staff support and technical advice. It also had the unenviable task of deciding whether to grant permits for activities in the coastal zone at the same time that the basic resource inventories and regulations were being drawn up. Nevertheless, this appointed Council representing heterogeneous political and economic interests weathered its first shakedown years successfully.

Although the Council had to deal with the first permit applications that came to it on an *ad hoc* basis, it did have the technical advice available in the Department of Natural Resources, the Coastal Resources Center of the University of Rhode Island, and the Statewide Planning Program. The Council is able to function, therefore, primarily as a politically and environmentally sensitive body that ratifies the technical analyses prepared for it by its staff and other state agencies that review permit applications. Council members, however, also have professional experience or intimate knowledge of local situations that gives them valuable insights into

the probable consequences of approving individual applications.
Although it might appear that a Council composed of state legislators, local officials, and public members who serve part-time and
represent diverse interests would not be likely to deal expeditiously
with the volume of permit applications that come before it, operating experience proves it to be successful in Rhode Island.

Planning and Management

The Coastal Resources Management Council has responsibility
by law for making studies of conditions, activities, and problems
of the coastal zone and for preparing coastal management plans
and programs. The latter are to be based on criteria and standards
that include:

1. The need and demand for various activities and their impact
   on ecological systems;
2. The degree of compatibility of various activities;
3. The capability of coastal resources to support various activities;
4. Water quality standards set by the Department of Health;
5. Consideration of plans, studies, surveys, inventories, and so
   forth prepared by other public and private sources;
6. Consideration of contiguous land uses and transportation
   facilities; and
7. Consistency with the state guide plan.[19]

The law creating the council established it as an independent
unit, but its staff was to be a constituent part of the Department
of Natural Resources. The name of the Division of Rivers and
Harbors was changed to the Division of Coastal Resources, and
some of its operating functions were transferred to other DNR
divisions. The Division of Coastal Resources remained in DNR for
administrative supervision, but it was to function as the staff for
the Council. Two other DNR divisions were designated to assist
the Council, but were not placed under its control. The Division
of Planning and Development would provide land acquisition and
engineering services, and the Division of Enforcement was charged
with enforcing all laws and regulations of the Department of
Natural Resources. Technical planning assistance for the Council

was also made available from the Coastal Resources Center of the University of Rhode Island and from the Statewide Planning Program. The Council, therefore, has several sources of professional and technical assistance for carrying out its planning and management functions.

It would appear that the DNR Division of Coastal Resources is in a difficult position in terms of institutional structure, for it must serve two masters, the director of the Department of Natural Resources and the chairman of the autonomous Coastal Resources Management Council. In the first years of Council existence this was an organizational problem. There were some personality conflicts between the DNR director and the Council chairman and turnover in the incumbents of these offices. The problem of inter-organizational relations has been partly solved by the appointment of a former state representative, John A. Lyons, to hold simultaneously the offices of Chairman of the Council and staff director of the Division of Coastal Resources. This has helped to establish a pattern of accommodation between the Council, DNR, and the Division of Coastal Resources.

Implementation

To carry out its policies and plans, the Council is authorized to adopt regulations for the entire seaward side of the coastal zone and for activities specified by law on the landward side. On the seaward side, this means that no private or public initiative for any development or operation within, above, or beneath the state's tidal waters may occur without complying with Council regulations and first obtaining a permit. These waters are defined as extending from the mean high water line to the extent of the state's three-mile jurisdiction. The Council may approve, modify, set conditions for, or reject any application for a permit. The applicant would have to demonstrate that the proposal would not (a) conflict with any resources management plan or program, (b) make any area unsuitable for any uses or activities to which it is allocated by a resources management plan or program, or (c) significantly damage the environment of the coastal region.[20]

Council regulation of the landward side of the coastal zone is limited to these specified uses and activities:

1. Power generating and desalination plants;
2. Chemical or petroleum processing, transfer or storage;
3. Minerals extraction;
4. Shoreline protection facilities and physiographic features being shaped and modified by tidal waters;
5. Intertidal salt marshes; and
6. Sewage treatment and disposal and solid waste disposal facilities.

The Council has the authority to "approve, modify, set conditions for, or reject the design, location, construction, alteration, and operation" of these activities. It does not matter where on land they are located as long as they affect any water area under the Council's jurisdiction as defined above. Nevertheless, its authority is limited to situations in which there is a reasonable probability of conflict with a plan or program for resources management or damage to the coastal environment. Implementation of Council plans and resource management programs includes these operations:

1. Issuing, modifying, or denying permits for any work in, above, or beneath the water areas in its jurisdiction, including any form of agriculture;
2. Issuing, modifying, or denying permits for dredging, filling, or any other alteration of intertidal salt marshes;
3. Licensing the use of coastal resources, which are held in trust by the state for all its citizens (sand and gravel extraction, for example) and imposing fees for private use of such resources;
4. Determining the need for and establishing pierhead, bulkhead, and harbor lines;
5. Developing, leasing, and maintaining state piers and other state-owned property assigned to the Council by the Department of Natural Resources, the governor, or the General Assembly; and
6. Investigating complaints alleging violations of state laws or riparian rights in the state's tidal waters.[21]

Coordination

It has already been noted that one of the problems of managing the Rhode Island coastal zone was the multiplicity of state and local governments and agencies pursuing their individual interests and programs. To assure coordination of state and local activities and avoid conflicts, the Coastal Resources Management Council is empowered by law to act as a "binding arbitrator in any matter of dispute involving both the resources of the state's coastal region and the interests of two or more municipalities or state agencies."[22] The Council regards this as one of its most important management powers.

Enforcement

Violations of the regulations of the Coastal Resources Management Council may be brought to its attention by officers in the Enforcement Division of the Department of Natural Resources, other agencies, or private citizens. The Council is authorized to order violators to stop their activities or initiate legal proceedings against them.

> In any instances where there is a violation of the coastal resources management program, or a violation of regulations or decisions of the council, the council shall have the power to order the violator to cease and desist or to remedy such violation. If the violator does not conform to the council's order then the council, through its chairman, may bring prosecution by complaint and warrant, and such prosecution shall be made in the district court of the state. . . . It shall be the duty of the attorney general to conduct the prosecution of all such proceedings brought by the council.[23]

Work Program

The important role played by the Statewide Planning Program and its chief, Daniel Varin, in the Governor's Technical Committee on Narragansett Bay and the Coastal Zone and in the establishment of the Coastal Resources Management Council has already been described. As a follow-up to these activities, the Statewide Planning Program prepared a prospectus to guide the new Council in getting its work started.[24]

The prospectus recommended a three-phase program that would attempt to deal with immediate pressing problems of the coastal zone and also initiate short-range and long-term technical studies and planning activities. Priority could be given either to preparing an inventory of coastal resources, which is the essential information base for resources management, or to specific problems that were of significance for the people and resources in the coastal zone. The Statewide Planning Program recommended that the latter objective be given priority attention.

> Either of these approaches would be extremely useful but . . . [dealing with immediate problems] could have the added value of permitting the Coastal Resource Management Council to produce recommendations on a subject of broad public interest within a relatively short period of time. This would be extremely helpful to the new Council and its staff in making itself known to the General Assembly, the press, and the public and in generating financial and other support for its future activities. . . . Inventory data has little impact on the public and would barely scratch the surface of what will have to be an effort of several years duration.[25]

Two urgent problems were recommended for immediate attention. One was to devise a permit system to carry out Council responsibilities for regulating all changes in the state's coastal water areas and for the major installations on land that might affect those waters, as specified in the law. This task would involve formulating procedures for receiving and acting on permit applications, standards for evaluating applications, criteria for separating applications for routine staff processing from those requiring consideration by the full Council, and procedures for hearings. The second urgent problem was the siting of a nuclear power generating station in the coastal zone.

The Statewide Planning Program recommended that parallel with these immediate activities a short-range technical program should begin. This would include the studies and resource inventories necessary for the Council's long-term responsibilities for coastal zone planning and resources management. These studies would include not only ecological and geomorphic analyses, but also identification of the public and private activities and interests competing for coastal resources. Conflicts, gaps, overlaps, and problems in the various public and private plans and programs should also be identified.

The recommended long-range work program would aim at providing information and assistance to policy-makers at all levels in dealing with coastal resources problems. It would also aim at fostering cooperation between governmental units and the private sector in achieving conservation and optimum utilization of the state's coastal resources. Some of the elements in such a long-range program would be:

1. Continuous monitoring of all key aspects of coastal waters;
2. Formulation and administration of regulatory measures;
3. Allocation of areas under the Council's jurisdiction to various uses or combination of uses; and
4. Special studies, such as identification of legal jurisdictions in the coastal zone, methods of improving public access to the shore, and the effects of various types of land use on adjoining water areas, port development, and marine commerce.

Plans, Policies, and Regulations

With a major input of technical studies by the Coastal Resources Center of the University of Rhode Island and the cooperation of the Statewide Planning Program, the official custodian of the Rhode Island coastal zone management program is the Coastal Resources Management Council. This is the program prepared to meet the requirements of the federal Coastal Zone Management Act. The procedure for adoption of the management plan includes review by the Council's Planning and Policy Subcommittee and citizens advisory committees. After acceptance of plan elements by the full Council, policies and regulations are formulated from them. After formal adoption by the Council, the regulations are filed with the Secretary of State. They then form part of the legal foundation for implementing the coastal management program.[26]

The published manual of regulations contains the Council's policies for the coastal zone. They are broad general statements that must be given operational definition and implementation in Council regulations. They contain statements such as these:

> The Council shall encourage programs and proposals which encourage programs and proposals which encourage access to the shore . . .

It shall be the policy of the Council to promote public participation in the preparation of its plans, programs, policies, and regulations . . .

It shall be the policy of the Council to cooperate with other government agencies in all matters of mutual interest . . .[27]

The Council's regulations describe how it will conduct its business and how persons and their representatives may appear before it in hearings, action on complaints, and other procedures. Permit requirements are spelled out in each chapter of the regulations. Their headings indicate the scope of the regulations.

1. Procedural rules
2. Fees
3. Chemical or petroleum processing, transfer, or storage
4. Power generating and desalination plants
5. Cables and pipelines
6. Harbors, port facilities, and marine transportation
7. Piers, docks, and wharves
8. Dredging and filling
9. Minerals extraction
10. Fishing and agriculture
11. Marine recreation
12. Riparian rights
13. State-owned property
14. Shoreline protection facilities and physiographic features
15. Intertidal salt marshes
16. Natural areas of particular concern
17. Pollution control

The procedure for obtaining a permit from the Coastal Resources Management Council actually begins with obtaining permits for the proposed project or activity as required by state and local regulations from the town where it would take place and from the Department of Health or other appropriate state agencies. Processing of applications by the Council begins with a site visit by staff members, who are in the Division of Coastal Resources of the Department of Natural Resources, and at least one Council member. Public notice of the application is then given. If no objections are raised by citizens or government agencies during a 30-day waiting period, the Council may grant the permit. If there are objections, the chairman of the Council appoints a subcommittee to hold a hearing which is held after notice and a further 20-day waiting period. The full Council reviews the subcommittee report and the hearing transcript and makes its decision to grant, deny, or modify the application. If approval is to be granted, a final 30-day waiting period is required so that objectors to the project or activity may appeal the Council's decision to the Superior Court.

The Coastal Resources Management Council and its regulatory powers and procedures have withstood their first court tests. Among its management successes are strict regulation of sand and gravel mining in coastal waters and a halt to building on undeveloped barrier beaches. A suit was brought in Washington County Superior Court against Nancy Filmore, who was refused a permit by the Council to build on an undeveloped barrier beach. The defendent had a valid local building permit and had begun construction. The Superior Court ruled the Council decision to prevent building on these beaches was a valid exercise of the state's police power. Filmore appealed to the state Supreme Court and was allowed to continue construction, but only on the ground that it had begun before the 1971 law creating the Council had been enacted. The courts have also upheld the Council in refusing to grant a permit even though a local building permit had been obtained, as long as actual construction did not start before passage of the 1971 Act[28] (Figures 13 and 14).

THE DIVISION OF COASTAL RESOURCES

The Division of Coastal Resources is one of the major components of the state Department of Natural Resources. Nevertheless, its function is to serve as the staff for the Coastal Resources Management Council. The administrative head of the Division reports to the chairman of the Council through the director of the Department of Natural Resources. Yet the Division of Coastal Resources is supposed to be under the complete control of the Coastal Resources Management Council. This appears to be a complicated arrangement that requires the Division to serve two

Figure 13. Barrier Island at East Beach between the Atlantic Ocean and Charlestown Pond. Development with beach houses tends to destroy the dunes, and owners demand measures to protect their property from storm damage. (Photo courtesy of the University of Rhode Island.)

Figure 14. Sign at Napatree barrier beach warns of legal prohibitions against vehicles on the dunes and beach and restrictions on foot traffic. (Photo courtesy of the University of Rhode Island.)

masters. Although this arrangement may appear contrary to the principles of organization and management, it seems to work. In any case, as long as the chairman of the Council and the director of the Division of Coastal Resources are the same person, there should be no problems of coordination or responsibility.

The Division of Coastal Resources provides administrative support for the Coastal Resources Management Council. The staff receives and processes all applications for permits required by Council regulations and notifies interested parties, investigates proposals, assembles evidence, arranges for hearings, issues responses to applicants, and maintains all files and records. The Division staff also coordinates services on behalf of the Council that are performed by the Division of Enforcement and the Division of Planning and Development in the Department of Natural Resources and by other agencies outside the Department.

THE COASTAL RESOURCES CENTER, UNIVERSITY OF RHODE ISLAND

Although by law the Coastal Resources Management Council is "the principal mechanism for management of the state's coastal resources," it has no technical planning or scientific resources of its own. When the federal coastal zone management program was established, its requirements for planning and resource analysis led to the designation of the Coastal Resources Center as the scientific component of the coastal management team. The Center carries out a series of studies, each of which becomes part of the state's coastal resources management plan. They include policy documents as well as management procedures for particular marine resources. A study element typically includes a description of the resource; its uses; its locations, limits, and other characteristics; a recommended management program; and proposed regulations.

To provide this service to the Coastal Resources Management Council, the Center has a nucleus staff within the Graduate School of Oceanography, and it may also call on the expertise of other members of the University of Rhode Island faculty. The work of the Center is supervised by an executive committee, which includes the University provost for marine affairs, the directors of the

Coastal Resources Center, the New England Marine Information Program and Marine Advisory Service, the Marine Experiment Station, and the International Center for Marine Resources Development, and the coordinator of the Sea Grant Program. The Statewide Planning Program also works with the Center so that scientific and planning resources may be integrated. This arrangement assures compatibility of coastal planning with statewide land use planning.

The coastal resources inventory is being prepared by the Center as the major information base for coastal resources planning and management. Its main components are:

1. Marine geology of Narragansett Bay and the sea floor below Rhode Island waters;
2. Hydrography of Narragansett Bay and coastal waters;
3. Chemical properties of coastal waters;
4. Climate;
5. Biological features of the coastal zone, land and marine;
6. Fish and fisheries;
7. Shoreline features, land use, and land ownership;
8. Environmental quality and sources of pollution;
9. Recreation;
10. Public facilities and utilities;
11. Commercial and industrial activities;
12. Regulation of coastal resources;
13. Management of Rhode Island coastal resources; and
14. Rhode Island in relation to southern New England

THE STATEWIDE PLANNING PROGRAM

The Statewide Planning Program was formally established during the January, 1970 session of the General Assembly. The law governing the state Department of Administration was then amended to include among its functions "to administer a statewide planning program including planning assistance to the state departments and agencies."[29]

Pursuant to this legislative mandate, Governor Frank Licht by executive order declared that

1. The Statewide Planning Program shall be the principal staff agency of the executive branch for coordinating plans for the comprehensive development of the state's human, economic, and physical resources.
2. The Statewide Planning Program shall prepare, continuously evaluate, extend, and prepare revisions to a long-range state guide plan. . . .
3. A state planning council is hereby established to provide policy advice and guidance to state planning activities.[30]

The State Planning Council membership was to consist of the director of the Department of Administration as chairman, nine heads of state agencies appointed by the governor, five officials of local government appointed by the Rhode Island League of Cities and Towns, and representatives of federal and regional agencies who might be invited to serve as nonvoting members. Council membership was expanded by Governor Philip W. Noel in 1975 to include 10 public members appointed by the governor.[31]

When the state decided to apply for a federal grant for program development under Section 305 of the Coastal Zone Management Act, Governor Noel designated the Statewide Planning Program to be the lead agency. The Coastal Resources Management Council was already in existence and might have been chosen for this role. Nevertheless, this was a new organization involved in getting ready to formulate coastal regulations and permitting procedures. The Statewide Planning Program had already experienced the application for and administration of federal grants and assembling the technical resources to use them. It is anticipated, however, that when program planning has been completed and approved by the Secretary of Commerce, federal administrative grants to implement the program under Section 306 of the Coastal Zone Management Act will be received and allocated among supporting state agencies by the Coastal Resources Management Council.

State law requires that all coastal management plans ". . . shall be developed around basic standards and criteria including . . . consistency with the state guide plan."[32] Much of the work of the Statewide Planning Program, as it relates to coastal management, involves coordinating coastal resources planning with state land use planning. A key document for carrying out this function is the *State Land Use Policies and Plan.*[33] This report is an element of the state guide plan. It lists these planning goals specifically for the Rhode Island coastal zone:

1. Preserve, develop and where possible, restore the resources of the coastal region in order to benefit from its variety of assets.

2. Reduce pollution and protect marine life, and enhance the natural qualities of the marine environment.

3. Prevent the deterioration of the shoreline.

4. Improve anchorages, harbors, and docks.

5. Reduce the potential loss of life, health hazard, and property damage caused by flooding and extreme tidal action.

6. Provide employment opportunities in the coastal region, consistent with other goals.

7. Increase and enhance recreational opportunities in the coastal region.

8. Reduce conflicts in the coastal region between different uses and between government jurisdictions.[34]

The land use guide plan includes a map entitled "Land Use Plan 1990," indicating the generalized allocation of state lands to various intensities of residential, commercial, industrial, and institutional use and to reserves for open space. Achievement of this land use pattern would require implementing state legislation, local land use regulations that conform to the guide plan, financial resources to extend and improve the transportation, utilities, and services infrastructure, and promotion of economic enterprise and population settlement patterns that follow the land use allocations in the state guide plan.

The graphic plan is supplemented by a detailed statement that spells out the policies that would have to be adopted if state and local governments in Rhode Island were to seriously support the state land use guide plan. Policies for the coastal zone are summarized as follows:

1. Develop resource management plans for the shore region that are compatible with the needs of the people of Rhode Island,

while preserving and enhancing as far as possible the natural qualities of the marine environment.

2. Examine proposals for changes in the coastal region in terms of their economic, recreational, aesthetic, and environmental importance to all of the people of the state in common rather than to individual communities or to small special interest groups.

3. Support programs to abate pollution and examine all proposals for use of the state's marine resources in relation to the degree of pollution which may result.

4. Encourage the development of both sport and commercial fisheries both inshore and offshore up to level of maximum sustainable yield providing such development does not curtail other more important uses.

5. Prevent filling of coastal waters and wetlands except when necessary to the health or welfare of the people of the state and there is no other alternative.

6. Protect selected areas from the effects of flooding and extreme tidal action; limit the intensity of development of unprotected areas.

7. Cooperate with local governments in all matters of mutual interest . . . and encourage municipalities to make full use of the powers available to them.

8. Extend the jurisdiction of the state over offshore waters to the maximum extent possible and work closely . . . with the federal government to insure that federal agencies exercise their authority in a manner consistent with the interests of Rhode Island.[35]

These statements in the *State Land Use Policies and Plan* are so general as perhaps to be meaningless to the casual reader. They lack operational definition and criteria or standards by which to evaluate achievements. These details are not being ignored in the state coastal resources management program, however. They are provided for in the very specific regulations of the Coastal Resources Management Council and the water quality standards of the Department of Health.

The Statewide Planning Program and the
Coastal Resources Management Council

It has already been noted that the Statewide Planning Program was instrumental in the establishment of the Coastal Resources Management Council and that it is the lead agency in administering the federal grant for program development under Section 305 of the Coastal Zone Management Act. This leadership role is expected to pass to the Council when program administration gets underway under Section 306 of the federal Act. The Statewide Planning Program will continue to maintain close working relationships with the Council. In its prospectus for the Council's initial work program, the Statewide Planning Program offered its full cooperation.

> The Statewide Planning Program will cooperate with the Coastal Resources Management Council in all planning activities of joint interest. This coordination will involve the exchange of data, procedures, and proposals so that both agencies are in reasonable agreement on the location and timing of future development and the new or improved facilities needed to serve this development. Extremely close working relationships between the staffs of the Statewide Planning Program and the Division of Coastal Resources are essential to achieve this objective.[36]

REFERENCES

[1] 15 CFR Sec. 920.45, *Federal Register* 40: (73) (April 15, 1975).

[2] 15 CFR Sec. 920.42.

[3] 15 CFR Sec. 923.42, *Federal Register* 40: (6) (January 9, 1975).

[4] Natural Resources Group. *Report on Administration of Narragansett Bay* (January, 1969). p. 1.

[5] Rhode Island, Governor's Technical Committee on Narragansett Bay and the Coastal Zone. *Report of the Governor's Technical Committee on the Coastal Zone*, Providence (March, 1970), p. 2.

[6] *Ibid.*, p. 3.

[7] *Ibid.*, p. 15.

[8] *Ibid.*, p. 110–112.

[9] Varin, D. W. "Remarks to the Second New England Coastal Zone Management Conference," Durham, New Hampshire (September 23, 1971) (mimeo).

[10]*Ibid.*

[11]"Executive order No. 19" (November 23, 1970).

[12]Rhode Island Statewide Planning Program. *Program Prospectus for the Coastal Resources Management Council*, Providence (September, 1971); "Appendix D, Minutes of the Meeting of the Governor's Technical Committee on the Coastal Zone on December 30, 1975.

[13]"General Laws of Rhode Island," Sec. 2-1-13 to 2-1-17.

[14]Rhode Island Statewide Planning Program. *State Land Use Policies and Plan,* Report No. 22, Providence (January, 1975), pp. 182–83.

[15]"General Laws of Rhode Island," 11-46.1.

[16]Rhode Island Statewide Planning Program. *State Land Use Policies and Plan,* p. 183, Providence (January, 1975).

[17]"General Laws of Rhode Island," Title 46, Chapter 23.

[18]*Ibid.*, Sec. 46-23-1.

[19]*Ibid.*, Sec. 43-26-6.

[20]*Ibid.*

[21]*Ibid.*

[22]*Ibid.*

[23]*Ibid.*, Sec. 46-23-7.

[24]Rhode Island Statewide Planning Program. *Program Prospectus for the Coastal Resources Management Council*, Providence (September, 1971).

[25]*Ibid.*, p. 18.

[26]Rhode Island Coastal Resources Management Council. *Plan, Policies and Regulations*, Providence (undated), pp. 3–4.

[27]*Ibid.*, p. 5.

[28]"Statement by counsel to the Coastal Resources Management Council at a public information meeting in the State House," Providence (March 8, 1976).

[29]"Rhode Island General Laws," Sec. 42-11-2.

[30]Executive order No. 10 (June 22, 1970).

[31]Executive order No. 23 (February 7, 1975).

[32]"General Laws of Rhode Island, Sec. 46-23-6.

[33]Rhode Island Statewide Planning Program. *State Land Use Policies and Plan,* Report No. 22, Providence (January, 1975).

[34]*Ibid.*, p. 18.

[35]*Ibid.*, pp. 159–162.

[36]*Program Prospectus for the Coastal Resources Management Council*, p. 15.

CHAPTER X

COASTAL ZONE MANAGEMENT PROGRAM

The usual practice in public environmental programs has been to plan first and then try to implement the plan. Planning and implementation usually have also been responsibilities of different governmental organizations. As a consequence, there seems to have been a great deal of state and local planning but not too much implementation. The Rhode Island General Assembly took a different approach to coastal resources management. It created the Coastal Resources Management Council and gave it responsibility for both functions. With help from its staff in the Division of Coastal Resources and technical support from the Statewide Planning Program and Coastal Resources Center of the University of Rhode Island, the Council has from its inception been concerned about planning and management together.

> Both its legislative charge and the press of events have required that these responsibilities be exercised concurrently. As a result the Council adopted and subsequently refined a set of broad management policies and guidelines to direct its permitting actions while more detailed plans and management programs could be developed and adopted. The order in which management problems have been studied in depth and for which detailed policies and regulations have been formulated has been determined in large part by necessity. As these detailed regulations are formulated they are reviewed by appropriate local, state and federal agencies, by appointing citizen and technical review committees and by the public at large before they are formally adopted as elements of the *CRMC Plan: Policies and Regulations.* The Plan therefore, continues to grow in scope and detail as additional planning increments are studied, appropriate regulatory

responses are adopted and existing plan elements are reexamined
and modified to reflect evolving problems and priorities.[1]

This statement in the Council's draft *Management Program*
clearly sets out Rhode Island's approach to coastal zone management. It is oriented to immediate action to protect, conserve, and
manage the state's coastal resources, using available knowledge. As
the technical information base expands, more detailed public action
programs and regulations for private activities are formulated. This
is an evolutionary, developmental approach that aims at taking
immediate action, where this is appropriate and justified, and expanding the scope of management as technical resources become
available. This approach has been incorporated into the draft
Management Program, which is presented at information meetings
and hearings.

Rhode Island's flexible evolutionary approach to coastal resources
management differs in some important respects from the management program visualized in the Coastal Zone Management Act and
its related rules and regulations. The federal requirements visualize
a complete and detailed program with a mapped coastal zone
boundary, mapped areas of particular environmental concern, categories of permissible uses and where they may be located, priorities
for use in the various areas, and locations for uses of state and
national interest. Rhode Island coastal resources management
planners, however, followed their own legislative mandate, which
was enacted before the federal program came into being, regarding
management objectives, coastal boundaries, and regulation of land
and water uses. Whether this approach will be accepted by the
Office of Coastal Zone Management is uncertain at this time.
Nevertheless, Rhode Island is committed to it and is already managing its coastal resources according to its own lights.

COASTAL ZONE BOUNDARY

Rhode Island state law defines the coastal zone as the area over
which it gave jurisdiction to the Coastal Resources Management
Council.[2] This includes jurisdiction over any development or operation within, above, or beneath the tidal waters below the mean

high water line and extending seaward to the limit of state jurisdiction. There is no comparable mapped boundary for the landward side of the coastal zone. Instead, state law gives the Council jurisdiction over particular land features and uses wherever they occur.

1. *Shoreline protection facilities:* breakwaters, bulkhead, groins, jetties, rip-rap walls, filled areas and other structures or results of construction customarily employed to correct, control, or prevent erosion.[3]

2. *Coastal physiographic features:* natural geologic features above mean high water that are being shaped and modified by tidal waters. These include, but are not limited to, beaches, barrier beaches, sand spits, bluffs, cliffs, and scarps directly inland of the mean high water mark or of a beach or a coastal wetland.[4]

3. *Intertidal salt marshes:* any land which borders or lies beneath tidal waters and upon which grow one or more kinds of specified salt marsh vegetation.

4. *Land uses:* the following land uses and activities, regardless of their location, where there is a reasonable probability of conflict with a resources management plan or of damage to the coastal environment. (Figure 15).

   (a)   Power generating and desalination plants

   (b)   Chemical and petroleum processing, transfer, or storage

   (c)   Minerals extraction

   (d)   Sewage treatment and disposal and solid waste disposal facilities[5]

5. *Sources of pollution:* land uses that introduce pollutants into freshwater bodies, rivers, streams, or aquifers, or into the atmosphere fall within the statutory definition of the coastal zone. Although the Coastal Resources Management Council does not have responsibility for pollution control, cooperative institutional arrangements between the CRMC and other state agencies with authorities over air and water pollution control and freshwater wetlands management augment these [CRMC] regulations and standards and ensure their implementation in a manner supportive of and integral to the state's coastal resources management program.[6]

Some federal lands are excluded from state jurisdiction over its coastal zone. Considerable land in Rhode Island is owned or leased

Figure 15. Land use regulation must accommodate competing demands for
transportation, residence, and open space in the coastal zone. (Photo
courtesy of the University of Rhode Island.)

by the Navy, the Coast Guard, the Fish and Wildlife Service, and
the National Marine Water Quality Laboratory. There are some unresolved federal and state differences over jurisdictional boundaries,
however. The Department of the Navy and the Office of Coastal
Zone Management at the federal level are still negotiating the determination of which Navy holdings will be excluded from state jurisdiction. Meanwhile Rhode Island considers that federal lands
subject to state jurisdiction include all Navy holdings where the
activities are nonmilitary in nature or private and nonmilitary users
have leases or other agreements with the Navy. All other federal
holdings are also subject to state jurisdiction under Rhode Island
law.[7]

COASTAL INVENTORY AND RESOURCE
CAPABILITY ANALYSIS

Coastal resources inventory and assessment is a basic data component of any resources management program. It provides the scientific and technical justification for identifying permissible uses, geographic areas of particular concern, and high and low priority of uses. The federal approach to these aspects of the coastal management program is to expect states to make lists of uses that are appropriate or inappropriate for particular mapped geographic areas in the coastal zone. Rhode Island planners have not found this approach applicable to their own task of developing a coastal management program. The Rhode Island approach will be described in sections following this summary of coastal resources inventory and analysis procedures.

The University of Rhode Island Coastal Resources Center has major responsibilities for preparing the coastal resources inventory. The objective of the inventory is not simply to map and measure the resources but to identify coastal ecosystems and assess their vulnerability to environmental changes. Ecosystems are complex patterns of interrelationships between biotic (plant and animal) and abiotic (physical and chemical) components. These patterns are relatively stable in the natural state of the system. Where there is disturbance by man, his works, and his activities, the physical characteristics of the environment and the numbers and relationships of plant and animal species change. In the Rhode Island inventory, ecosystems dominated by human modifications are described and analyzed not only for their natural biotic and environmental components, but also for their social and economic characteristics.[8]

> Coastal ecosystem analysis in Rhode Island has focused on identification and analysis of the defining characteristics of components of individual ecosystems and the complex interrelationships which exist between these components. A special effort has been made to assess each system's sensitivity and response to environmental changes, and to trace (in as much detail as existing knowledge allows) interactions between specific environmental changes and identified system characteristics. Resource capability, then, is

seen as an ecosystem's ability to accommodate externally induced
environmental changes without serious disruption or alteration
of its distinctive internal components, functions and interactions.
This ability is a primary management concern of the CRMC under
state law which mandates that preservation and restoration of
ecological systems shall be the primary guiding principle upon
which environmental alteration of coastal resources will be
measured, judged and regulated[9] (Figure 16).

Figure 16. Marshes at Quonochontaug Pond support a wide variety of birds
and aquatic animals. (Photo courtesy of the University of Rhode
Island.)

The Rhode Island coastal resources inventory has identified,
mapped, and analyzed 53 types of natural and human-dominated
ecosystems for both marine and terrestrial environments. Where
human activities are significant, demographic, economic, and social
factors have been analyzed as well as the natural features. In spite

of the complexity of social and economic factors in the coastal
zone, available information is considered adequate for preliminary
evaluation of the effects of future changes, in the intensity or
scale of resource use.

Having described the natural and socioeconomic characteristics
of identified coastal ecosystems, the next step was to define categories of potential changes in marine and terrestrial environments
and the atmosphere due to further human activity. The categories
of changes include various forms of pollution, removal or deposi-
tion of materials affecting the physical environment, addition or
removal of organisms, and changes in habitat. For marine environments, 35 categories of potential changes have been identified, 16
categories for terrestrial environments, and three for the atmosphere.

The effects of these potential environmental changes on identified
coastal ecosystems may be assessed by a matrix, with ecosystems
and their characteristics in the vertical dimension and the potential
changes in the horizontal dimension. This matrix facilitates identification of the likely sensitivity of each ecosystem to any of the 54
kinds of potential environmental change.

The third step in the process of resources inventory and assessment of resources use capability was to identify categories of land
and water uses such as agriculture, industry, commerce, residence,
transportation, recreation, shipping, and fishing. Thirty-three distinct types of land and water uses have been identified, and for
each one the characteristic combination of activities involved that
may generate environmental or socioeconomic changes in each
coastal ecosystem. Thirty kinds of physical and eight kinds of
socioeconomic activities have been identified for the various land
and water use categories. Additional matrices reveal potential correlations between the 30 kinds of activity resulting from land and
water uses, and the economic changes.

The coastal resource inventory and assessment provides the information base for evaluating land and water use proposals. It
identifies the sensitivity of designated ecosystems and human systems to a list of specified environmental and socioeconomic changes.
The potential for inducing such changes is correlated with particular
categories of land and water use. The value of this inventory and
assessment procedure for resources management is that it provides

information for making trade-off judgements between conserving environmental values and promoting socioeconomic development. Permit applications cannot be evaluated by the Coastal Resources Management Council on the basis of environmental costs alone or socioeconomic benefits alone. Both sets of values must be considered, and some reasonable trade-off determined for each proposal.

The Council would follow a decision-making procedure on permit applications somewhat in this manner:

1. The natural and human systems at the site of the proposal are identified from coastal maps.

2. Ecosystem characteristics and sensitivity to environmental or socioeconomic change are identified from the coastal resources inventory and assessment.

3. The activities associated with the proposed land or water use are identified as well as the potential of these activities for generating environmental or socioeconomic change.

4. The change generating potential of the proposal is then compared to the sensitivity to change of the ecosystem at the site and possible problem impacts are identified.

5. Management attention is focused on the potential problem impacts of the proposal, and management decisions that reflect a realistic appraisal of environmental and socioeconomic trade-offs are made.[10]

PERMISSIBLE LAND AND WATER USES

Section 305 of the federal Coastal Zone Management Act requires that a state coastal zone management program must include ". . . a definition of what shall constitute permissible land and water uses which have a direct and significant impact on the coastal waters." This is an example of what appears to be the hard and fast federal approach to coastal management program development. The demand is for a list of uses, but the Rhode Island coastal resources managers were not in a position to meet it in the form prescribed.

The first task was to arrive at an operational definition of "direct and significant impact on coastal waters." The Rhode Island managers had difficulty doing this because they acknowledge

having insufficient information about the marine environment and
the complex interactions between marine ecosystems. Furthermore, the most important concern in measuring environmental impact is *change*. The coastal inventory and analysis process has
afforded some information about the types of changes most likely
to affect the integrity and vitality of coastal ecosystems. It could
not, however,

> . . . readily, consistently or confidentially distinguish between
> those types and/or levels of change which are 'significant' and
> those which are not. We must, therefore, treat every change as
> of potential management concern. . . .

> In pursuit of its responsibilities under law, the Coastal Resources
> Management Council . . . adopts the following definition: The
> term 'direct and significant impact on coastal waters' shall in-
> clude any and all appreciable or detectable change(s) to the
> physical, chemical or biological parameters of any marine or
> intertidal ecosystem(s).[11]

In addition to defining significance of impact in terms of environmental change, it was also necessary to designate land and water
uses that have such an impact on coastal waters. Rhode Island did
not find it useful for management purposes to designate such uses
a priori, because a particular use may have different impacts depending on the specific activities it generates, the characteristics
of the ecosystem affected, the unique conditions at the site, the
magnitude, intensity and duration of the use, and the manner in
which the use is carried out.

> While the state of Rhode Island questions the management value
> of designating specific land and water uses as the primary indi-
> cator of impacts on coastal waters, we agree most emphatically
> with the implicit intent of this requirement. . . .

> Our primary management concern will, therefore, be for the
> probable physical consequences . . . of land and water uses and
> their associated activities as *actually* implemented or proposed
> at specific sites. . . .

> The Coastal Resources Management Council, therefore, con-
> cludes that all land and water uses and their associated activities
> demonstrate a latent potential for exercising direct and significant

> impacts on coastal waters; provided that such uses and activities
> (a) are undertaken under, in, on, or over tidal and intertidal
> waters, salt marshes or coastal physiographic features; or (b)
> introduce or cause to be introduced any substance or pollutant
> into any river, stream, freshwater wetland or aquifer or into the
> atmosphere which may thereby and subsequently be introduced
> into and cause alteration of a marine ecosystem.[12]

Having presented the reservations discussed above about making
too general a definition of "direct and significant impact" or too
broad a designation of uses that may cause such impacts, the coastal
managers declared that "The state of Rhode Island finds generally
applicable designations of permissible land and water uses [to be]
of limited management significance."[13] Therefore, they also
adopted a more flexible and site-specific approach to "permissi-
bility" than is apparently required by the federal law and regulations. Instead of permitting or excluding designated categories of
use, the Rhode Island approach is to develop standards and criteria
by which "a logical, systematic and thorough examination of consequences [may] be made before new or additional uses are introduced into the coastal environment."[14]

The geographic and permitting jurisdictions of the Coastal Resources Management Council have been described in earlier sections
of this report. State law created the Council and gave it police
power authority to regulate all activities affecting coastal waters
from the mean high water mark out to the edge of the state's territorial sea. Salt marshes and other physiographic features are under
similar protection; and the Council has established management
criteria and performance standards for power-generating and desalination plants; chemical or petroleum processing, transfer or storage;
shoreline protection facilities; minerals extraction; sewage treatment
and disposal and solid waste disposal facilities. Furthermore, any
proposed action that has potential impact on coastal waters through
the introduction of substances or pollutants into rivers, streams,
freshwater wetlands, aquifers or the atmosphere is subject to state
and federal regulations and standards established under the Air and
Water Pollution Control Act of 1972, the Clean Air Act, and the
Environmental Policy Act. The Rhode Island Departments of
Health and Natural Resources cooperate closely with the Coastal

Resources Management Council in administering these regulations, to protect coastal resources.

AREAS OF PARTICULAR CONCERN, USE PRIORITIES, AND NATIONAL AND REGIONAL INTERESTS

In these aspects of coastal resources management, the Rhode Island approach also differs from federal requirements. Federal law and regulations demand geographic mapping of areas of particular environmental concern, designation of high and low priority uses in various parts of the coastal zone, and designation of sites for uses of national and regional concern. The Rhode Island coastal resources management program has identified 23 different types of natural and developed areas as of particular concern, and these have been mapped in the coastal resources inventory and assessment. They include natural areas, such as wetlands, barrier islands, dunes and beaches; flood-prone and hazardous areas; and developed areas, such as ports, heavy industrial sites, military installations, and areas of urban concentration[15] (Figure 17).

Regional and National Interests

Military installations are of declining importance in Rhode Island. Uses of greater than local concern that will probably become of greater importance along Rhode Island's coast are recreation, energy production and related activities, and industrial and commercial activities. The coastal resources inventory and assessment permits identification of those coastal areas likely to undergo continued developmental pressure, but it has not been found possible to equate specific uses with designated sites.

> Indeed, because of the many variables involved, very few *a priori* management decisions can be made on the suitability of undertaking specific uses in designated sites. . . . It has rather been found more useful to develop and apply procedures for assessing the resource capability of individual coastal ecosystems, identifying probable impacts of various resource uses on these systems,

Figure 17. The Napatree barrier beach was hit by the 1938 hurricane that
completely destroyed the summer houses crowded on it. In its present
natural state it protects Little Narragansett Bay and its shoreline.
(Photo courtesy of the University of Rhode Island.)

and applying these insights on a site- and situation-specific basis
to the management process. This is accomplished through the
application of appropriate management criteria and performance
standards to [Coastal Resources Management Council] permit
programs and responsibilities.

A priori consideration of the national interest as it relates to
utilization of specific coastal zone sites is even more difficult
than assessing statewide and regional needs. With very few
exceptions, national interest as set forth by federal agency policy
is insufficiently detailed to allow for site-specific application to
Rhode Island's coastal zone. . . .

It is already CRMC's policy to manage coastal zone usage on the
basis of the unique characteristics of Rhode Island's coastline

and marine waters. This, rather than subjective judgements on the adequacy of existing contributions to national and regional needs appears to be the most reasonable basis for decision-making. . . .

It is the state's belief, therefore, that it can best discharge its responsibilities to the nation as a whole by applying and enforcing management criteria and standards . . . through CRMC permit programs. [16]

Use Priorities

This is another federal requirement that the Rhode Island coastal managers find difficult to comply with by specifying high and low use priorities for each coastal zone area. Instead, the effect of particular uses at specific sites on coastal or marine ecosystems is their major management concern. The coastal resources inventory and assessment, and the matrix showing the probable effect of each of 33 different types of use on the 53 identified types of ecosystems helps reviewers spot the kinds of changes that would be considered acceptable or unacceptable.

> . . . priorities of use which must as a minimum reflect relative permissibility are also difficult to establish on a broad and generally applicable basis. It would, in fact, be misleading and potentially counterproductive to establish priority guidelines without considerable qualification of their true significance. The CRMC finds this significance to be more as a decision-making aid than as any binding guide to how specific land and water use decisions should be made. [17]

Instead of listing hard and fast orders of priorities, the Rhode Island management program indicates for each of several types of ecosystems the relative potential that various uses have for generating destructive environmental changes. Management decisions will be made only on a site-specific basis for each use application; but as a concession to federal requirements the management program lists generally applicable use priorities in various types of ecosystems to "focus management attention on proposed activities most likely to cause unacceptable environmental alterations." [18]

REFERENCES

[1] Rhode Island Coastal Resources Management Council. *Management Program* (draft), Providence (March 3, 1976).

[2] "General Laws of Rhode Island," Sec. 46-23-1.

[3] Rhode Island Coastal Resources Management Council. *Policies and Regulations,* Sec. 15-4-1.

[4] *Ibid.*, Sec. 15-4-2.

[5] "General Laws of Rhode Island," Sec. 46-23-6.

[6] Rhode Island Coastal Resources Management Council. *Management Program*, p. 48.

[7] *Ibid.*, pp. 49-50.

[8] *Ibid.*, pp. 6-7.

[9] *Ibid.*, p. 7.

[10] *Ibid.*, pp. 20-23.

[11] *Ibid.*, p. 31.

[12] *Ibid*   pp. 33-34.

[13] *Ibid.*, p. 35.

[14] *Ibid.*

[15] *Ibid.*, pp. 6-4 to 6-10.

[16] *Ibid.*, pp. 6-11 to 6-14.

[17] *Ibid.*, Chapter 6, pp. 6-16.

[18] *Ibid.*

PART IV

COASTAL RESOURCES MANAGEMENT
IN THE STATE OF WASHINGTON

CHAPTER XI

LEGISLATIVE BACKGROUND

Washington was one of several coastal states, including Maine and Rhode Island, that enacted coastal management programs before Congress passed the Coastal Zone Management Act of 1972. Concern over coastal resources in Washington was recognized by the state government during the middle 1960s, and the Shoreline Management Act was passed in 1971. Two events precipitated state legislative action. One was a legal case arising from the action of property owners to deposit fill in Lake Chelan. The other was a proposal to the governor from the Washington Environmental Council for a Seacoast Management Bill.

The Lake Chelan Case (*Wilbour v. Gallagher,* 77 Wash. Dec. 2d 307) was decided in 1969. It was brought to abate fill being placed in Lake Chelan for a trailer court. The lake level was controlled by the Chelan Electric Company, and the owners of the property in question had filled it to five feet above the 1100-foot legal high water level. Part of the fill covered vacated streets and alleys; and when the property was under water it had been used by the public for recreation. The fill, therefore, eliminated public access to that part of Lake Chelan and also interfered with navigation. The court found that when the water fluctuates in a body of navigable water, "The public has a right to go where the navigable waters go, even though the navigable waters lie over privately owned lands."[1] The case was interpreted by the governor's office as making fills in navigable waters illegal unless permitted by state legislation. The governor, therefore, froze all permits for public or private shoreland projects that required filling navigable waters.[2]

The Seacoast Management Bill suggested to the governor by the Washington Environmental Council failed to pass in the legislature in 1970. The Council then drafted a Shorelines Protection Act and obtained a record number of petition signatures, enough to place it in the legislature as Initiative 43. In Washington, legislative options on an initiative are either to pass it, refer it for an electoral referendum, or propose an alternative measure. In the case of the third option, both the initiative and the legislature's proposal go on the ballot. The voters must then decide if they want that kind of legislation at all, and if so, which proposal they prefer. The legislature's proposal was the Shoreline Management Act passed in 1971.[3]

The main difference between Initiative 43 and the Shoreline Management Act was the management structure proposed. Under the Washington Environmental Council initiative, the state Department of Ecology would be entirely responsible for the development of a shorelines plan and for the issuance of permits. Under the legislative act local governments would be responsible for planning and regulation subject to Department of Ecology guidelines and approval. The Council was apparently skeptical that local governments would give priority to environmental values over economic values, so their Initiative 43 proposed to give shoreline management responsibility to the state. It was questionable, however, whether the financial and personnel resources of the Department of Ecology, then only one year old, could cope with the tasks that would be imposed on it by Initiative 43.[4] The legislature, on the other hand, obviously preferred the emphasis to be on local responsibility. The electorate did decide in the referendum that it wanted some kind of coastal management program, and it overwhelmingly chose the legislature's Shoreline Management Act.

Two documents provide the legal foundation as well as detailed directions for organizing and carrying out the Washington coastal resources management program. One is the referendum-approved state law noted above, known as the Shoreline Management Act of 1971. It has been incorporated into the Revised Code of Washington (RCW) as Chapter 90.58. To implement the provisions of this law, regulations were promulgated by the director of the state Department of Ecology under the Washington Administrative Code (WAC). These regulations constitute Chapter 173-16 and serve as guidelines to local governments for the development of master programs to regulate the uses of the shorelines of the state.

The guidelines point out that the purpose of shorelines management is to plan for and foster all reasonable and appropriate uses.
State policy is concerned with enhancement of the shorelines, not
restriction of uses. The guidelines were to provide state criteria
for the development of local shorelines master programs, but they
note that the effectiveness of shorelines management will depend
on the way in which local governments interpret and use the guidelines. Judgment and good faith are required of both levels of
government, for the guidelines recognize that available knowledge
about the coastal zone is not yet complete or sophisticated enough
to determine precisely the nature and interrelationship of the physical, biological, chemical, and esthetic factors that influence management decisions.[5] The Shoreline Management Act of 1971 visualized
immediate regulation of shoreline development. The Department
of Ecology guidelines were also intended, therefore, to serve as
guides for interim shoreline use regulation by local governments
until shoreline master programs were prepared and adopted.

A third document supplements the Shoreline Management Act
and the guidelines by describing the legally established shorelines
management program in terms compatible with federal coastal zone
legislation and regulations. This document is the state of Washington
Coastal Zone Management Program. Its objective is to demonstrate
that the Washington program, established before federal action,
meets all federal criteria and will achieve the purposes of the Coastal
Zone Management Act of 1972.

INTERGOVERNMENTAL RELATIONS IN
SHORELINE MANAGEMENT

The Shoreline Management Act seems to put primary responsibility for resources management and shoreline regulation on local
governments. They must inventory their shoreline resources, prepare shoreline master programs, and establish permit procedures.
The Act establishes

> ... a cooperative program of shoreline management between
> local government and the state. Local government shall have the
> primary responsibility for initiating and administering the regula-
> tory program.... The department [of ecology] shall act

primarily in a supportive and review capacity with emphasis on
insuring compliance with the policies and provisions of this
chapter.[6]

Nevertheless, many state agencies in Washington other than the
Department of Ecology are involved in shoreline resources management. Coordination of their activities required the establishment
of a State Agency Advisory Committee for the Department and
passage of the state Environmental Coordination Procedures Act.

The Department of Ecology is the single agency designated responsible for coastal zone planning and implementation under the
federal Coastal Zone Management Act. Other state agencies also
have responsibilities in the coastal zone, however. The Departments of Fisheries, Natural Resources, and Parks and Recreation
have direct management responsibility for various coastal resources.
The Departments of Agriculture, Commerce and Economic Development, Highways, and Social and Health Services also carry out
activities that significantly affect the coastal zone. A State Agency
Advisory Committee helps the Department of Ecology coordinate
development plans of these state agencies in the state shoreline and
federal coastal zone management programs (Figure 18).

Various state agencies had statutory authority to regulate private
and public activities in the coastal zone before local governments
were given their own regulatory responsibilities under the Shoreline
Management Act. State statutes granting regulatory powers in the
coastal zone to state agencies include the following.

State Environmental Policy Act, 1971
(RCW 43.21c)

This state law was patterned after the National Environmental
Policy Act of 1969. It requires all Washington state agencies to
prepare environmental impact statements for proposed activities.
The law originally designated the Department of Ecology and the
Ecological Commission as the administering agency, but it was
later amended to establish the Council on Environmental Policy.
The Council is composed of the Pollution Control Hearings Board,
which is responsible for implementation of the Act. Environmental
impact review, pollution control, and shorelines management are

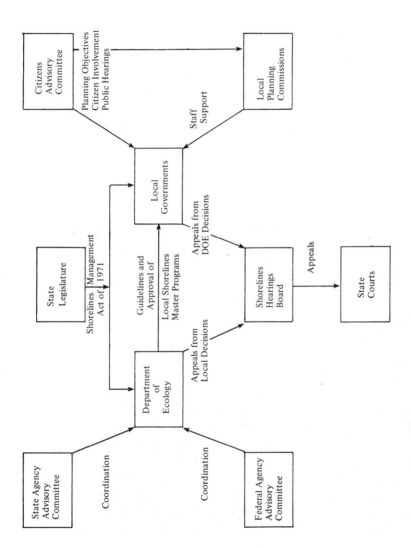

Figure 18. Washington Organizational Structure for Coastal Zone Management

related institutionally by common membership of the Pollution Control Hearings Board on both the Council on Environmental Policy and the Shorelines Hearings Board.

Thermal Power Plant Site Evaluation Council Act, 1970 (RCW 80.50)

This Council consists of designated state department and agency directors or administrators. It reviews applications for the siting of thermal power plants and recommends approval or rejection to the governor. Permits are issued only after final decision by the governor.

Forest Practices Act, 1974 (RCW 76.09)

The Act established a Forest Practices Board consisting of designated state agency heads and public members appointed by the governor. The Board promulgates rules and regulations governing the growing, harvesting, and processing of timber. The regulations are administered and enforced by the Department of Natural Resources.

Washington Clean Air Act, (RCW 70.94)

A state air pollution control program was first enacted in 1967. The State Air Pollution Control Board and the Department of Health were the responsible state agencies, but operational responsibility was vested in county air pollution control authorities. In 1970 the Department of Ecology was created and all of the powers and functions of the two state agencies were transferred to it. The Department of Ecology later adopted general regulations for air pollution sources as Chapter 18-04 of the Washington Administrative Code. County or multicounty air pollution control authorities operate within these state standards, but have their own boards, control officers, regulations, and administrative and appeals procedures as provided in the state Clean Air Act.

Water Pollution Control, (RCW 90-48)

Water pollution control is particularly important for coastal resources management because all the extensive water basins west of the divide of the Cascade Range drain into Washington's coastal waters. State legislation originally vested responsibility for pollution control to the state Water Pollution Control Commission. This responsibility was transfered to the Department of Ecology when it was created. This Department adopted state water quality standards as Chapter 173-201 of the Washington Administrative Code. It has also formulated annual strategies for implementing the federal water pollution abatement programs and the state water quality monitoring program.

**Environmental Coordination
Procedures Act, 1973**

This legislation was enacted to relieve the burden on developers caused by requirements to obtain numerous permits and related documents from various state and local agencies. The legislature also found that procedures for obtaining public views on proposed projects were cumbersome and thwarted public opportunity to make objections or to support proposals. The Act was intended to overcome these problems as well as to better inform developers about federal and state legal requirements for projects and give them a greater degree of certainty about action on their permit applications. The procedures established under the Act would also foster better coordination and understanding between state and local agencies in the administration of the various state programs relating to air, water, and land resources. Provisions of the Act and its implementing regulations will be discussed in the section on shorelands regulation.

DEFINITION OF COASTAL ZONE
BOUNDARIES

Shoreline Management Act Provisions

State law defines the Washington shorelines as consisting of:

1. *Shorelines:* all water areas of the state, including reservoirs, and their associated wetlands, except shorelines of statewide significance.

2. *Shorelines of statewide significance:* geographically defined reaches of the Pacific Ocean and Puget Sound shores to the seaward limit of state jurisdiction and certain bays, canals, and deltas; lakes with a surface area over 1,000 acres; natural rivers having a mean annual flow of 1,000 cubic feet per second, if they are west of the Cascade range, and 200 cubic feet per second if they are east of the divide.

3. *Lakes:* over 20 acres in area.

4. *Streams:* downstream from the point where mean annual flow is more than 20 cubic feet per second.

5. *Wetlands:* all lands extending 200 feet in all directions from the ordinary high water line of the shorelines, lakes, and streams defined above, as well as all marshes, bays, swamps, floodways, river deltas, and floodplains associated with tidewaters, lakes, and streams.[7]

There is a legal difference between the Washington definition of shorelines and the concept of the coastal zone in the federal Coastal Zone Management Act. The state definition is more comprehensive as it includes freshwater bodies. It also designates shorelines of statewide significance, but these do not include all coastal zone areas of particular concern to be identified under the federal Act. Areas of particular concern will be discussed in the section on the coastal management program.

To meet federal requirements for coastal zone boundary definition, the Washington coastal zone management program identifies two tiers. The first tier is defined in terms of direct and significant impact of land and water uses on coastal water. The boundary established by the Shoreline Management Act defines this first tier, which is considered sufficient to control the direct impacts of development, resource harvesting, and pollution. For federal purposes, the first tier boundary will stop at the limit of saltwater intrusion, which is defined as one part saltwater per thousand parts of freshwater.

Coastal planning, administration, and regulation require an intermediate second tier boundary. In Washington, this has been established as the eastern boundary of the 15 coastal counties. These counties and their municipalities on the shoreline have primary shoreline management responsibility under the Shoreline Management Act. The local governments also have land use planning and zoning authority and other development regulations to administer along with their shoreline master programs. A broader coastal boundary concept is required to take into account indirect impacts on coastal waters, those that come from freshwaters that drain into the coastal waters or from air that floats over them. The third tier is essentially the rest of the state, from which air and water changed by private and public activity may affect the coastal waters.[8]

REFERENCES

[1] Court decision as quoted in Susan F. Morry, *1970 Seacoast Management Bill: Background and Analysis,* Division of Marine Resources, University of Washington, Seattle (October 1971), p. 7 (mimeo).

[2] *Ibid.*

[3] Spencer, W.H. *Environmental Management for Puget Sound: Certain Problems of Political Organization and Alternative Approaches,* Division of Marine Resources, University of Washington, Seattle (November 1971), p. 33.

[4] *Ibid.*

[5] Washington Department of Ecology. *Final Guidelines: Shoreline Management Act of 1971,* Olympia (June 20, 1972), p. 1.

[6] "Revised Code of Washington," Section 90.58.050, 1971.

[7] "Revised Code of Washington," Section 90.58.030, 1971.

[8] Washington Department of Ecology, *Washington Coastal Zone Management Program,* pp. 25, 26, February 14, 1975.

CHAPTER XII

SHORELINE MASTER PROGRAMS

The Washington focus is on local governments as the primary source of coastal resources management programs. They are required to prepare master programs, which are comprehensive use plans for their shoreline jurisdictions, together with statements of development objectives, standards, and implementing regulations. These local programs, as has already been noted, were to be prepared in accordance with state guidelines adopted by the Department of Ecology.

The Washington approach to coastal management appears to be based on the premise that the state shorelines do not constitute a single ecologic or geomorphic system that can be planned for all in one piece. Conditions vary along different reaches of the shoreline, so the master programs are expected to reflect the unique shoreline and development requirements for each community. Local governments can identify local shoreline problems and seek solutions that will meet their own needs.

Nevertheless, there would appear to be a need for a state master program that embodies statewide concerns. The Shoreline Management Act does provide for a state master program, but defines it simply as "the cumulative total of all master programs approved or adopted by the Department of Ecology."[1] But is a state coastal management program just the sum of its local parts? Is there not some statewide view of objectives for coastal resources management that would be more comprehensive than the view from city hall or county court house? Are there perceived differences in the way shoreline resources should be managed and used by adjacent jurisdictions, so that local master program objectives and regulations could conflict with one another?

The Shoreline Management Act does provide ways of asserting state interests and resolving conflicts. These will be described in some detail later, but they may be noted here. First, the local master programs must be reviewed and approved by the Department of Ecology. If a master program is not considered satisfactory, the Department may itself prepare and adopt one for the local jurisdiction. Where adjacent municipalities share ecologic or geomorphic systems, the director of the Department may take the initiative in designating regions for the preparation of regional master programs that cover two or more jurisdictions. Then "it shall be the duty of the designated units to develop cooperatively an inventory and master program."[2] Moreover, the Shoreline Management Act designates by geographic description certain "shorelines of statewide significance," which must be given special consideration in local master programs. The federal Coastal Zone Management Act and its implementing regulations encourage states "to exercise their full authority over the lands and waters in the coastal zone" and to develop "unified policies, criteria, standards, methods, and processes for dealing with land and water use decisions of more than local significance."[3] Meeting federal requirements is, therefore, another incentive for the Department of Ecology to demonstrate to the federal authorities that the local master programs do reflect statewide objectives and unified policies.

MASTER PROGRAM CHARACTERISTICS

The state guidelines declare that for local master programs to retain their validity for a reasonable period in spite of changing conditions they should be general, comprehensive, and long-range. These characteristics are defined as follows:

> 'General' means that the policies, proposals and guidelines are not directed towards any specific sites.

> 'Comprehensive' means that the program is directed towards all land and water uses, their impact on the environment and logical estimates of future growth. It also means that the program shall recognize plans and programs of the other government units, adjacent jurisdictions and private developers.

'Long-range' means that the program is to be directed at least 20 to 30 years into the future, look beyond immediate issues, and follow creative objectives rather than a simple projection of current trends and conditions.[4]

SHORELINE INVENTORY

Local shoreline master programs are the essential elements of the Washington coastal zone management program. The information base for regulating land and water uses and managing coastal resources is the shoreline inventory of physical and biological characteristics and existing land use and ownership patterns. The Shoreline Management Act placed the burden of preparing inventories on the local governments and gave them 18 months to do it. One of the elements of the Department of Ecology package of guidelines for local governments was the Procedures for Shoreline Inventory.

The shoreline inventory guidelines presented a series of categories by which to classify segments of shoreline. There was no attempt to describe and analyze ecologic or geomorphic systems. The major categories to be used were: (a) existing land and water uses, (b) ownership, (c) river shorelines, (d) lake shorelines, (e) marine shorelines, (f) physical elements, (g) biota, (h) plans and programs for public works and private development.

The land and water use categories followed the traditional breakdown into classes of residential, commercial, industrial, agricultural, and public uses. Shoreline land ownership categories were concerned with identifying parcels owned by the various levels of government, and they distinguished private lands as small parcels with less than 1000 feet of water frontage and large parcels with frontage of more than 1000 feet.

River shorelines were categorized into four zones. These were required to be applied to rivers of statewide significance, but were suggested for inventory of shorelines of lesser streams as well:

Zone I   —   Estuarine Zone—negligible gradient, branched stream course, bed material composed of silts and mud;

Zone II — Pastoral Zone—gradient less than five feet per mile, meandering stream course, bed material composed of sand and silt;

Zone III — Floodway Zone—gradient between five and 25 feet per mile, braided stream course, bed material composed of sand and gravel;

Zone IV — Boulder Zone—gradient greater than 25 feet per mile, fixed stream course, bed material composed of cobbles and boulders.[5]

Lake and marine shorelines were classified as natural or modified by seawalls, bulkheads, or other protective works. Natural shorelines were further classified according to the type of beach or bank, or whether they were swamp (freshwater) or marsh (saltwater). Physical elements of the shorelines to be mapped and described were: (a) topography, (b) soil characteristics, (c) beach characteristics, (d) mineral resources, (e) shore defense works, and (f) water level fluctuation.

Shoreline biota were to be categorized according to the types of plants and animals present. Maps of vegetation should show homogeneous upland areas of forest (deciduous or evergreen), marsh grass, shrubs, grasslands, or the various proportions of these types present in areas of mixed vegetation. Major wildlife species and populations of mammals, birds, fish and shellfish, reptiles, and amphibians were also to be described.

It should be pointed out that the Department of Ecology guidelines require the shoreline inventory to be carried out with a focus on the narrow 200-foot strip abutting marine shores, lakes, and rivers, and the associated wetlands, that the Shoreline Management Act legally defines as the state shoreline. The guidelines suggest that "consideration should also be given to including those land use facilities and activities lying outside of the 200-foot wetland zone if it appears that those uses have or may have a direct impact on the shoreline area."[6] Conversely, the area inventoried might include lands outside the 200-foot strip that might be affected by development within the official shoreland zone. Federal lands are not formally required to be inventoried either, but the guidelines suggest that information about them be obtained where federal developments might have an impact on state shorelines.

MASTER PROGRAM ELEMENTS

The Shoreline Management Act provided a detailed description of the content of local master programs. They were to contain the following elements:

1. An economic development element for the location and design of industries, transportation facilities, port facilities, tourist facilities, commerce and other developments that are particularly dependent on their location on or use of the shorelines of the state;

2. A public access element making provision for public access to publicly owned areas;

3. A recreational element for the preservation and enlargement of recreational opportunities, including but not limited to parks, tidelands, beaches, and recreational areas;

4. A circulation element consisting of the general location and extent of existing and proposed major thoroughfares, transportation routes, terminals, and other public utilities and facilities, all correlated with the shoreline use element;

5. A use element which considers the proposed general distribution and general location and extent of the use on shorelines and adjacent land areas for housing, business, industry, transportation, agriculture, natural resources, recreation, education, public buildings and grounds, and other categories of public and private uses of the land;

6. A conservation element for the preservation of natural resources, including but not limited to scenic vistas, esthetics, and vital estuarine areas for fisheries and wildlife protection; and

7. An historic, cultural, scientific and educational element for the protection and restoration of buildings, sites, and areas having historic, cultural, scientific, or educational values.[7]

CLASSIFICATION OF ENVIRONMENTS

The Department of Ecology guidelines offer detailed criteria that may be applied in preparing each of these master program elements. Economic development, public access, transportation, recreation, land uses, and conservation activities and facilities should be located and designed to be compatible with the particular shoreline environments that exist within each planning jurisdiction. Five broad categories of shoreline environment are defined as: (a) natural, (b) conservancy, (c) rural, (d) urban, and (e) shorelines of statewide significance. The last are specifically identified in the Shoreline Management Act. By classifying shorelines this way, policies and use regulations may be applied uniformly by all local governments.

> To accomplish this, the environmental designation to be given
> any specific area is to be based on the existing development
> pattern, the biophysical capabilities and limitations of the
> shoreline being considered for development, and the goals
> and aspirations of local citizenry.[8]

The state objective in putting forward these categories is to encourage uses in each type of environment that enhance its character; at the same time, local governments may formulate development standards to prevent degradation of that character. Here the Washington approach to coastal management is somewhat different from the federal legislation and regulations. The federal rules ask for the designation of permissible uses in the coastal zone and the specific geographic areas where different permissible uses may be located. The Washington guidelines suggest performance standards that will achieve locally defined environmental goals rather than exclude any particular use from any one environment.

These broad environmental categories are not meant as substitutes for local zoning and land use regulation. These are "umbrella" categories, within which detailed planning and zoning regulations may be formulated. Local planners are to classify their shorelines on the basis of inventories of resources that would help to identify those attributes that determine opportunities and limitations for development. The guidelines also address an important planning question, which is how management of shoreline resources is to be related to policies, plans, and regulations for adjacent lands and the entire area in the governmental jurisdiction. The Shoreline Management Act provides a specific directive in this regard:

> All state agencies, counties, and public and municipal corporations
> shall review administrative and management policies, regulations,
> plans, and ordinances relative to lands under their respective
> jurisdictions adjacent to the shorelines of the state so as to achieve

a use policy on said land consistent with the policy of this chapter, the guidelines, and the master programs for the shorelines of the state.[9]

Finally, classification of shoreline environments should consider local values and development objectives as determined through the process of citizen involvement.

Natural Environment

This category should be applied to shoreline reaches that are relatively free from human influence and where the objective would be to preserve and restore the natural systems. Regulation should be concerned with preserving the characteristics that make the areas unique and valuable by imposing restrictions on types and intensities of use.

Conservancy Environment

This category is appropriate for areas where the regulatory objective would be to "protect, conserve, and manage existing natural resources and valuable historic and cultural areas to ensure a continuous flow of recreational benefits to the public and to achieve sustained resource utilization."[10] Preferred uses are those that can maintain a sustained yield of existing natural resources and would not preclude opportunities for future use of these resources. Conservancy areas would also be characterized by severe limitations on development, such as steep slopes with erosion or slide hazards, flood-prone areas, and sites that cannot provide adequate water supply or sewage disposal.

Rural Environment.

Designation of an area as a rural environment would tend to protect prime farming lands from urban expansion and contain sprawling development by maintaining open space buffers between urban areas. New development would be regulated to limit residential density, retain permanent open space, and require adequate setbacks from waterfronts to conserve the shoreline. Public recreation facilities should be located and designed to minimize conflict with agriculture. Farm management practices should be encouraged that would prevent erosion and subsequent siltation of water bodies and minimize the flow of polluting wastes and chemicals into water courses.

Urban Environment.

This category is for areas of high-intensity land use, where there is pressure for intensification of residential, industrial, or commercial development; it is also for areas planned to accommodate future urban expansion. Regulations should encourage development to take place within areas already urbanized and give priority for industrial and commercial sites to uses that depend on waterfront locations. Master programs should also provide for public access to the waterfront in intensively developed urban areas.

Shorelines of Statewide Significance

Designation of these shorelines is made by the state legislature, and their descriptions are included in the Shoreline Management Act. As they benefit people in the entire state, local master programs must give preference to uses on these shorelines that favor public and long-range goals. The Act specifies the following order of priorities for uses on shorelines of statewide significance. Preferred uses:

1. Recognize and protect the statewide interest over local interest;
2. Preserve the natural character of the shoreline;
3. Result in long-term over short-term benefit;
4. Protect the resources and ecology of the shoreline;
5. Increase the public access to publicly owned areas of the shorelines; and
6. Increase recreational opportunities for the public on the shorelines.

These priorities are set forth in the legislative findings in the Act
and are elaborated in the Department of Ecology guidelines. The
legislative findings also state these policies for use of shorelines of
statewide significance:

> Uses shall be preferred which are consistent with control of pollu-
> tion and prevention of damage to the natural environment or are
> unique to or dependent upon use of the state's shoreline. Alter-
> ations of the natural condition of the shorelines of the state, in
> those limited instances when authorized, shall be given priority
> for single-family residences, ports, shoreline recreational uses
> including but not limited to parks, marinas, piers, and other im-
> provements facilitating public access to shorelines of the state,
> industrial and commercial developments which are particularly
> dependent on their location on or use of the shorelines.[11]

NATURAL SYSTEMS

A section of the Department of Ecology guidelines is devoted to
general descriptions of various natural areas along Washington shorelines. It is intended to help local governments in the preparation
of shoreline master programs. The master programs will designate
particular shoreline areas for various uses and regulate public and
private activities on them. Therefore, the guidelines pay particular
attention to those natural systems that are susceptible to damage
from development. The shoreline systems described are:

Marine beaches
    Sandy beaches
    Rocky beaches
    Muddy shores
Spits and bars
Dunes
    Primary dunes
    Secondary dunes
    Back dunes
Islands
Estuaries
Marshes, bogs, and swamps

Lakes
Rivers, streams, and creeks
Flood plains
Puget Sound
Pacific Ocean[12]

Local government decision-makers, who will be responsible for
policies incorporated in shoreline master programs, will be laymen
elected to local governing bodies and citizen advisory committees.
Some of these people are knowledgeable about shoreline biophysi-
cal systems and processes and their values for food production,
recreation, and ecosystem maintenance. Others regard some of
these natural areas simply as wastelands to be exploited for the
economic benefit of property owners or business. Such decision-
makers need orientation to shoreline environmental processes and
values.

USE ACTIVITIES

Local shoreline master programs designate areas for various kinds
of uses and regulate the manner in which these uses may be carried
on and the way in which the buildings and facilities necessary for
them may be located and constructed. The Department of Ecology
guidelines provide a general description of various classes of uses
and suggest criteria on which regulations for these uses may be
based. Particular attention is paid to the destructive effects of permitted uses on existing natural systems. In developing master
programs,

> ... local government should identify the type or types of natural
> systems ... within which a use is proposed and should impose
> regulations on those developments and uses which would tend to
> affect adversely the natural characteristics needed to preserve the
> integrity of the system. Examples would include but would not
> be limited to proposed uses that would threaten the character of
> fragile dune areas, reduce water tables in marshes, impede water
> flow in estuaries, or threaten the stability of spits and bars.[13]

These guidelines recognize that there must be some flexibility in
their application to local master program development and the

processing of permit applications. Nevertheless, they do specify parameters for planning, regulation, and environmental protection. Master programs must be approved by the Department of Ecology, which scrutinizes all development permits granted in the shorelines of the state. The guidelines provide criteria for planning and regulating these categories of land and water use: agriculture, aquaculture, forest management, commercial development, marinas, mining, outdoor advertising, signs, and billboards, residential development, utilities, ports and water-related industry, bulkheads, breakwaters, jetties and groins, landfill, solid waste disposal, dredging, shoreline protection, road and railroad design and protection, piers, archaeological areas and historic sites, and recreation.

TIME SCHEDULES AND DEADLINES

Washington state law does not limit itself to general instructions; it imposes a timetable. And local governments were not given a choice of planning for shoreline management; the law mandated it. June 1, 1971 was established as the starting time for state and local action.

State Guidelines

The Department of Ecology had four months to prepare and circulate master program guidelines to local governments. The latter were to send the Department written comments on the draft guidelines within two months. Four months later proposed final guidelines were to be completed, public hearings were to be held two months thereafter, and final guidelines were to be adopted by the Department three months after that. This whole procedure was to be accomplished in 15 months, or by August 31, 1972. The Department beat the deadline by almost three months, for the final guidelines were adopted on June 20, 1972.

Local Master Programs

Local governments were to complete comprehensive inventories of their shorelines within 18 months, or by November 30, 1972, and complete their shoreline master programs within 24 months after the adoption of the state guidelines, at the end of June 1974. In any case, by November 30, 1971, local governments were to submit to the Department of Ecology letters of intent to complete shorelines inventories and master programs within the legal deadlines.

Because the Shoreline Management Act was to be implemented, in effect, by local governments, the law required that if any of them failed to submit letters of intent or to adopt shoreline master programs within the mandated time frame, then the Department of Ecology would do it for them.14

Thus the legislated shorelines management program in Washington was to be essentially complete by the latter part of 1974. Most other states would have waited until the federal Coastal Zone Management Act of 1972 made grants available before initiating coastal zone programs; and it would be several years thereafter before their programs would be ready for submission to the Office for Coastal Zone Management. Nevertheless, in spite of legislative intent and its early start, the Washington coastal zone program had not received federal approval at the time this is being written, in April 1976.

To prepare such comprehensive master programs, local governments were required by law to inventory their shoreline resources within 18 months after the Shoreline Management Act was passed in 1971. Master programs would also require detailed and accurate analyses of the local population and economic structures as well as future changes. Economic-demographic forecasts are difficult to make for small areas, especially those affected by external influences at the metropolitan, regional, national, or even international scale. Comprehensive area analysis and planning at the scope and detail specified in the Act is costly and requires personnel that are expert and sophisticated in the various scientific and technical fields from which information must be drawn. It is not likely that most local governments would have available the necessary financial and personnel resources. Having imposed the legal requirement that localities must assume primary responsibility for coastal management, it would appear incumbent upon the state to make the necessary resources available. The state has, in fact, accepted half of this responsibility. Matching grants are to be made available by the Department of Ecology from state appropriations upon application by the local governments.[15]

PUBLIC PARTICIPATION

The Shoreline Management Act enjoins the Department of Ecology and local governments "to insure that all persons and entities having an interest in the guidelines and master programs . . . are provided with a full opportunity for involvement in both their development and implementation." DOE and local governments are to "make reasonable efforts to inform the people of the state about the shoreline management program . . . [and] shall not only invite but actively encourage participation by all persons and private groups and entities, showing an interest in shoreline management programs."[16]

The law requires that at least one public hearing be held in each county affected by a master program before it may be approved by the Department of Ecology. The Department guidelines go further and insist that the general public must be involved early in the process of planning for and formulating the master program.

> The extent of citizen involvement in the formulation of the master program will be considered by the department in the review of the program. A failure by the local government to encourage and utilize citizen involvement, or to justify not having done so, may be noted as a failure to comply with the Act.[17]

The Department guidelines do not specify a method for public participation, but encourage local governments to follow detailed suggestions. The first step would be to establish a citizen advisory committee to represent business as well as environmentalists. Existence of the committee alone is not evidence of public participation; its main function would be to encourage broad citizen involvement by holding a series of evening meetings and at least one public hearing. The guidelines suggest there should be at least three evening meetings, for which there should be advance notice,

free discussion, and resource persons from the local government to
provide information about coastal resources management. The
advisory committee, in cooperation with the local government,
should publish a newsletter about activities in connection with
development of the master program and also take advantage of
radio, television, and newspapers to publicize the program.

The committee would hold a formal public hearing after at least
three evening information meetings. The method of public notice
is specified in the guidelines, and the proposed master program
should be available for public inspection at the local government
offices. But publicity, evening information meetings, and a formal
hearing would not satisfy all the requirements of the guidelines.
They also want evidence of public agreement on the master
program.

> Prior to adoption of the master program, all reasonable attempts
> should have been made to obtain a general concurrence of the
> public and the advisory committee. The method of obtaining or
> measuring concurrence must be established by the local govern-
> ment and must provide a clear indication of how citizen input
> is utilized.

> If the level of concurrence on the master program is not consid-
> ered adequate by the advisory committee at the conclusion of
> the public hearing, the local government should hold subsequent
> public meetings and public hearings until such time as adequate
> concurrence . . . is reached.[18]

When it examines local master programs submitted for approval,
the Department of Ecology will review the written record of public
meetings and citizen involvement and how local concurrence on
the program was measured. Public participation was also to have
a specific impact on the master program document. This would
take the form of a statement of policies regarding shoreline development, which would provide a foundation for developing shoreline
use regulations and relating them to the goals identified by the
citizen involvement process.

> In summary, the policy statements must reflect the intent of the
> [Shorelines Management] Act, the goals of the local citizens, and
> specifically relate the shoreline management goals to the master
> program use regulations.[19]

REFERENCES

[1] Revised Code of Washington, Section 90.58.030 (3) (c), 1971.

[2] Revised Code of Washington, Section 90.58.110, 1971.

[3] *Coastal Zone Management Act of 1972*, Section 302(h).

[4] Washington Administrative Code, 173-16-040, 1972.

[5] Washington Department of Ecology. *Procedures for Shoreline Inventory: Shoreline Management Act of 1971*, February 29, 1972, p. 5.

[6] *Ibid.*, p. 1.

[7] Revised Code of Washington, Section 90.58.100, 1971.

[8] Washington Administrative Code, 173-16-040 (4), 1972.

[9] Revised Code of Washington, Section 90.58.340, 1971.

[10] Washington Administrative Code, 173-16-040 (4), 1972.

[11] Revised Code of Washington, Section 90.58.010, 1971.

[12] Washington Administrative Code, 173-16-050, 1972.

[13] Washington Administrative Code, 173-16-060, 1972.

[14] Revised Code of Washington, Section 90.58.070 and 90.58.080, 1971.

[15] Revised Code of Washington, Section 90.58.250, 1971.

[16] Revised Code of Washington, Section 90.58.130, 1971.

[17] Washington Administrative Code, 173-16-040 (1), 1972.

[18] *Ibid.*

[19] Washington Administrative Code, 173-16-040 (2), 1972.

CHAPTER XIII

SHORELINES REGULATION

After approval or adoption by the Department of Ecology, local master programs constitute use regulations for the shoreline within the jurisdictions covered by them. Permit systems are developed to implement the regulations. By a requirement of the Shoreline Management Act, they would allow for conditional uses or variances "only if extraordinary circumstances are shown and the public interest shows no substantial detrimental effect."[1]

STATE GUIDELINES

The Department of Ecology guidelines for preparing local shoreline master programs include a section on conditional uses and variances, WAC (Washington Administrative Code) 173-16-070, which will be discussed later in this section. The WAC was also amended to include sections concerning permitting procedures: WAC 173-14-010 to 120.

The permit procedure guidelines define "substantial development" following provisions of the Shoreline Management Act, establish exemptions from permits for developments started before the effective date of the Act, and give deadlines for starting and completion of projects before permits expire. They also give procedures and forms for notice, applications, and permits.

The applicant is required by the guidelines to publish notices that the application has been made, at least once a week for two weeks in a newspaper of general circulation within the county in which the development is proposed. Interested parties have 30 days after final publication of the notice to make their views on the application known to the appropriate local government. Local governments may, if they wish, establish a mandatory or optional public hearing procedure that would come before the decision on whether to issue or deny the permit. Both the application and the local ruling on it must be sent to both the Department of Ecology and the Office of Attorney General.

DEFINITION OF SUBSTANTIAL DEVELOPMENT

The legal definition of development is crucial to an understanding of the Washington approach to regulating uses in the coastal zone. Development is defined as any construction, dredging, drilling, or mining that interferes with normal public use of the surface waters and underlying lands designated as shorelands of the state. Nevertheless, not all development is subject to regulation. Only "substantial development," whose cost or market value is over $1000 or that materially interferes with normal public use of state waters or shorelines, is regulated. This is not as stringent as it seems, for not included in the definition of substantial development, and therefore excluded from regulation, are the following classes of projects that would require special permits in most other state coastal zones:

1. Construction on wetlands by an owner, or lessee, of a single-family residence for his own use that is not more than 35 feet above average grade level.
2. Construction of a barn or other similar structure on wetlands.
3. Construction of a dock for pleasure craft and noncommercial use by a property owner or lessee that does not cost more than $2500.
4. Construction of protective bulkheads for single-family residences.
5. Normal maintenance of existing development or emergency measures to protect property from damage by the elements.
6. Construction of navigational aids.[2]

DEVELOPMENT PERMITS

Development on the shorelines of the state is permitted by law only after local master programs have been approved by the Department of Ecology, but in any case, it must be consistent with the objectives and policies stated in the legislative findings in the Shoreline Management Act. Once their master programs have been approved, local governments establish programs for the administration and enforcement of permit systems to implement them. These permit systems must be consistent with Department of Ecology guidelines; but once established, local governments have exclusive authority over development decision.[3] The Department of Ecology has no power to intervene in local shoreline permit procedures or decisions. If DOE believes a permit was granted that was inconsistent with state policy or not authorized by law, its only recourse is to appeal within 30 days to the Shorelines Hearings Board. This puts the Department in the same position as any private person aggrieved by a local permit decision. The Department can review all permit rulings, however, for they must not only be communicated to the applicant, they must also be filed with the Department of Ecology and the attorney general.

The applicant must prove that the proposed "substantial" development is consistent with state and local criteria for alteration of the shoreline. Appellants for review of permit decisions likewise have the burden of proof, not the state or local agencies. Local governments may rescind a permit if the developer has not complied with its conditions. If the Department of Ecology finds that a developer is violating permit conditions, it can intervene only by an appeal to the Shorelines Hearings Board, after written notice to the developer and the local government. There is, however, one exception to the exclusive authority of local governments over shoreline development permits. Applications for a variance or conditional use must be submitted to the Department of Ecology for approval or disapproval before the local government may act.[4]

CONDITIONAL USES AND VARIANCES

It has already been noted that local master programs must provide for conditional uses and variances. These are regulatory safety valves that assure that owners may use their property in a reasonable manner while protecting the public interest in environmental values.

Conditional Uses

Specified in master programs, these are permitted only after special consideration by the local government and by meeting explicit performance standards so that the conditional uses will be compatible with other permitted uses in the same area.

Conditional use permits will be granted only after the applicant can demonstrate all of the following:

1. The use will cause no unreasonably adverse effects on the environment or other uses.
2. The use will not interfere with public use of public shorelines.
3. Design of the site will be compatible with the surroundings and the master programs.
4. The proposed use will not be contrary to the general intent of the master program.[5]

Variances

These are quite different from conditional uses. The latter are permitted in specific areas by master programs if they meet certain performance standards. Variances, however, are permits to do what is otherwise prohibited by master programs. The rationale for such departures from the strict application of the regulations is that property owners cannot make any reasonable use of their property, and therefore suffer practical difficulties or unnecessary hardship. Hardship does not mean that property owners could make more money by using the property in a manner not permitted by the master program.

A variance will be granted only after the applicant can demonstrate the following:

1. The hardship which serves as the basis for granting of variance is specifically related to the property of the applicant.
2. The hardship results from the application of the requirements of the Act and master program and not from, for example, deed restrictions or the applicant's own actions.
3. The variance granted will be in harmony with the general purpose and intent of the master program.
4. Public welfare and interest will be preserved; if more harm will be done to the area by granting the variance than would be done to the applicant by denying it, the variance will be denied.[6]

SHORELINES HEARINGS BOARD

The six-member Shorelines Hearings Board is established as a quasi-judicial body. Three of its members are to be members of the State Pollution Control Hearings Board, and the chairman of that board is also to be chairman of the Shorelines Appeals Board. One member is to be appointed by the Association of Washington Cities, and another by the Association of County Commissioners. The sixth member is the state land commissioner or his designee. Final decisions by the Shorelines Hearings Board require agreement by at least four members.[7]

The Board has considerable power, for it must arbitrate all disagreements between state and local governments, as well as between applicants and objectors, with regard to shoreline management. Persons who feel aggrieved by the issuance, denial, or rescinding of a permit may appeal for review of the local decision within 30 days, with copies to the Department of Ecology and the office of the attorney general. These agencies, however, may veto the requested review by the Board, if they do not both support it.

> If it appears to the Department or the attorney general that the requestor has valid reasons to seek review, either the Department or the attorney general may certify the request within 30 days after its receipt to the Shorelines Hearings Board following which the Board shall then, but not otherwise, review the matter.[8]

Nevertheless, even if such a veto is exercised, the appellant may go directly to the Superior court for review of the local permit decision. The Department and the attorney general may intervene in the court proceeding, however, to protect the public interest and insure compliance with state shoreline policies.

It has already been noted that the Department of Ecology and the attorney general must voice any objections they may have to a local permit decision by appealing to the Shorelines Hearings Board. Local governments may, in turn, appeal to the Board for review of any rules, regulations, guidelines, or determinations by the Department of Ecology; and they may also object to decisions by the Department to approve or disapprove a shoreline master program. The Hearings Board makes final decisions in disputes about the validity of local master programs, but these determinations, as well as the Board's decisions on rules, regulations and guidelines, are subject to review by the Superior Court.

It might be expected that the Shorelines Hearings Board would accumulate a heavy docket of requests for reviews of local or state agency decisions. Administrative and clerical assistance in handling its cases is provided by the staff of the Pollution Control Hearings Board. Nevertheless, the Board would seem also to require technical assistance in evaluating permit decisions or the validity of master programs. No provision for such assistance is made in the Shoreline Management Act.

ENFORCEMENT

The Shoreline Management Act is to be enforced by legal action, at the request of state and local agencies or on their own initiative, by the state attorney general or by attorneys for local governments. They may bring "such injunctive, declaratory, or other actions as are necessary to insure that no uses are made of the shorelines of the state in conflict with the provisions and programs" of the Act.[9]

Violators of state law or of local master programs, rules or regulations may incur civil liabilities and may be judged guilty of a gross misdemeanor, which is punishable by fine, imprisonment or both. Violators may be liable for damage to public or private property resulting from their actions and may also be required to pay the cost of restoring the affected area to its condition prior to the violation.

ENVIRONMENTAL PERMIT COORDINATION

The Environmental Coordination Procedures Act of 1973 established an optional system for centralized handling of permit applications and hearings. The system was to be developed by the
Department of Ecology in cooperation with other state agencies
that have environmental regulatory programs and with local governments, which regulate land and water uses according to their
shoreline master programs. The regulations adopted by the Department of Ecology to implement the Act list the agencies and permit
programs involved:[10]

Department of Natural Resources
Burning permits	RCW 76.04.150 and 170
Dumping permits on forest lands	RCW 76.04.242
Operating permit for machinery	RCW 76.04.275
Cutting permit	RCW 76.08.030
Surface mine reclamation permit	RCW 78.44.080
Right-of-way clearing	RCW 76.04.310
Drilling permit	RCW 78.52.120
Log patrol license	RCW 76.40.030

Regional Air Pollution Control Authorities
New source construction approval	RCW 70.94.152
Burning permit	RCW 70.94.650
Burning of field and turf grown for seed	RCW 70.94.650

Incorporated Cities and Counties
Substantial development permit (shoreline management permit)	RCW 90.58.140

Department of Ecology
Surface water rights permit	RCW 90.03.250
Dam safety approval	RCW 90.03.350
Reservoir permit	RCW 90.03.370
Approval of change of place or purpose of use or point of diversion—surface water code	RCW 90.03.380
Groundwater code	RCW 90.44.100
Groundwater permit	RCW 90.44.050

New source construction—approval	RCW 90.94.152
Burning of field and turf grasses grown from seed	RCW 70.94.650
Flood control zone permit	RCW 86.16.080
Waste discharge permit	RCW 90.48.180
National Pollution Discharge Elimination System permit	WAC 173-220
Sewage and industrial waste treatment facilities approval	RCW 90.48.110
Weather modification permit	RCW 43.37.110

Department of Fisheries

Hydraulic project approval	RCW 75.20.100
Salmon aquaculture permit	RCW 75.16.100

Department of Parks and Recreation

Park and recreation facilities	RCW 90.08.260
Safe and adequate facilities and equipment	RCW 70.88.010
Permits for improvement of parks	RCW 43.51.130

Department of Game

Hydraulic project approval	RCW 75.20.100

Department of Social and Health Services

Public sewage	WAC 248-92
Public water supplies	WAC 248-54

The coordinated permit procedures system provides a single place where developers may obtain permit forms, submit them after completion, and receive the results of permit reviews. Some projects require more than one of the permits listed above, and in some cases permit applications for the same project must be reviewed by more than one agency. The system is optional, however, and the developer may apply to each agency separately instead of using the master application procedure.

The developer may begin the master application procedure by obtaining a master application form from the Department of Ecology main office in Olympia, from one of the Department's regional offices, or from a county master application office. Completed forms may be filed at any of these offices, but they are all forwarded to the Department of Ecology Master Application Center in Olympia. A completed master application form must be accompanied, however, by a certification from the local government that the proposal complies with all zoning ordinances and associated comprehensive plans. The local certification must include a statement as to whether the project falls within the jurisdiction of the Shoreline Management Act.[11]

Copies of the master application form are forwarded from the DOE Master Application Center to all participating agencies. The agencies must respond within 15 days as to whether they have an interest in the project, a permit application should be filed with them, or a public hearing held. The Master Application Center then notifies the applicant of the permit requirements of the various agencies, and provides appropriate blank application forms. Completed forms and appropriate application fees are returned to the Center and forwarded to the agencies concerned. At the same time DOE prepares a notice of application, which the applicants must publish at their own expense for three successive weeks in accordance with prescribed procedures. The Master Application Center or any agency reviewing a master application may call for a public hearing. The applicant, the public, and interested agencies may all be heard. The hearing officer conducts formal proceedings and then establishes the date by which all state agencies must forward their final decisions on the applications to the Department of Ecology. These decisions must give reasons for the determination reached and include a final order granting the permit or denying it, possibly subject to conditions that the agency may have power to impose. The DOE Master Application Center then incorporates these final decisions into one document and forwards it to the applicant. Applicants who wish to contest permit denials have access to appropriate appeals boards or the state courts.

REFERENCES

[1] Revised Code of Washington, Section 90.58.100, 1971.

[2] Revised Code of Washington, Section 90.58.030, 1971.

[3] Revised Code of Washington, Section 90.58.140, 1971.

[4] *Ibid.*

[5] Washington Administrative Code, 173–16–070 (1), 1972.

[6] Washington Administrative Code, 173–16–070 (2), 1972.

[7]Revised Code of Washington, Section 90.58.170, 1971.

[8]Revised Code of Washington, Section 90.58.180, 1971.

[9]Revised Code of Washington, Section 90.58.220, 1971.

[10]Washington Administrative Code, 173–08–030, 1972.

[11]Washington Administrative Code, 173–08–060, 1972.

CHAPTER XIV

COASTAL MANAGEMENT PROGRAM

According to federal requirements, state coastal zone management programs should: (a) define coastal zone boundaries, (b) identify permissible land and water uses that have direct and significant impact on coastal waters, (c) delineate areas of particular concern, (d) contain priorities for land and water uses, (e) designate coastal areas for preservation and restoration, and (g) accommodate local regulations to uses of regional benefit. Coastal zone boundaries and the permitting system have been discussed in previous sections, but they do not discuss the Washington approach to determining permissible land and water uses in the coastal zone.

PERMISSIBLE LAND AND WATER USES

The federal Coastal Zone Management Act requires states to identify land and water uses that would have a direct and significant impact on coastal waters, and then determine which of those uses would be permissible. After an elaborate attempt to conceptualize these requirements, Washington's coastal zone management program defines as having direct and significant impact "all development along the shorelines as governed by the Shoreline Management Act."[1] It then goes further and declares that implementation of the state Act by Department of Ecology guidelines and supervision and by local preparation of shoreline master programs provides the procedural and technical basis for determining which land and water uses are permissible.

It may be of general interest to follow the Washington attempt to explore the meaning of the phrase "direct and significant impact."

> It seems, from the Coastal Zone Management Act and its offspring regulations, that the substance seawater forms the basis for an operational definition of direct and significant impact on the coastal waters. If any of the characteristics of seawater, specifically the seawater of Washington state, are altered then an impact has occurred. Significant impact would have to be related to the degree of the impact, its relative permanency. So, a 'land or water use having a direct and significant impact on the coastal waters' is 'an activity caused by man, to which is clearly traceable a permanent alteration in the character of the seawaters of the state.'
>
> 'Permanent' means that the alteration will not be erased by natural causes in a reasonable amount of time.
>
> 'Alteration' means a change in any of the following characteristics of seawater: chemical properties, depth, currents, tides, surface area, color, temperature, odor, sediment load, fresh-to-saltwater ratio, bottom configuration, and patterns of movement.[2]

The determination of permissible uses is not made at the state level. There is no official list of permissible uses in the state coastal zone management program. Permissible and prohibited uses on Washington shorelines are determined by each local government or regional combination after coastal inventory, planning, public participation and hearings, and state review. Such determinations are included in each shoreline master program.

AREAS OF PARTICULAR CONCERN

Although there is no statewide map of coastal areas of particular concern, such areas are designated in connection with a variety of state and local activities. From the Washington point of view, the entire coastal zone is an area of particular concern. This concern extends to all government levels.

> Within the zone there are certain areas of particular concern to the state as a whole and worthy of state intervention. And, also within the zone are areas of particular concern to the local

intervention supported by the state. Finally, the zone contains areas of particular concern to federal agencies and worthy of state cooperation with federal agencies in the management and maintenance of such areas.[3]

In the Shoreline Management Act, the state legislature designated by name and geographic description "shorelines of statewide significance" as areas of particular concern. Data for more detailed designations of such areas are being compiled in the preparation of coastal inventories by local governments, the Department of Natural Resources, the Oceanographic Commission of Washington, and the Department of Ecology. These provide the basic information for the preparation of local shoreline master programs. According to DOE guidelines, shorelines must be identified in one of four different environment categories: (a) natural, (b) conservancy, (c) rural, or (d) urban. Each of these environments is considered to be of special concern, and the objective of shoreline master programs is to maintain their environmental values and, where appropriate, guide development to be in harmony with them. Areas placed in "natural" environment designations are recognized as having unique features, such as physical instability or ecologic fragility, historical significance, or extreme natural systemic importance. As master programs are further refined, more detailed designation of areas of particular concern will be made.

PRIORITY OF USES

The Shoreline Management Act has established general priorities for use of the state coastal zone:

> Uses shall be preferred which are consistent with control of pollution and prevention of damage to the natural environment or are unique to or dependent upon use of the state's shoreline. Alteration of the natural condition of the shorelines of the state, in those limited instances when authorized, shall be given priority for single-family residences, ports, shoreline recreational uses including but not limited to parks, marinas, piers, and other improvements facilitating public access to shorelines of the state, industrial and commercial developments which are particularly dependent on their location on or use of the shorelines of the

state and other development that will provide an opportunity for substantial numbers of the people to enjoy the shorelines of the state.[4]

This state legislation is supplemented by Department of Ecology guidelines for the preparation of local shoreline master programs. It has been repeatedly noted that the guidelines direct local governments to classify shorelands into one of four categories of environments and the special class of shorelines of statewide significance. The guidelines designate use priorities for each type of environment, and the shoreline master programs apply these in their detailed regulations.

Natural Environment

Priorities are to preserve and restore the natural environment. The main emphasis of regulation in these areas should be on severe restriction of intensities and types of use, to maintain the environment in its natural state.

Conservancy Environment

Preferred uses are those that can use environmental resources on a sustained yield basis. Activities and uses of a nonpermanent nature that do not substantially degrade the existing character of the area are appropriate.

Rural Environment

This type is for active agriculture and intensive recreational development. New developments should be of limited residential density, provide permanent open space, and maintain building setbacks from the shoreline adequate to avoid destroying it. Public recreation facilities that can be located and designed to minimize conflicts with agricultural activities are recommended.

Urban Environment

The objective in these areas is to ensure optimum use of shore-lines in urban areas by providing for high-intensity residential, commercial, and industrial development. Emphasis should be given to water-dependent industrial and commercial uses requiring frontage on navigable waters. Priority should also be given to planning for public visual and physical access to water.[5]

NATIONAL INTEREST IN THE SITING OF FACILITIES

The Washington coastal zone management program notes that the state's coastal zone "provides a significant amount of resources to meet state, national, and regional needs for recreation, food, military installations, petroleum refining, export and import facilities, and maintenance of essential natural systems."[6] Guidance is sought from federal agencies about their needs for sites, but the state cannot adequately program for them until the federal agencies themselves have formulated their own requirements. Meanwhile, a task force has been established to provide federal review of local shoreline master programs.

The Navy already has nearly two dozen bases, installations, and operating areas in the state coastal zone. There are also many national parks and monuments. An important element of the national interest is power generation to meet increasing demand for energy. In creating the Thermal Power Plant Site Evaluation Council, the state legislature established a special process for evaluating power plant sites. It provides for hearings and the consideration of all interests in power plants and guarantees appropriate sites, design, and operation.

AREA DESIGNATION FOR PRESERVATION AND RESTORATION

The state Departments of Fisheries and Game already acquire, preserve, and restore areas in the coastal zone as part of their ongoing programs. In addition, local shoreline master programs designate "natural environment" areas, according to state guidelines, which are to be protected in their natural state or preserved and restored. However, coordination of state activities, mapping of areas for preservation and restoration, and establishment of priorities will have to be delayed until additional financial resources become available, presumably during the first year of program administration. Nevertheless, the Department of Ecology has formulated a method and criteria for identifying areas for preservation and restoration.

1. Such areas must be part of a designated area of particular concern.
2. They must be of biological, natural systemic, cultural, or scenic importance, as agreed upon by expert evaluation, and ranked in this order:
   (a) Critically important— indispensable
   (b) Very important—unique, but not indispensable
   (c) Moderately important—neither unique nor indispensable, but a strong link that would be missed
   (d) Minor importance—easily replaceable, not unique, not a major contributor
3. They must be ranked as to degree of urgency:
   (a) Quite urgent—destruction beyond possibility of restoration within one year
   (b) Moderately urgent—destruction within five years
   (c) Urgent—destruction in ten years
   (d) Not urgent—destruction unlikely
4. They must be relatively well-preserved at present, as determined by these criteria:
   (a) Pristine
   (b) Noticeably intruded
   (c) Heavily intruded
   (d) Not restorable

LOCAL REGULATIONS AND USES OF REGIONAL BENEFIT

Uses of regional benefit are defined as facilities to meet requirements other than local in nature. They may be considered as unreasonably restricted or excluded by local governments if it can be demonstrated that such uses would not cause an adverse environmental impact; or that the costs of changes to the local community would not outweigh gains or benefits.

The state has a variety of means to assure that a local government will not unreasonably or arbitrarily exclude uses of regional benefit. The Shoreline Management Act designates most of the coastal zone as "shorelines of statewide significance." The law mandates that for these shorelines, the statewide interest shall be paramount over the local interest. The substantial development permit system also has safeguards to protect the regional interest. Local permit decisions must be made according to legally established procedures, which require state review by the Department of Ecology and the attorney general. Local permit decisions considered to exclude uses of regional benefit can be appealed by the state to the Shorelines Hearings Board and, if necessary, to the state courts.

PROGRAM APPROVAL

The Secretary of Commerce in Washington, D.C. approved the Washington coastal zone management program on June 14, 1976. This was the first state coastal management program to win federal approval. Program development under Section 305 of the Coastal Zone Management Act has been formally completed, and Washington is eligible to receive continuing federal grants to implement the coastal program under Section 306 of the Act.

A Draft Environmental Impact Statement (DEIS) on the Washington program was prepared by the Office of Coastal Zone Management based on program information submitted by the Department of Ecology. The DEIS was submitted to the federal Council on Environmental Quality and made available to the public March 21, 1975. As might be expected, agency and public response to the DEIS was mixed. Government programs almost invariably adversely affect some individual property owners, citizens, and various interest groups. The most serious comments were focused on the concern that program approval would be premature. Critics believed that more work should have been done on refining and clarifying the Washington program, for the following reasons:

1. There was inadequate federal consultation and coordination;
2. All local shoreline master programs should be completed and approved by the Department of Ecology before federal approval is granted;
3. The organizational network for coastal management is weak;
4. The specific interests of various federal agencies were not adequately considered;
5. The Washington program did not meet all Coastal Zone Management Act requirements and guidelines.[7]

With a time extension and supplementary program development grants, the Department of Ecology continued work on coordinating with federal agencies, clarifying its organizational network, encouraging local governments to complete their master programs, and improving the technical and information base for the state program. DOE completed program revisions in January 1976, and in April the Office of Coastal Zone Management submitted a Final Environmental Impact Statement (FEIS) to the Council on Environmental Quality. OCZM evaluation of the revised Washington program was expressed in the FEIS in these terms:

> While much of this work has been accomplished, there are some elements that require continued efforts on the parts of state, federal, local and public participations. While the CZMA requires that the management system be 'in place,' it does not require nor can it be expected that a system is perfected or running at 100 percent efficiency at the time of approval.
>
> DOC [Department of Commerce] has determined that Washington has established the policies and procedures for implementing a management program that is consonant with the objectives of CZMA [Coastal Zone Management Act]. Time, effort, and resources are needed to bring the program to total fruition.[8]

The Office of Coastal Zone Management approach to evaluating program submissions from the states is indicated in this paragraph from the FEIS:

> The main changes that have occurred in the Washington CZMP
> [Coastal Zone Management Program] are additions, refinements
> and expansion to respond to comments and have not affected
> the basic policies and processes that the DEIS [Draft Environ-
> mental Impact Statement] was based on. . . . A coastal zone
> management program should not be viewed as a final product.
> The CZMA allows for amendments. What is important is that
> the state has an adequate process that can handle changes and
> conflicts. The state of Washington has such a process.[9]

Natural Resources Defense
Council Comments

Federal approval of the Washington state coastal program is likely
to set a precedent for action on other state programs. If the OCZM
was willing to approve the Washington program because there was
a process for improving and refining it, even though some of the
requirements may not have been completely satisfied, other states
would expect the same treatment. But some environmental groups
were not satisfied that the Washington coastal program had been
developed to the point where it would prove effective. The Natural
Resources Defense Council (NRDC) in reviewing the Final Environmental Impact Statement claimed there were too many loose ends
in the Washington program and that it did not really meet federal
objectives for effective management.

NRDC examined separately Washington proposals for managing
the first tier of the coastal zone, the strip of land 200 feet from
the shoreline, and the second tier, which has been established as
the eastern boundaries of the 15 coastal counties.

Criticism of First Tier Planning

Primary reliance for coastal resources management in the first tier
is placed on local governments. However, federal approval has been
granted before some local shorelines master programs have been
completed. Moreover, neither the state program nor the Final
Environmental Impact Statement describes or evaluates the local
plans. After adoption of local programs by the Department of
Ecology, the local governments become entirely responsible for

regulating their shorelines. Before approving the Washington program, therefore, the Office of Coastal Zone Management should
themselves review the local master programs. DOE guidelines are
too general to assure local management effectiveness. Furthermore,
there is no statewide planning framework for the local programs.
A state management program that is simply the cumulation of local
programs does not ensure consistency in resources management
from one local jurisdiction to another. The Washington program
therefore appears not to meet the Coastal Zone Management Act
requirements of a unified program for the whole state.[10]

Criticism of Second Tier Planning

The Natural Resources Defense Council holds that in order to
meet the criteria of the Coastal Zone Management Act a state
management program must contain two essential elements: (a)
a comprehensive land and water use plan or set of unified criteria
for regulating development, and (b) for implementing the plan, a
final arbiter with authority to disapprove proposed developments
that are inconsistent with the plan and to resolve conflicts among
state agencies. NRDC claims, however, that

> Washington's management program does not purport to establish
> a simple, new comprehensive land use plan for the second tier.
> Nor does it rely on one state agency for the 'authorities' required
> under the Act. Rather, the management program makes reference
> to a plethora of single purpose land and water use plans in varying
> stages of development and relies on what it describes as a 'managerial
> network' comprised of 'a variety of formal and informal complex
> interrelationships among agencies.' Unfortunately the actual con-
> tents of these plans, and the means by which they are to be im-
> plemented, are described only in the most vague terms in the
> program document. Accordingly, there is no basis for concluding
> that Washington's proposed management program is adequate to
> carry out the purposes of the Coastal Zone Management Act.[11]

NRDC believes that federal approval of a state coastal management program should be based on a demonstration that it stands a
very good chance of protecting environmental values in the coastal
zone. The Office of Coastal Zone Management appeared to take a

more tolerant view. It was willing to accept Washington's own policy regarding the allocation of management responsibility between state and local governments. It also recognized that there were political and technical constraints on working out a perfect coastal program.

Only continuous monitoring of the Washington coastal management experience will reveal whether the federal government was justified in approving a process rather than a finalized plan; or whether the Natural Resources Defense Council was justified in claiming that program approval should be based on evidence of vigorous planning and that an effective management structure is in place.

REFERENCES

[1] *Washington Coastal Zone Management Program,* p. 37, February 14, 1975.

[2] *Ibid.,* p. 36.

[3] *Ibid.,* p. 41.

[4] Revised Code of Washington, Section 90.58.020, 1971.

[5] Washington Administrative Code, 173-16-040, 1972.

[6] *Washington Coastal Zone Management Program,* p. 53, February 14, 1975.

[7] U.S. Office of Coastal Zone Management. *Final Environmental Impact Statement, State of Washington Coastal Zone Management Program,* Department of Commerce, Washington, D.C. (April 9, 1976), p. i.

[8] *Ibid.,* p. iii.

[9] *Ibid.,* p. v.

[10] Jamieson, B., Jr. and R. Beers. *Comments of the Natural Resources Defense Council, Inc., on the Washington State Coastal Zone Management Program,* Palo Alto, California (May 21, 1976), pp. 2-7.

[11] *Ibid.,* p. 8.

PART V

ANALYSIS

CHAPTER XV

STATE MANAGEMENT STRUCTURES

INTRODUCTION

Two contrasting approaches to designing an institutional structure for coastal resources management may be identified. One
would be to start with an *a priori* concept, establish the organization by law, and then let it make its way by developing working
relations with the existing institutional structure of state and local
government. This is what may happen when legislators in one
state wish to start up a coastal program by imitating the structure
in another that had pioneered in the field. The consequent proliferation of state agencies may be inefficient and costly, however,
and the new organization may find itself hampered by obstacles
put in its way by agencies that have some resources management
responsibilities and authority vested under earlier state laws.

The opposite approach would be to analyze the substantive concerns of the new coastal management function, identify the existing
distribution of related functions among state agencies, and then
consider how the new management responsibilities may best be
carried out. Various aspects of coastal resources management are
long-established functions in many coastal states. It is only participation in a new federal program under the Coastal Zone Management Act of 1972 that requires states to focus their attention on
this field and create an institutional structure that will satisfy
federal criteria.

Once the substantive concerns of coastal resources management
have been identified, consideration may be given to the suitability
of existing agencies for assuming new responsibilities. If this would
not be completely satisfactory, then reorganization may be in

195

order to reassign or consolidate responsibilities. Using this procedure, if it is determined that a new agency or management mechanism is necessary, it may be established within the context of a
broader reorganization plan.

Organization or reorganization for coastal resources management
does not involve state agencies only. Local governments also are
concerned. State law long ago delegated powers over land use and
other development regulations to local government. Planning,
zoning, and issuing building permits are regarded, along with home
rule, as the sacrosanct domain of local officials. Allocation of
coastal resources management responsibilities must therefore also
take into account their distribution between state and local agencies. This would involve deciding which aspects of coastal resources
management are of statewide concern and should be assumed by
state government, and which are of local or regional concern and
might best be left to local determination.

Since the federal Coastal Zone Management Act became law in
1972, coastal resources management has been considerably developed and defined as a field of government responsibility. Areas of
statewide concern have been identified as including: (a) definition
of coastal zone boundaries, (b) identification of areas of particular
environmental concern, (c) siting of power plants and major energy
production facilities, (d) siting of petroleum, chemical and other
heavy industrial plants that have substantial impact on environmental quality and the use of adjacent lands, (e) ports, rail yards,
airports, and other major transportation facilities, and (f) regional
recreation facilities. These and other aspects of coastal resources
management, as major policy concerns for state-level decision,
would conceivably be incorporated as elements of a state coastal
plan. Within this kind of policy framework, state guidelines might
then be established for local planning, zoning, and other development regulations. It would be presumed that once statewide
coastal resources management objectives had been identified, local
and regional coastal concerns should be left to the discretion of
the appropriate jurisdictions.

The problems of intergovernmental coordination with which a
coastal resources management structure will have to deal are not
limited to those within the state. Interstate and federal–state

relations are also involved. The New York Bight demonstrates the need for interstate coordination. New York, New Jersey, and Connecticut share these shores. Some crucial coastal resource management decisions must be made with the participation of all three states. They must certainly cooperate to avoid polluting one another's shores. An even more sensitive area for decision-making is the location of sites for new installations of regional significance, such as offshore petroleum drilling and its transportation, refining and storage. For these kinds of decisions as well as those involving military installations and international commerce, federal–state coordination is also necessary. An example is the issue of whether to permit the Concorde SST to land at Kennedy Airport. Landing and take-off of these aircraft would have a significant impact on the New York coastal zone. The federal government has decided to allow the landings over the protests of the state government. New York and New Jersey must act together to try to nullify this decision because both states are parties to the compact that established the Port of New York Authority that operates Kennedy Airport. Intergovernmental coordination at all levels is, therefore, a significant task for state coastal resources management institutions.

Resources management institutions include both policy-making and administrative functions. These are inseparable aspects of government activity, but one or the other may predominate in any particular entity. The legislature, the governor, and advisory boards, for example, are primarily concerned with policy. Permitting and appeals boards have both policy and administrative concerns. Staffs for processing permit applications and performing technical analyses of coastal resources have more administrative than policy concerns. The important point is that all these entities are components of the institutional structure for coastal resources management.

This brief survey of the federal coastal zone management program and three early state approaches to meeting Coastal Zone Management Act objectives indicates the broad scope and complexity of managing coastal resources. A simplified but perhaps useful broad overview of state responsibilities may be obtained from Figure 19. There are two major management objectives: (a) economic development, and (b) conservation and environmental

	Objectives	
Methods	**Economic Development**	**Conservation and Environmental Quality**
Regulation of Private Action	Determination of permissible land and water uses and priorities; zoning and land use regulations to allocate land for residential, industrial and commercial use to provide for population increase and economic development; regulation of fisheries; siting of energy facilities.	Regulation of areas of particular concern; restrictions on use and physical alteration of wetlands, fragile ecological systems, areas of unstable soils, flood plains; regulation of point and non-point sources of air and water pollution; regulation of sand and gravel mining; refining, transfer, and storage of petroleum products.
Government Action	Construction of transportation and utility networks; service networks for residential population and business firms; siting of facilities of regional and national concern; construction of ports, piers, marinas; harbor and channel dredging; placement and maintenance of navigational aids.	Governmental purchase of wetlands and other areas of particular concern; purchase of or otherwise obtaining scenic, recreational, and other easements to limit development; construction of solid waste disposal and sewage treatment facilities; fish and wildlife conservation.

Figure 19. Coastal resources management.

quality. These are complementary social objectives, but also involve conflicts between different interest groups. Concern for expansion of employment opportunity, business activity, and state and local tax resources motivate some public and private groups to emphasize economic development. The inevitable results, however, are conversion of natural areas to urbanization, depletion of some resources, and additions to the solid waste and water and air pollution load on the environment. Conservation and recreation groups, therefore, tend to oppose development and advocate strong public action to conserve open space, expand recreation facilities, and require municipalities and business firms to construct facilities to remove air and water pollutants from the environment. The management problem, and ultimately the task of political decision-making, is to determine the trade-offs between economic and environmental values: how much of the benefits derived from development are worth how much cost to the environment.

To pursue both the economic and environmental objectives, government has available two basic methods. These are regulation of private activities and direct public action. Permit and licensing procedures comprise the regulatory mode. They are established by laws that determine the kinds of activities to be regulated, the organizations responsible, procedures and standards for evaluating applications, penalties for violation of the law, and how appeals may be taken from administrative decisions. Building permits, zoning, dredging permits, effluent discharge permits, and fishing licenses are familiar examples. These are the procedures for determining and regulating permissible land and water uses, activities on wetlands and other areas of particular environmental concern, and the location and waste discharge practices of industrial and commercial activities.

Government action to achieve economic or environmental objectives involves investment in public works and the physical facilities that make possible provision of public services. Highway and port transportation facilities are investments in support of economic development. Water supply and sewage treatment facilities also are necessary for urbanization and economic expansion; but disposal of solid and liquid wastes by public systems also maintain or improve environmental quality. Parks, wildlife refuges, and purchase of lands and easements for open space and resources conservation also contribute to achieving environmental objectives.

Conceptualization of planning for public action and regulating private activities may be helped by considering yet another pair of aspects of such programs. These aspects are: (a) *substance* or content of the programs, and (b) the *process* by which they are carried out. The Coastal Zone Management Act of 1972 might convey the impression that Congress was prepared to let the states decide *what* they wanted to do, but wanted assurance that the states would follow national guidelines on *how* to do it. A manual on the federal coastal zone management program, whose preparation was financed by OCZM, states that: "the requirements of the Act appear to focus on *process* and leave the substance of the management programs to the states to define."[1] This point of view was emphasized by the assistant director of OCZM, who pointed out that federal review procedures for the program development stage (under Section 305 of the Act) focused on the management process proposed by the various coastal states. The substantive aspect of coastal management would be more closely examined during the administrative stage under Section 306.[2]

PLANNING AND REGULATION

Regulation of private activities and direct public action are tied together within the more general function of planning. Public works and service programs must certainly be planned. But physical and service delivery systems are designed to serve residential, commercial, and industrial activities that are spatially distributed in various patterns of use and density. Planning land use in conjunction with public facilities and services networks aims at providing the most efficient service within the constraints of available financial resources. The planning aspect of public management anticipates a planned rather than random pattern of land uses and densities. Implementation of the complete management plan for the area, therefore, includes regulation of the location and quality of development by the private sector.

The logic of this process would appear to have planning come before implementation. Highway, water supply, and sewerage systems, for example, would certainly have to be planned before construction may begin. But this is not necessarily the case with the regulatory function. Land use regulations should presumably implement a carefully prepared land use plan. Resources management, however, especially when there are problems of depletion or degradation, may require immediate steps to prevent irreparable loss or damage before plans for land use, public facilities, or public land acquisition may be prepared. Water resources management may be faced with similar problems.

It is not surprising, therefore, that in each of the three coastal management programs described earlier, regulatory measures were devised and put into operation before the coastal zone planning process was completed. In Maine, the Site Location of Development Law was enacted in 1969 before there was any federally aided coastal zone management program. It does not even contemplate operation on the basis of a statewide land use plan. Instead, developers take the initiative to select sites for their proposed activities within the constraints of local zoning and other regulations, if any; then the state Board of Environmental Protection applies legally adopted performance standards to the proposal. The Board may approve or reject the developers' proposal or approve it subject to specified conditions.

In 1967 Maine law also mandated wetlands regulation. Applications for permits to alter wetlands had to be reviewed and approved by both local and state agencies, but apparently would be considered on an *ad hoc* basis rather than in relation to a statewide plan for wetlands conservation or conversion for various uses. The 1971 Mandatory Shoreland Zoning and Subdivision Control Act required all organized municipalities with legally defined shorelines to adopt zoning controls and subdivision regulations following state guidelines, within two years. As many municipalities in Maine had either no land use planning or rudimentary programs, it was apparently expected that the zoning and subdivision regulations would be drafted without benefit of extensive land use planning studies.

Early coastal zone management experience in Rhode Island also put regulation ahead of planning. The Coastal Resources Management Council was established in 1971. It was expected to decide whether to grant permits for activities in the coastal zone at the same time that the basic resource inventories and regulations were being prepared. Permit decisions had to be made on an *ad hoc* basis with technical advice from the Department of Natural Resources, the University of Rhode Island, and the Statewide Planning Program.

In Washington, operational responsibility for shoreline planning and regulation was assigned by state law to local governments. These already had planning and zoning powers, so their shorelines management would be a special focus of attention. While their shoreline inventories and master programs were in preparation, however, they would continue to issue building, zoning, and other development permits. During this period, local governments were to use the state DOE guidelines as the interim basis for evaluating applications for development on their shorelines.

PATTERNS OF ORGANIZATIONAL STRUCTURE

When addressing the problem of designing a coastal management structure, several questions may help to identify alternatives from which to choose:

1. What shall be the role of the state planning organization?
2. What shall be the role of the natural resources department or the environmental protection agency?
3. Should responsibility be placed in a new coastal management board or commission? If so, how should it be staffed?
4. What kind of coastal regulations should be adopted and what kind of permit application and review procedures established? Should the state or local governments regulate the coastal zone?
5. How should appeals be brought from administrative decisions made during the regulatory process?
6. Should the traditional pattern of the distribution of land use planning and regulation powers between state and local governments be changed?
7. How will management of coastal zone resources be related to management of other state resources beyond the coastal boundary?

No two state governments have identical structural features. It is therefore to be expected that adaptations or changes to

accommodate the new federally aided coastal program would likewise vary. Organizations are not always designed according to
theories of administration, for they must usually be related to the
constitutional and statutory framework and the distribution of
powers, responsibilities, and political support among existing agencies. Generalizations about coastal management structure, because
it is so varied, must be confined to a few obvious characteristics,
with considerable variation in detail between the extremes:

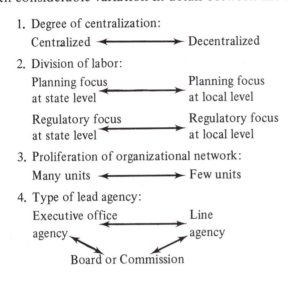

1. Degree of centralization:

   Centralized ◄――――――► Decentralized

2. Division of labor:

   Planning focus ◄―――――― Planning focus
   at state level ――――――► at local level

   Regulatory focus ◄―――――― Regulatory focus
   at state level ――――――► at local level

3. Proliferation of organizational network:

   Many units ◄―――――► Few units

4. Type of lead agency:

   Executive office ◄――――― Line
   agency ―――――► agency
   ↘   ↙
   Board or Commission

Maine

It appears virtually impossible to diagram the relationships of all
the state and local organizational actors that participate in coastal
resources management in Maine. Figure 20 shows only a few of
these participants and their ties. It is evident that this is a very decentralized structure. Policy-making, planning and regulation have
a kind of piebald pattern. Some Maine laws focus power and responsibility on the state, others focus on local government. There
are many separate units in the network, many taking the form of
boards or commissions. The State Planning Office, an executive
staff agency, is the lead agency for the coastal management program, but its power to shape the program and coordinate the activities of the various actors is not clear. The SPO itself described its
role in these terms:

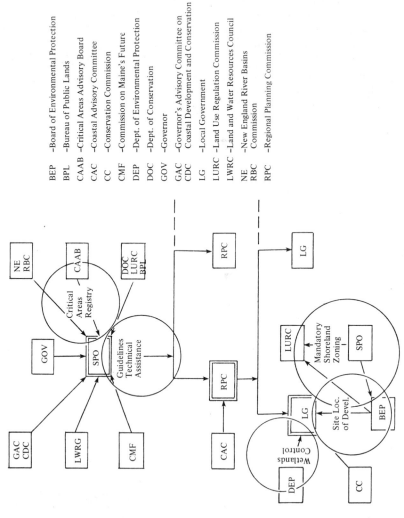

BEP – Board of Environmental Protection
BPL – Bureau of Public Lands
CAAB – Critical Areas Advisory Board
CAC – Coastal Advisory Committee
CC   – Conservation Commission
CMF – Commission on Maine's Future
DEP – Dept. of Environmental Protection
DOC – Dept. of Conservation
GOV – Governor
GAC – Governor's Advisory Committee on
CDC   Coastal Development and Conservation
LG   – Local Government
LURC – Land Use Regulation Commission
LWRC – Land and Water Resources Council
NE   – New England River Basins
RBC   Commission
RPC – Regional Planning Commission

Figure 20. Partial Maine Coastal Management Network

The State Planning Office's Coastal Planning Group will serve
primarily as an intermediary between the regulatory agencies and
the various units of government providing technical assistance
and communicating and developing executive department policy
whenever appropriate. The State Planning Office's role will continue to be primarily with the coordination and integration of
land resource use management not with direct regulation or enforcement activities.[3]

It has been noted that four state laws provide the basic legal foundation and establish management programs for coastal resources:

1. The site location of development process involves regulation
   at the state level (Board of Environmental Protection).
2. Wetlands control is shared by a state agency (Department
   of Environmental Protection) and local government.
3. Shoreland zoning and subdivision control is a local responsibility, aided by the state (State Planning Office) and re-
   regional planning bodies.
4. The critical areas register is maintained by a state agency
   (SPO and Critical Areas Advisory Board).

This is a complex network that would appear to be difficult to administer and for the public to understand. This may be one of the
reasons why the Maine program has been held back by the governor. Where there are long and strongly held traditions of personal
liberty, the sacredness of property rights, and preference for local
self-government, the establishment of new programs that involve
the transfer of power from local to state government must be expected to be viewed with suspicion by the public. It would appear,
then, that the simpler the structure and the greater the allocation of
responsibility to local government, the more readily popular support
may be found for the program.

Rhode Island

The organizational structure for coastal resources management is
relatively simple in Rhode Island. It is fairly well centralized in the
state, there are few units in the network, and the state is responsible for planning and regulation. The Statewide Planning Program,
in the governor's executive department, is the lead agency during

the stage of program development. After the program has received federal approval, the Coastal Resources Management Council, the state coastal regulatory agency, will become the lead agency. Figure 21 shows the organizational network stripped to its essentials. Power for regulating all activities in, on, or under the coastal waters is vested in the Coastal Resources Management Council. It also regulates wetlands, shoreline protection structures, and topographic features shaped and influenced by the tides and marine processes. Major energy and industrial facilities are regulated by the Council regardless of location.

Staff services to the Council for processing permit applications are provided by the Division of Coastal Resources in the Department of Natural Resources (DNR). Technical services for coastal planning and permit application review are provided by the University of Rhode Island Coastal Resources Center, the Statewide Planning Program, and other divisions in DNR. Administrative services for the Council are provided by the office of the director of DNR. The Division of Coastal Resources is therefore supervised by both the Coastal Resources Management Council and DNR.

The Statewide Planning Program played a key role in the conception and establishment of the Coastal Resources Management Council. During coastal program development, it allocates federal coastal zone management funds among the participating organizations and coordinates their efforts. The Statewide Planning Program also must prepare the formal coastal program submission to Washington and nurse it through the process of review and approval.

The coastal management structure in Rhode Island is fairly simple. Responsibility for operating the program is clearly to be focused in the Coastal Resources Management Council. This is the state regulatory agency for the coastal zone as defined by state law, and does not share its powers with other state agencies or local governments. Therefore, it also has full responsibility and must take the full heat of disagreements with its decisions or failures in resources management.

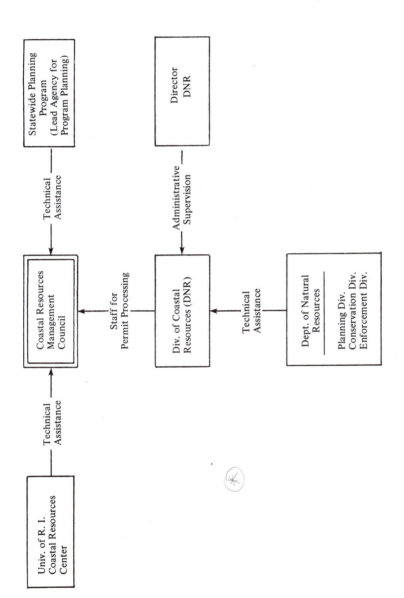

Figure 21. Rhode Island coastal management structure.

Washington

The state of Washington has the simplest organizational structure for coastal management of the three discussed here. It is decentralized in the sense that local governments are responsible for both planning and implementation. Nevertheless, there is strong centralized state supervision of the planning process by the lead agency, the Department of Ecology, which is an operating department. The Department also monitors the regulatory activities of local governments in the coastal zone, but it must intervene in local decisions by appealing to the Shorelines Hearings Board. Relationships between the Board, the Department, and local governments are diagrammed in Figure 18, page 149.

There are many individual units in the coastal management network because so many local governments are involved. Planning and regulation may tend to be uneven in the sense that local policies and objectives for shoreline conservation and development may vary considerably. Nevertheless, because of the strong state supervision of planning and regulatory activities, local variations in the management process may be contained within limits established by state policy in the Shorelines Management Act and the Department of Ecology guidelines.

It should be noted that the effectiveness of coastal management may not bear any relationship to the elegance, simplicity, or complexity of paper organization diagrams. It would appear that simplicity would allow ease of coordination and efficient communication between units. Public participation and access to the decision process as well as awareness of the focus of responsibility for success or failure would also be favored by structural simplicity. These propositions will have to be tested empirically, however, before valid judgements may be made about the influence of organizational structure on management performance. There are undoubtedly other variables, such as political climate, public support, attitude of the courts, and financial resources for management that also affect the fate of coastal resources and the quality of development in the coastal zone. The difficulties of categorization are exemplified in the three state structures described in preceding chapters.

An important point to keep in mind in considering the Maine, Rhode Island, and Washington coastal management programs is that they were established by state laws before the federal program was enacted. Coastal management is already in operation in these states, and it is not likely they will be modified in any major respect to satisfy federal requirements. The Office of Coastal Zone Management in Washington may, in fact, find deficiencies in the formal management programs submitted by these states and delay granting approval. Even though this may mean withholding federal implementation grants, these states probably will not be forced to repeal or drastically amend their coastal management statutes. These programs are already in being, regulations have been adopted, and private developers as well as public agencies are following established permit application procedures. It should not be expected that these will become prototype programs for other states. Nevertheless, they have been in operation for several years, and the experience gained may benefit developing programs.

REFERENCES

[1] Armstrong, J., *et al. Coastal Zone Management: The Process of Program Development,* p. 1, November 1974.

[2] Interviews with Richard Gardner, Washington, D.C. (May 14, 1976).

[3] Maine State Planning Office. *An Introduction to the Maine Coastal Plan,* Augusta (November 20, 1974), p. 49.

CHAPTER XVI

STATE-LOCAL RELATIONS IN
RESOURCES MANAGEMENT

One of the major administrative and political tasks that has to be carried out by a state coastal management structure is the reconciliation of local, regional, and state interests in coastal resources. Some or all of these jurisdictions may have been granted constitutional or statutory powers for regulating public and private activities in coastal lands and waters. They may also have responsibility for building public facilities and providing services in the coastal zone.

The coastal management structure has to cope with both administrative and adjudicative aspects of resources management. The administrative problem concerns rationalizing the procedures for reviewing permit applications by developers, who must sometimes obtain permits from a half dozen or more different state and local agencies. The adjudicative problem involves the reconciliation of differences between jurisdictions. State agencies or local governments may be able to veto each other's proposals unless there is some mechanism for assuring needed development of regional value or preventing development in areas of particular environmental concern. Such a mechanism will be required to define statewide and local interests and arrive at equitable trade-off decisions.

Local government autonomy is fostered by state constitutional or statutory provisions for home rule and by delegation of police power authority to regulate land use and development. Municipal governments are understandably suspicious of any state action that may infringe on their established rights to self-determination. State designation of areas of particular environmental concern imposes development limitations on these areas, thereby reducing land values, investment potential, and local taxes. On the other hand, local concern is also aroused by state proposals to locate facilities to serve region-wide needs, such as power plants, major parks, sewage treatment plants, or housing for low-income families in the community.

State coastal management structures will have to be sensitive to local interests and assure local participation in goal setting and management. It may be necessary to discover ways to compensate local governments for the costs of either limiting development in certain areas or accepting unwanted facilities of regional benefit. In the past, local governments often seemed to regard land within their jurisdiction not as a resource to be conserved and developed carefully, but rather to be exploited for profit and tax revenues. The federal coastal zone program may require a change in both state and local attitudes toward land development regulation. Instead of permissive state laws enabling local governments to zone and regulate development if they choose to, states may find they must require localities to adopt and enforce such regulations.

Coastal zone management may well be the leading edge of a new wave of state action to recover regulatory power and responsibility for managing environmental resources. This may well be disturbing to local governments, but it may also force them to strengthen their own capability for resource management. It should encourage them also to participate fully in the preparation of state coastal management programs to safeguard their own interests.

ISSUES IN STATE–LOCAL RESOURCE MANAGEMENT RELATIONS

It has been noted that states have delegated zoning and other land use regulatory powers to local governments. Most land use decisions should perhaps properly remain within local jurisdictions. Nevertheless, accelerating urbanization and the large scale of technological systems that have emerged for transportation, resource extraction, manufacturing, and energy production cause land use decisions made in one locality to have important consequences for other communities. Land use issues of greater than local significance should be resolved by a process that includes a regional or state authority. In this way the broader community affected by land use decisions may have some influence over them.

Greater state involvement in land regulation may help to overcome the all too prevalent "beggar thy neighbor" attitude of local governments. Exclusive control by local jurisdictions permits them to compete for favored types of development, such as non-nuisance industries and shopping centers that produce high land values and tax revenues; but they may also exclude what are considered unfavorable projects, such as housing for low-income families, which may place financial and social costs on the community. Two experts in the field of land use regulation, Fred Bosselman and David Callies, called the reaction to this situation a "quiet revolution in land use control." They write that

> the *ancien regime* being overthrown is the feudal system under which the entire pattern of land development has been controlled by thousands of individual local governments, each seeking to maximize its own tax base and minimize its social problems, and caring less what happens to all the others.[1]

Changing Concept of Land

While the United States still had a seemingly endless frontier and inexhaustible land resources, ownership of land was considered to convey the right to make as much money out of it as possible. Land was regarded as a commodity whose value was to be protected. Zoning was even originally justified on the ground that it would conserve and enhance land values.

> The promoters of these land use regulations in the 1920s made no attempt to conserve land for particular purposes or to direct it into a specific use, but only sought to prevent land from being used in a manner that would depreciate the value of neighboring land. The traditional answer to the question, 'Why regulate land use?' was 'to maximize land values. . . .' Where development would not harm property values it went unregulated. Zoning permitted residential uses to be built in the most polluted industrial districts on the theory that any development which did not reduce the value of the surrounding land should not be prohibited.[2]

In recent years new attitudes toward land have emerged. We have entered an age of resource scarcity; and land, formerly thought of as abundant, is now coming to be appreciated as a resource in increasingly short supply. It may be difficult for most people to conceive of a land shortage in the United States. Nevertheless, national and state reservations have had to be established to protect our seemingly vast desert and wilderness areas. Land scarcity is more obvious in the urban areas where most people now want to live. Competition for urban land has driven up land values, and since most urbanization has taken place on or near the marine and Great Lakes coasts, development pressure on the coastal zone is enormous. There is a new recognition that land formerly thought to be worthless has value if left in its natural state. Wetlands and sand dunes along the shore, for example, were regarded as nuisances to be filled in or leveled for development. Now we know that wetlands are among our most biologically productive areas and that shoreland dunes protect upland areas from inundation during severe storms.

The Role of the State

The distribution of coastal management responsibilities between state and local governments involves three major functions: (a) planning, (b) regulation of private activities, and (c) provision of public works, services, and programs. For each function, the alternatives are: (a) to vest all powers and responsibilities in the state, (b) to delegate them all to local governments, or (c) to share them, giving some powers to local units and retaining some for the state.

The most obvious choice is the last alternative whereby powers and responsibilities are shared in one way or another. It would not be politically feasible to deprive local governments of powers they have exercised for many years, and the state would find it difficult and costly to exercise all management and regulatory functions itself. The variety of state legal and administrative structures precludes the possibility of devising a perfect scheme that would suit all states. Each state, therefore, seeks its own organizational solution adaptable to its political and administrative realities.

The consequence of sharing regulatory powers is that dual regulatory systems are established, one for state permits and the other
for local permits. In some states, for example, zoning is a local
function, but a state permit is also required for any proposed alteration of a wetland. In such a dual system of shared regulatory
responsibility, some states have taken the initiative to provide
guidelines for local zoning and shorelines regulation as well as to
organize a centralized permit application service in which the private developer may apply at a central location for all required
permits.

ALTERNATIVE MANAGEMENT
TECHNIQUES

The federal Coastal Zone Management Act of 1972 sets out
alternative techniques by which state and local roles in coastal
management may be organized. Section 306 (e) of the Act states
that an approved state coastal program must provide

> for any one or a combination of the following general techniques
> for control of land and water uses within the coastal zone;
> (a) state establishment of criteria and standards for local imple-
>   mentation, subject to administrative review and enforcement
>   of compliance;
> (b) direct state land and water use planning and regulation; or
> (c) state administrative review for consistency with the manage-
>   ment program of all development plans, projects, or land and
>   water use regulations, including exceptions and variances
>   thereto, proposed by any state or local authority or private
>   developer, with power to approve or disapprove after public
>   notice and an opportunity for hearings.

The three states whose coastal management programs have been
described here have chosen to combine the first two of these arrangements, but emphasize one or the other.

State Standards for Local Implementation

State promulgation of standards to guide local implementation appears to be the managerial approach adopted by most coastal states. The state legislature enunciates coastal policy and goals in state law and assigns responsibility to a state agency. This agency promulgates guidelines and criteria to be followed by local governments in implementing state policy. Local governments are *required* by state law to adopt and enforce coastal land and water regulations. The state agency reviews local plans and programs for compliance with state guidelines, and it may be authorized to enforce its decisions by adopting a plan and regulatory program for the locality if the latter fails to do so.

Washington

The Washington coastal management program fits this model almost exactly. The Shoreline Management Act of 1971 clearly defined state objectives for coastal management and the priorities that were to be given to public access and use. The Department of Ecology was designated as the responsible state agency. Local governments were required by state law to prepare shoreline master programs, which had to conform to guidelines adopted by the Department of Ecology. If the Department was not satisfied with the local effort, it was authorized to itself prepare a master program for local enforcement.

The Department of Ecology does not exercise any shoreline regulatory power itself. It does monitor all permit rulings by local governments, but it has no power to intervene directly in local permit procedures or decisions. It must oppose local shorelines actions by appealing to the state Shorelines Hearings Board. Nevertheless, the Washington system does provide a mechanism for state supervision of local shorelines decisions. This is reassertion by the state of its position as the constitutional source of all regulatory powers, which was advocated by Bosselman and Callies; but it applies in Washington only to the shorelines, not to zoning in general.

Maine

The Maine coastal program is a mixture of state and local regulation, but in one respect it incorporates the technique of promul-
gating state guidelines and mandating local regulation. A principal
element of its state legislative foundation for coastal management
is the Mandatory Shoreland Zoning and Subdivision Control Act.
It requires all organized municipalities to adopt zoning and subdivision controls following State Planning Office guidelines for the
coastal strip 250 feet inland of the high water mark. The state
Board of Environmental Protection and the Land Use Regulation
Commission, coordinated by the State Planning Office, were directed by law to adopt ordinances for municipalities that failed to do
so themselves by the legislated deadline.

Rhode Island

The Rhode Island approach does not give local governments a
direct role, under state supervision, in coastal management. Local
governments may exercise zoning and other land use controls
under state enabling laws, but they are not required to do so. Local
governments also apply in coastal areas the traditional building permit procedures that cover their entire area of jurisdiction. These
are not coastal resources management activities as conceived by the
federal Coastal Zone Management Act, however. The Rhode Island
program relies entirely on direct state regulation by the Coastal Resources Management Council.

Direct State Land and Water Regulation

Rhode Island

Four organizations have been designated by Rhode Island law or
executive order as the coastal zone management team. They are all
at the state level. The Coastal Resources Management Council has
central responsibility, and is assisted by the Division of Coastal
Resources in the Department of Natural Resources, the University
of Rhode Island Coastal Resources Center, and the Statewide
Planning Program. Drawing on the other organizations in the

management team, as well as other state agencies, for staff and technical assistance,the Coastal Resources Management Council has responsibility by law for making technical studies and inventories of coastal resources; analyzing activities, conditions and problems in the coastal zone; and preparing coastal resources management plans and programs.

To carry out its policies and plans, the Council is authorized to adopt regulations for the entire seaward side of the coastal zone below the mean high water line. No private or public activity or development covered by Council regulations may take place on, within, or under the state's tidal waters without first obtaining a permit from the Council. This is complete centralization of management authority, which the Council does not share with any other state agency or local governments. The Council may approve, modify, set conditions for, or reject any application for a permit.

There is no legal definition for the landward side of the coastal zone in Rhode Island. The Council does have power, however, to regulate specified coastal areas and uses that will affect the condition of the coastal waters and the ecological systems within them. The areas under the Council's jurisdiction are intertidal salt marshes, shoreline protection facilities, and physiographic features being shaped and modified by tidal waters. Activities regulated by the Council are power generation and desalination plants; chemical and petroleum processing, transfer, and storage; minerals extraction; sewage treatment and disposal facilities; and solid waste disposal facilities. The Council has authority to approve, modify, set conditions for, or reject the design, location, construction, alteration, or operation of these activities anywhere in the state if they will affect the water areas under the Council's jurisdiction, or if they will probably conflict with a resources management program or damage the coastal environment.

The Council does not share these operational responsibilities with any state agency or local government. It also enforces its own regulations. Violators are to be brought to a district court of the state by the chairman of the Council, and the complaint would have to be prosecuted by the state's attorney general. By the same token, however, developers whose permit applications have been denied or who feel aggrieved by any action of the Council may also appeal to the state courts to remedy their grievances.

Maine

The coastal management structure in Maine, as has already been noted, has both state and local elements with direct responsibility for regulating coastal lands and waters. The State Planning Office is the lead agency for the coastal zone, but its responsibility is limited to state planning, assistance to regional and local planning bodies, and preparation of planning guidelines. The SPO is primarily concerned with identifying state concerns and objectives and coordinating the formulation of state coastal management policies. It has no regulatory powers or functions itself.

Direct state regulation is carried out by the Board of Environmental Protection, with staff assistance from the Department of Environmental Protection, for major development projects under the Site Location of Development Law. The Department also regulates wetlands, in partnership with local governments, under the Wetlands Control Act. Permit application, review, and appeals procedures follow the pattern common to most states. These are limited state regulatory functions compared to the Rhode Island structure, however, for in Maine they are shared with local governments under the Mandatory Shoreland Zoning and Subdivision Control Act. There is a State Register of Critical Areas, but the register is not established by regulation of private properties. Instead, private lands are included in the register by negotiation or purchase.

Washington

In this state, regulation of the shorelines is entirely in the hands of local governments. The lead coastal management agency, the state Department of Ecology, establishes guidelines for local shoreline master programs, and monitors local permit decisions. Under the Shoreline Management Act, however, the Department of Ecology has no regulatory powers. Some state agencies do have regulatory powers and issue permits under air and water pollution control laws and to meet state health regulations, but these are not exclusively concerned with coastal management.

THE ROLE OF THE COURTS

There is a long history of state and federal court adjudication of disputes involving zoning and other development regulations. With the validation of zoning by the U.S. Supreme Court in the case of the *City of Euclid v. Ambler Realty Co.*, 272 U.S. 365 (1926), courts have mostly been concerned with the adequacy of local legislative standards for guiding local zoning decisions and with the niceties of legal procedure. More recently, however, the courts have become involved in evaluating local development policies as expressed in zoning and land use regulations. The courts seem to be doing judicially what Bosselman and Callies in their *Quiet Revolution* book thought the states should do legislatively or administratively; that is, to strengthen state supervision over local regulatory decisions. The role of the courts in this field has been thoroughly explored in legal treatises, but a few cases may be noted here. They do not concern coastal management specifically, but they indicate the potential for court intervention in state–local relations in coastal land and water use regulation.

One area of controversy that has received considerable attention in recent years is exclusionary zoning. This is the attempt by communities in the more affluent suburbs to keep out people with low incomes, which also means excluding blacks and other minority groups. To accomplish this purpose, zoning ordinances have been drawn to raise housing costs beyond the reach of such families. These ordinances require large lots, large lot frontage, and large building floor areas; and they exclude multi-family rental housing.

There have been many state court decisions that struck down exclusionary zoning, but the "Mount Laurel" case has drawn attention recently. It was decided in the New Jersey Supreme Court. The contrast of this decision with earlier trends is indicated by the following quotation from a 1971 article:

> Zoning is above all supposed to promote general welfare; clearly
> something has gone very wrong. . . . In New Jersey, the pattern
> of exclusionary zoning has been successfully rationalized in court
> on a highly parochial basis, by relying on the odd notion that the
> statutory reference to the 'general welfare' refers to the general
> welfare of each individual municipality. Yet in recent years the

New Jersey Court has cut the logical basis out from under this whole line of precedent by deciding explicitly that the 'general welfare' should be interpreted on a regional basis.[3]

The regional interpretation is exactly what the New Jersey Supreme Court gave in 1975 upholding the decision on *Southern Burlington County NAACP, et al. v. Township of Mount Laurel,* 119 N. J. Super. 194, 290 A. 2d 465 (1972), which was handed down by the Superior Court. This decision found that the Mount Laurel Zoning ordinance effectively excluded housing for people with low or moderate incomes. This kind of zoning prevented people from moving to new locations in search of employment opportunity and concentrated the burden of providing housing for such families on older communities. Since every community should share in taking care of housing needs in the entire region, the court required Mount Laurel to revise its land regulations to permit the township to accommodate families from every social and economic stratum represented in the region.

Court action on exclusionary zoning indicates the role of the judiciary in reaffirming state concern with the local development process. Another issue, with perhaps greater significance for coastal zone management, is whether local governments may establish legal limits to community growth. Such limits may be expressed in terms of population, building permits per year, or physical limits to development. Perhaps the leading case on this issue was brought in the federal rather than state courts, but the "Petuluma" case provides a precedent that is likely to influence state court decisions.

The city of Petaluma, a suburb of San Francisco, enacted its "Petaluma Plan" in 1971 in response to rapid population growth. Improved transportation facilities had reduced commuting time to San Francisco. The five-year plan limited building permits for multiple-unit housing to 500 units each year. It also established a 200-foot wide greenbelt around the urbanized area as a boundary for development. The response of real estate developers was to sue the city of Petaluma. The decision in *Construction Industry Association v. Petaluma* (No. 75-923 April 1974) by the U.S. District Court for Northern California found the Petaluma plan unconstitutional. The court found that the plan excluded substantial numbers of people who would otherwise have moved into the city and there-fore infringed upon the constitutional right to travel.

The Ninth Circuit Court reversed this decision, holding that the Petaluma plan was rationally related to the social and environmental welfare of the community. The Appeals Court took the position that the city had not acted arbitrarily or unreasonably in establishing limits to growth; and it was not for the courts to question the wisdom of local legislative decisions. The U.S. Supreme Court refused in February, 1976 to review the decision of the Appeals Court, thus giving legal sanction to the Petaluma Plan.

Municipalities in the coastal zone will find this case an important guideline for planning. Development pressures are greatest on coastal communities for permanent residence as well as for vacation homes. Uncontrolled development has tended to convert wetlands, barrier beach islands, estuarial flood plains, shoreline bluffs, and other environmentally sensitive areas into sprawling subdivisions or crowded beach housing. Local ordinances limiting population and physical growth may complement wetlands regulation, flood plain zoning, and other legal devices to protect areas of particular concern as elements in coastal resources management programs.

A third land regulation issue that is likely to change both state and local powers in zoning has recently been decided by the U.S. Supreme Court. It is difficult to foresee the full effects of this case, but it could significantly influence zoning as a tool for coastal management. The case of *City of Eastlake v. Forest City Enterprises, Inc.* (No. 74-1563) was decided June 21, 1976. It concerns the validity of voter referendums as a way of deciding proposed amendments to a zoning ordinance.

The city charter of Eastlake, Ohio, requires that proposed zoning amendments must be ratified by at least 55 percent of the voters in a referendum. A developer who had requested a zoning change for a high-rise apartment building, which was denied after a referendum, alleged in his suit that the city charter was invalid. He claimed that the charter unconstitutionally delegated legislative power to the voters. The Ohio Supreme Court agreed with the developer on the ground that the popular referendum requirement in the charter does not provide standards for guiding the

voters in deciding on the zoning issue involved. This would permit
the police power to be exercised in an arbitrary or capricious manner. That is to say, the voters could reject a zoning change, on
political or narrow self-interest grounds, even if it had been approved by the local governing body after technical study as being
in the public interest.

In a six-to-three decision, the U.S. Supreme Court reversed the
Ohio Supreme Court. The majority opinion held that a referendum
is a means for direct political participation in the form of a veto
over enactments of the local legislature. The decision stated that

> Since the rezoning decision in this case was properly reserved to
> the people of Eastlake under the Ohio constitution, the Ohio
> Supreme Court erred in holding invalid, on federal constitutional
> grounds, the charter amendment permitting the voters to decide
> whether the zoned use of respondent's property could be altered.[4]

This decision appears to alter the entire philosophical basis of
zoning. The concept of zoning that was built up over many decades of technical study and court review was that a zoning
ordinance should be based on a city plan. The plan would provide
the factual justification for using government police powers to
regulate private property and incorporate the legislative standards
that justify the pattern of permissible land uses incorporated in
the zoning ordinance. Deciding whether to regulate private property by zoning would be a political act that could properly be
ratified by a referendum. But having decided in favor of zoning,
establishing and changing the zoning district boundaries should
properly be based on technical criteria of efficiency, economy,
safety, health, and other aspects of the public interest rather than
purely political considerations.

The U.S. Supreme Court either was not aware of or rejected
this theory of zoning and regarded it basically as a political process subject to the vagaries of popular opinion. This may be expected to have a profound effect on coastal management eventually.
Regulation of land and water uses in the coastal zone is crucial to
the implementation of a coastal management program. It is evident
from the accounts of coastal planning in Maine, Rhode Island, and
Washington that enormous effort and money must be poured into

the scientific and technical studies that underlie coastal management regulations. The U.S. Supreme Court appears to have vitiated this entire effort and possibly nullified the possibility of having comprehensive and coherent state coastal management programs, because implementation can now be subject to the whims of local political controversy.

REFERENCES

[1] F. Bosselman and D. Callies. *The Quiet Revolution in Land Use Control: Summary Report* (Washington, D.C.: U.S. Government Printing Office, 1971), p. 1.

[2] *Ibid.*, p. 23.

[3] N. Williams and T. Norman. "Exclusionary Land Use Controls: The Case of North-Eastern New Jersey," *Syracuse Law Review,* 22: 503 (1971).

[4] *Commerce Clearing House, Urban Affairs Reports, No. 429* (June 24, 1976), p. 1.

CHAPTER XVII

INTEGRATION OF COASTAL AND
INLAND RESOURCES MANAGEMENT

Regardless of how the coastal zone is defined, it is set apart from the rest of the state only by a line on a map. The coastal zone is a long narrow strip of land and water, and the landward side has no organic unity. Depending on how it is determined, the artificial coastal boundary may cut across watersheds, upland ecosystems, political jurisdictions, and integrated economic areas. Designation of the coastal boundary is a political/technical issue, and the other aspects of coastal management are similar in character: (a) designation of areas of special concern, (b) determination of high and low priorities for use and development, and (c) siting of facilities of regional and national concern.

All these management concerns involve policies about where to encourage and where to limit population and economic growth and its concomitant physical development in the coastal zone and in the rest of the state. All these aspects of coastal management have implications for the design of the organizational structure. If a new organization is to be created to manage the coastal zone, how will it relate to the existing agencies that have planning, public services, and resource management responsibilities in the rest of the state? If an existing agency is to be given responsibility for coastal management, how will it organize special programs for that zone, especially those designed to meet federal requirements? There is not now an empirical or conceptual basis for a definitive answer to these questions. What is most appropriate as a coastal management structure will likely vary from state to state. It may be useful, however, to explore some of the issues involved and see how they have been handled by the states whose programs have been described here.

THE COASTAL BOUNDARY AND
MANAGEMENT STRUCTURE

The coastal zone boundary is an artificial barrier between parts of organic, physiographic, political and economic wholes. Land uses and economic activities inland will impact across the boundary on the coastal zone. Drawing a new line for development and economic use regulations will influence market decisions. Development and activities excluded from the coastal zone may tend to locate just over the boundary line; and regulatory agencies whose jurisdictions may meet at this line will have to resolve problems arising from the effect of adjacent uses on one another. Boundary designation may produce three kinds of consequences:

> First would be the phenomenon of over-the-boundary boom—where future development locates just beyond the boundary of a state's coastal zone, but still is close enough to the coastline to profit from the location. . . .
>
> Second, the development may locate in an adjacent state with a more narrowly defined coastal zone. In these situations where a shared resource is involved . . . problems might transfer into the state with the wider coastal zone. . . .
>
> Third, the development may locate in the interior of the state. . . . In this case the state may still have problems. . . . To deal with such potential problems, a state may wish to establish statewide land use controls or utilize some other means of control and coordinate these activities with its coastal zone management program.[1]

The problem of regulating development across the coastal zone boundary appears to provide one reason why the coastal management function ought to be integrated with resources management statewide. Another reason is that there may be some uncertainty about where the boundary line should be drawn. The environmental, jurisdictional and management consequences of the location of the boundary may not be readily forseen. If problems arise after the boundary has been legally established and separate organizations given regulatory jurisdiction on either side, boundary adjustments may be difficult to make. A state agency entrusted with resources management statewide could make such adjustments

easily. Responsibility for coastal zone management to give it
visibility and satisfy federal requirements could be assigned administratively to a unit within the statewide agency.

GROWTH POLICY AND
THE COASTAL ZONE

It has already been noted that pressures for economic growth
and urbanization are greatest on the coastal zone. But not all
activities that people want to be there must be near the water's
edge. Resisting growth pressure to conserve and protect environmental, scientific, cultural or historic values requires the formulation of a state development policy for limiting growth in the
coastal zone and other threatened resource areas and for encouraging growth in locations where it would be beneficial. Growth
limitation issues may also cross state lines, in which case regional
and national development policies would appear called for.

Protecting coastal areas of particular concern implies the limiting
of growth there and encouraging it to locate in designated growth
areas in the coastal zone or elsewhere. This policy issue, however,
affects a great variety of public and private interests that have conflicting values and development objectives. Reconciling these
interests and resolving growth issues present a serious problem in
the design of a coastal management structure. The growth issue
also poses a political problem that may be difficult to resolve within the context of current American values.

It has proven very difficult for American governmental institutions to assume responsibility for planning at the regional, state
and national scales. Congress has considered and rejected bills to
formulate a national land use policy and provide assistance to the
states for statewide planning within a national policy framework.
Many states have organizations for statewide planning, but state
development policies and plans that can be implemented are not
very numerous. Although government consolidation and other
measures have produced a few metropolitan governments in this
country, regional planning has more form than substance. The
major obstacle to regional and statewide planning appears to be

interjurisdictional competition for economic advantage. Political
and business leaders are understandably reluctant to forego economic development to conserve environmental values if the consequence is that neighboring regions and states would receive the
rejected growth and its economic and fiscal benefits.

With by far the greatest proportion of economic growth taking
place in the coastal zone, a national policy framework may be
required to relieve development pressure there and encourage
growth in the interior. But efforts to formulate such a national
policy would run counter to market trends, consumer preferences,
and American values of limiting government interference in the
decisions of individual firms and households. Enormous problems
would probably be encountered in trying to arrive at a national
political consensus for a growth policy to protect environmental
resources in the coastal zone and direct away from it development
that does not absolutely require a coastal location. In fact, the
federal Coastal Zone Management Act states as one of the objectives of management programs, "wise use of land and water resources of the coastal zone giving full consideration to . . . needs for
economic development" as well as conserving environmental and
cultural values. The key problem, therefore, is to develop a policy
for selective development balanced by conservation and protection.

The formulation of such a policy, which is mandated by the
federal Act, would in its growth-inhibiting aspect impose loss of
economic efficiency on firms prevented from locating where their
production and distribution costs would be minimized in relation
to the market prices for their products. Coastal jurisdictions
would also be deprived of the presumed fiscal advantages of an
expanding tax base. A successful national land use and development policy would therefore very likely have to incorporate economic and financial incentives to both businesses and local
governments to act in accordance with such a policy.

James L. Sundquist has examined the efforts of Great Britain,
France, Italy, the Netherlands and Sweden to geographically re-
distribute their urban populations and economic activities. He
concludes that

> All those countries have growth policies intended to disperse the
> national population by stemming migration and thus retarding the

congestion of the biggest cities. Some of their plans are quite
specific. Some have quantitative population targets for regions,
or even communes. In each country, the dispersal policies enjoy
complete political support. Implementing measures are becoming
increasingly forceful and are clearly effective in slowing down, or
stopping altogether the movement from smaller places to larger
centers. There is of course, the usual squabbling over what the
policies should be—that is, where the growth should be directed—
but there is no significant political group or party in any of these
countries that advocates abandoning a national growth policy and
going back to laissez-faire.[2]

These European nations have employed the following controls
to implement their growth-distribution policies.

Incentives

Investment Subsidies

This is the basic incentive. It usually takes the form of capital
grants to investors to cover part of the cost of locating in areas where
growth is to be encouraged. Most subsidies are about 20 percent of
capital investment, but many countries have a kind of zoning whereby development in areas most in need of encouragement may get a
subsidy of up to 25%, or even 35-50% in the case of Italy.

Infrastructure Development

This takes the form of public investment in roads, ports, utilities,
and other infrastructure systems to serve development regions.
This form of incentive has also been used in the United States, of
course, in Appalachia and other regions. Nevertheless, our national
policy seems not to have kept up with the times. Federal investment has favored the South and West since the days when the
Northeast and Great Lakes states were most advanced economically.
Now New England and New York are falling behind, but national
policy has not reorganized this.

Tax Concessions

Income or property taxes are reduced for establishments that locate in development areas. This is another incentive that has been widely used in this country, but in a different policy framework from its application in Europe. The programs Sundquist describes follow national policies that designate particular development areas. In the United States, tax concessions are used by state and local governments to compete for enterprises without reference to a national rationale for a pattern of industry location.

Wage Subsidies

British policy offers a regional employment premium to reduce labor costs for firms locating in development areas. About $7.00 a week is paid to adult male employees, smaller amounts to women and youth, to offer firms cheaper labor than in other areas.

Controls

These are counterpart measures to incentives. They are intended to discourage private development investment in areas that have been under the greatest development pressure. These are by and large the great metropolitan areas on the seacoasts or on rivers that afford access to the sea.

Britain

Entrepreneurs who want to build industrial plants or even office buildings in the London region must prove that they cannot feasibly be located elsewhere.

France

Since 1955 special permits have been required for construction in the Paris region. A small penalty tax has also been imposed to discourage new development there.

Italy

Controls have been placed on industrial construction in large
northern cities. For example, Alfa Romeo was prevented from
locating a factory in Milan that would have created 11,000 new
jobs there.

Sweden

Investors who want to locate plants in the country's three largest
metropolitan areas must first consult with a national government
agency. Here, however, persuasion is used rather than tax or regulatory deterrents.

IMPLICATIONS FOR COASTAL MANAGEMENT POLICY

The primary objective of the European programs described by
Sundquist is to attract industry to economically depressed areas.
Reducing development pressure on already highly developed or
congested areas is a secondary objective. In the context of coastal
zone management, these priorities would be reversed in some states.
Environmental resources conservation for wetlands, barrier beaches,
estuaries and other coastal features, will be the focus of attention.
Incentives to attract development to economically depressed areas,
however laudable that may be, will be intended to complement
coastal zone development regulations intended to discourage development in areas of particular environmental concern. In some
states there might even be attempts to direct economic growth
away from congested urban centers on the coast to other locations.
It is not likely, however, that the United States will follow these
examples in Europe. These countries have a long tradition of
planning and acceptance of government controls. American values
favor competitive enterprise, although subsidies to private businesses have shown this to be frequently more myth than reality.
In any case, individual European countries are relatively small.

The attempt to formulate a national economic growth policy here would really be comparable to establishing such a policy for the entire Continent plus Great Britain.

Although we cannot expect a national economic growth policy to come out of Congress, its enactment of a national coastal zone program would imply that growth management problems will have to be confronted. These will not be concerned with the issue of economic growth vs. a steady state economy at the national level, but rather with selective limitation of growth in areas of particular concern. Coastal states would not be deprived of all growth opportunity; only particular designated segments of the coastal zone, including urbanized areas, would have specified limits to growth.

This is not an issue that affects the coastal zone exclusively. Other areas with unique environmental values may also be forced to endure development controls. In New York State a development plan, implementing regulations, and a management agency have been created by state law for the Adirondack Park. Property owners, local governments, and their representatives in the state legislature have vigorously protested the foreclosure of their depressed region to free economic growth and increase in employment opportunity. The Adirondack Park Agency has been a center of controversy since the day it was established. Coastal zone management agencies may have to be prepared for the same kind of political and economic pressure on their resource management programs.

ORGANIZATIONAL STRUCTURE FOR RESOURCES MANAGEMENT INTEGRATION

Resources management planners in Maine, Rhode Island and Washington have recognized the importance of integrating resources management statewide. Their state laws and the institutions and programs established by them provide for management integration in a variety of ways.

Maine

Shoreland zoning, wetlands regulation, and the register of critical areas are obviously three Maine management programs that are concerned particularly with the coastal zone. One major piece of legislation on which the state relies for coastal management, however, is the Site Location of Development Law. This law has already been described as regulating the location of major private developments. As it is applied statewide, without distinction between coastal and inland areas, the location of large subdivisions and industrial and commercial structures can be regulated to avoid negative environmental impacts. Under the law, developers must assure the Bureau of Environmental Protection that they are able to meet state air and water pollution controls and solid waste disposal and water supply standards. Provision must be made to move additional traffic stimulated by the development, and it must not adversely affect existing uses, scenic character, or natural resources of the surrounding areas.

These are negative controls, however, that act like zoning to prevent presumably undesirable things from happening in the environment. Such controls do not face the issues of the limits to growth, development-carrying capacity of particular environments, relief of development pressure on the coastal zone, or the encouragement of expanding or new firms to locate in economically depressed areas. In conjunction with laws to protect wetlands and other areas of particular concern, a management program that relies mostly on negative controls can go a long way to curb environmental damage that might otherwise occur. Nevertheless, its main thrust is to prevent abuses, not to promote a development policy based on explicit objectives for balanced economic expansion and environmental protection or a desired geographic distribution of population and economic activity. As already noted, it is probably unrealistic to anticipate a move toward this kind of regional, state or national planning in this country.

In the section on the Maine costal zone program (pp. 58-60) it was noted that Governor Longley established by executive order two new bodies for coastal policy and resources management coordination. They were the Governor's Advisory Committee on Coastal Development and Conservation and the Maine Land and Water

Resources Council. They were established primarily to provide an institutional focus for the decentralized and fragmented state structure for resources management. They also have potential, however, as an integrating mechanism for management of inland and coastal resources. Both bodies contain representatives of the state agencies responsible for resources management and the University of Maine. The Advisory Council also has public members. It is the common public agency membership on the Coastal Development and Conservation Committee and the Land and Water Resources Council that gives them the potential for management integration. The Council is concerned with land and water resources statewide and is primarily a cabinet mechanism for management coordination. Since almost all its members are also concerned with coastal policy as members of the Governor's Advisory Committee, statewide issues in resources management will have an institutional forum for discussion.

Washington

The Washington institutional structure does not have an obvious means for integrating coastal and statewide resources management. Primary responsibility is vested by state law in the individual municipalities that have designated shorelines; and the landward depth of this zone is only 200 feet. It is true that state Department of Ecology guidelines were to provide standards for individual local shorelines management programs. Department review and approval of these efforts would also provide quality control. Nevertheless, once management programs were approved, state supervision ended except by Department of Ecology complaint to the Shorelines Hearings Board.

Implementation of local management programs will provide the true test of coastal management effectiveness in Washington. It is in the admnistrative stage of the program that the institutional potential for integrating coastal and inland resources management will either become evident or prove disappointing. The 200-foot landward depth of the coastal zone is considered by the Department of Ecology to be only its first tier. To obtain a larger management perspective, the boundaries of coastal counties are

considered to constitute the second tier of the coastal zone. For
an even broader perspective, especially for control of air and
water pollution sources, the whole state makes up a third tier.

The same municipalities that are given responsibility by the
Washington Shoreline Management Act for coastal management
also have jurisdiction over planning, zoning, and other land use
controls for the entire local community. In some areas, several
coastal municipalities and the county in which they are located
have joined in a collaborative approach to developing coastal
management programs. All coastal counties, that conceptually
comprise the second tier of the coastal zone, can also design and
implement their programs to integrate shoreline and county-wide
environmental objectives. The same approach may be taken by
state agencies responsible for health, pollution control, and
forestry and other natural resources management to integrate
coastal and statewide environmental concerns.

Formal structure alone, therefore, will not determine how well
coastal and inland resources management are integrated. Program
planning and operations by municipal, county, and state agencies—
and the working relationships that develop between them—will
prove whether the potential for integrating resources management
and guiding the physical manifestation of the state's economic
and population growth can be realized.

Rhode Island

The Rhode Island coastal zone has no formally designated inland coastal zone boundary. Instead, the Coastal Resources
Management Council regulates legally specified kinds of industrial,
chemical, and fuel and energy operations wherever they are located in the state, if they might affect the quality of coastal
waters and ecosystems. This is a strong organizational means to
integrate the regulation of particular kinds of development in
the coastal zone and statewide.

This approach bears some resemblance to the Maine operation
of the Site Location of Development Law. But the Rhode Island
program goes much further in integrating coastal resources management and statewide land use planning. Rhode Island is not

relying solely on the initiative of developers to determine the location of major subdivision and construction projects. A statewide plan, if effectively implemented, will determine the essential pattern for the future distribution of population and economic activity. The state cannot determine its own rate of growth, but such economic expansion and population change as can be encouraged to take place will conform to a statewide guide plan.

One element in the guide plan has already been published. It is the State Land Use Policies and Plan. State law that established the coastal management plans must be consistent with the state guide plan. The Statewide Planning Program is proceeding with other elements in the state guide plan, and it has established good working relationships with other state agencies responsible for transportation, health, natural resources conservation, and other major networks of facilities and services. Equally important, it has the confidence and support of the governor.

One factor making for the considerable potential for state planning in Rhode Island is undoubtedly the small size of the state. This makes for easier comprehension of the state planning process and reduces the number of jurisdictions and organized interests involved in the political aspects of planning. In this relatively favorable environment the Statewide Planning Program has proposed an institutional reorganization intended to produce a more effective state planning process.

RELATION OF COASTAL AND STATEWIDE RESOURCES MANAGEMENT

The federal Coastal Zone Management Act has provided financial aid and a focus for state action to manage coastal resources. This program raises two policy issues that each state must resolve for itself as it develops its coastal management program. One is how to relate resources management in the coastal zone to resources management statewide. After all, a line on a map is only an artificial boundary between coastal lands and waters and the inland development of industry, commercial centers, and residential communities that place additional burdens of effluent discharge and recreation demand on the coastal zone. The other

important policy issue to be resolved is the distribution of land
and resources management authority between state and local
governments. Land use regulation has been delegated by states
to local governments for many decades. Implementation of state
concern for land and resources management will require states to
retrieve some of their delegated powers to give policy direction
to local governments and take over direct management of fragile
resources such as wetlands.

Rhode Island's experience with coastal resources management
has produced an institutional and policy model that is in part
applicable to dealing with the issues noted in the preceding paragraph. This model has been incorporated in a draft for a state
land management bill. The objective of the bill is to do for the
rest of the state what the coastal management program is doing
for shorelands and coastal waters. It should be pointed out that
coastal and statewide resources management are already integrated
to some extent by existing law. Earlier sections of this report
have noted that the Rhode Island Coastal Resources Management
Act of 1971, which created the Coastal Resources Management
Council, requires that Council plans, policies and regulations
conform to the state guide plans adopted on the recommendation
of the Statewide Planning Program. Another integrating device is
the authority granted to the Council to receive and decide on
applications for power and desalination plants, chemical and petroleum processing, transfer or storage, minerals extraction, and
sewage treatment and disposal and solid waste disposal facilities
wherever they are located if there is a reasonable probability of
conflict with a coastal management plan or damage to the coastal
environment.

Nevertheless, there are statewide problems of land and resources
management that cannot be effectively attacked with present
legal tools. These are:

1. Relating development to land capability;
2. Relating the intensity of development to the level of public
   services and facilities;
3. Recognizing the areawide impact of certain major development decisions;

4. Protecting valuable natural resources and areas;
5. Retaining a balance and distinction between the urban and the rural environments that establish the state's character;
6. Reserving suitable sites for needed economic development;
7. Providing adequate housing for all residents;
8. Improving the visual quality of development.[3]

Institutional Structure

For the state to cope with these land and resource management problems, a new institutional structure and new regulatory authority are proposed by the draft land management bill. The term Statewide Planning Program would acquire new meaning to cover several organizational components rather than just the present staff in the Department of Administration. Following the coastal resources model, a State Planning Council would be established that would have regulatory and rule-making authority similar to that exercised by the Coastal Resources Management Council. The State Planning Council would also be able to establish technical committees and subcommittees to provide representation of different interests and viewpoints on state planning issues. The State Planning Council would receive technical and administrative staff support from a new Division of State Planning, which would replace the Statewide Planning Program but remain in the Department of Administration.

A new institutional element would be a State Land Adjudication Board. This Board would add an intermediate adjudicatory review process between the State Planning Council and the superior court.

> The purpose of the State Land Adjudicatory Board is to serve as an independent review body to reconcile conflicts that arise in the implementation of the state land management program. The board will facilitate the resolution of land use disputes and would act as a buffer between the decisions of the State Planning Council and cities and towns in implementing state land management strategies.[4]

State Regulatory Powers

The draft Land Management Bill would give to the state planning structure the power to promulgate general land use standards and guidelines as well as special standards for critical areas. It could also issue nonbinding recommendations to local governments on development of regional impact.

The state general land use standards and guidelines would be based on the State Land Use Policies and Plan, which has already been adopted. They would apply to three broad categories of land use—urban, transitional, and rural—to direct growth statewide in a pattern based on land capability and the available level of public services, either existing or planned. The proposed Division of State Planning would recommend these general standards to the State Planning Council. The Council in turn would issue the specific rules to guide local development into the pattern established statewide. All cities and towns in Rhode Island now have some form of land use regulation, but under the new system they would have three years to adopt a land management ordinance consistent with the community's own guide plan as well as state land use regulations. This local land management ordinance would have to be reviewed and approved by the State Planning Council. If a satisfactory ordinance was not submitted, the Council would adopt general development regulations the local government would be required to follow.

Within the general land use pattern established for the state, critical areas would be identified and regulated under special standards. Such areas would include major public facilities, historic places, significant environmental resources, large economic development sites, and land not covered by a management ordinance. The Division of State Planning would recommend critical area designations and development standards to the State Planning Council. After modification or adoption of these standards by the Council, cities and towns would have six months to submit proposed local regulations for critical areas. If proposed regulations are not prepared or are inadequate, the Council could itself adopt regulations that would have to be enforced locally.

With regard to development of regional impact, the State Planning Council would make recommendations rather than mandate local action. Development of regional impact would include large-scale projects and major facilities that would affect more than a single community. Decisions on such projects should not be left entirely in the hands of the communities in which they would be located. The Division of State Planning would submit proposed categories of development of regional impact and standards for identifying them. These would be considered and adopted by the State Planning Council. Thereafter, an application to a local government for a development of regional impact would be forwarded to the proposed Division of State Planning. Within 60 days the Division would send back its recommendations on the proposal to the local government, which would not be bound by them, but would consider them before approving or denying the application.[5]

This draft Land Management Bill may appear to be a radical attempt by Rhode Island to return to the state some of its constitutional authority over land use regulation. Its provisions may indeed run counter to past trends, which delegated these state powers to local governments. Nevertheless, these proposals are not unusual, for several other states have adopted one or more of them. As additional states approach the time when they must submit their coastal zone management programs to Washington, and must have formulated proposals for coastal management institutional structures, they will also have to reconsider existing distribution of regulatory powers over land and natural resources between state and local governments. Such an institutional reassessment would include consideration of how management of coastal and inland resources could be integrated into a statewide program.

REFERENCES

[1] Armstrong, J., *et al. Coastal Zone Management: The Process of Program Development* (Sandwich, Massachusetts: Coastal Zone Management Institute, 1974), p. 17.

[2] Sundquist, J. L. "Europe Stops the Urban Swarm," *The Brookings Bulletin,* 12:8 (Winter 1975).

[3]Rhode Island Statewide Planning Program. *Proposed Land Management Bill: Summary and Draft Text,* Providence (January, 1976) (mimeo), p. 3.

[4]*Ibid.,* p. 6.

[5]*Ibid.,* pp. 5-6.

CHAPTER XVIII

PUBLIC PARTICIPATION

Introduction

The federal Coastal Zone Management Act states as one of the conditions for approval by the Secretary of Commerce that a state coastal zone program has been adopted

> after notice, and with the opportunity of full participation by relevant federal agencies, state agencies, local governments, regional organizations, port authorities, and other interested parties, public and private.

As part of its submission for program review the state must offer evidence of its efforts to involve all relevant public and private organizations in the participation process. The federal rules and regulations specify that the minimum evidence of participation required would be that:

1. A comprehensive listing of all federal and state agencies, local governments, regional organizations and public and private organizations likely to be affected by or have a direct interest in the development and implementation of a coastal program.
2. A listing of the specific interests of such organizations in development of the management program and identification of the efforts made to involve them in the development process.
3. Public hearings have been held after at least 30 days notice; documents associated with the hearings have been available for public review and study; hearings were held at times and places convenient to affected populations; all citizens of the state had an opportunity to comment on the management

243

program, and a report on each hearing was made available to
the public within 45 days.[1]

Participation activities involving local governments have already
been described in earlier sections of this book that dealt with state-
local relations in program development. Legal requirements for
coordination with federal agencies may be met by committees set
up for this purpose by the designated state coastal management
agency. Contacts are most easily maintained with regional offices
of the federal agencies involved. Further opportunity for federal
agency review is provided by the requirement that environmental
impact statements must be prepared for each proposed state coastal program and circulated to federal and other interested bodies for
review. The draft environmental impact statements are also available for review and comment by private organizations.

The existence of legal requirements for intergovernmental
coordination in coastal program development and the presence of
official communications mechanisms has made this aspect of participation less problematic than participation by citizen's organizations and private special interest groups. It is on the latter
component that attention is focused here regarding the process
called public participation.

Washington

Of the three coastal management programs examined, Washington
has given the most explicit attention to public participation. Local
shorelines master programs must be approved by the state Department of Ecology before shorelines regulation can be implemented.
This means that local government must provide evidence to the
state agency that they have followed its guidelines on public participation in the formulation of their master programs. The state
guidelines require citizen's advisory committees in each community.
These committees were to hold public information meetings, use
the news media, and hold local public hearings. Citizen input into
the master programs was to be related mostly to formulating goals
for shorelines management and to show evidence of public agreement on and support for the master programs finally adopted.

Rhode Island

In Rhode Island, the Coastal Resources Management Council has assumed major responsibility for public participation. It has prepared descriptive brochures and issued a periodic newsletter with help from the other institutional members of the state management team. It has also held public information meetings in several locations around the state and conducted the formal hearings required by the federal coastal zone Act and regulations. During the program development stage the Statewide Planning Program, as the Section 305 lead agency, has taken responsibility for intergovernmental coordination. It held a series of workshops for federal agencies and established a federal policy advisory committee. Federal agencies identified by the Office of Coastal Zone Management and the New England River Basins Commission, a federally sponsored organization, have been asked to participate in the coordination efforts of the committee.

Maine

The State Planning Office in Maine made a conscientious effort at public participation, but failed to convince enough residents in the coastal zone that they had made a sufficient input into development of the state coastal management program or that the program itself was a good idea. Public objections were loud enough to reach the ear of the governor, who withdrew the program from consideration by the federal government. The State Planning Office has intensified its public participation efforts, and the governor has given formal recognition to the need for a solid base of citizen support by establishing the Governor's Advisory Committee on Coastal Conservation and Development. Perhaps in response to these new institutional initiatives, perhaps because the major objectors to coastal management were satisfied that they had made their point, public attitudes have changed. There is evidence of wider popular support for coastal resources conservation and development regulation. It may be that dissatisfaction with the form that development of the Maine shoreline has taken, especially in the southwestern part of the state, has demonstrated the need for a system of regulations.[2]

CONCEPTS OF PUBLIC PARTICIPATION

The importance of public participation in and support for coastal management programs is evident from the Maine experience. Lacking popular support, presumably because the people of Maine affected by the proposed program felt left out of policy-making, Governor Longley withdrew the application for federal approval. Effective public participation, therefore, is more than superficial demonstration of compliance with formal requirements of federal or state law. It becomes evident only when there is enough public involvement in formulating the program to bring about widespread understanding and political support. Formulating a public participation program involves finding answers to at least these questions: What is meant by public participation and involvement? What are the mechanics and techniques? What does the public expect as the result? What do government agencies do with information obtained from the process?

What is Public Participation?

Three aspects of the activity called public participation are emphasized in literature. One is generally referred to as public relations. This is the effort by government agencies to publicize their programs, expand public awareness of them, and gain popular support. Another aspect is the attempt to sell a program or project to the public after all decisions have been made and formal hearing requirements must be met. Citizen organizations are dissatisfied with these definitions of public participation. By participation they mean real involvement in and influence on decision-making. This is the third and most significant aspect of the process. In this context, public participation means involvement in the early stages of program and project analysis so that individual citizens and groups can make informed judgements about them. They do not want simply to react to bureaucratic and political decisions after they have already been made. Participation means making input of citizen values and judgements into the planning process before alternatives have been discarded and choices made.

Part of knowing what is public participation is understanding what is meant by "the public." Is there any such thing as *the* public; and does it have a unitary "public interest?" Political experience has long indicated that there are many publics with a variety of competing and conflicting interests. Understanding public participation is made even more complicated by the existence of both organized and unorganized publics. Unorganized publics are often those most in need of having their interests made known to the government decision-makers. Unfortunately, such class or group interests are not articulated because the people involved lack the leadership and financial resources to organize. The consequence is that these people are often disregarded, and public participation is often conceived, even by its staunchest advocates, as the expression only of organized group interests.

This raises another question about the meaning of public participation, and this has to do with "representativeness." How well is the public, and its many interests, represented in the participation process? It has been noted that unorganized publics may not be represented at all; but even members or supporters of organized interest groups may not be well represented, for they are often led by self-selected elites. Memberships are rarely polled on issues that organization leaders express opinions about in the news media and at hearings. And how representative is the process by which groups compete for attention? Do confrontation tactics, noisy demonstrations, or slick propaganda give groups influence disproportionate to their size?

The requirement for public participation that has been incorporated into the Coastal Zone Management Act of 1972 and other federal and state laws is for a different kind of role than private interest groups have played in former years. In the "old" public participation, federal water development policy was

> based on interactions among three groups—congressional committees, agencies, and interest groups. Bureaus thus were encouraged to become relatively independent from the executive department hierarchy, becoming more responsive to the legislative committees. In addition, agencies solidified and sometimes institutionalized their relationships with particular interest groups that were supportive to the agencies' programs.[3]

For example, the Corps of Engineers received support from the National Rivers and Harbors Congress, which represented state and local officials, industrial organizations and construction contractors. The Bureau of Reclamation had close ties with the National Reclamation Association and its affiliates. The predominant influence of these pro-development interests tended to exclude conservationist and preservationist interests from decision-making. With the Coastal Zone Management Act and other laws, the decision rules for government agencies are changing. They now include non-economic critieria for project evaluation, and consideration of values and priorities in place of "objective" cost-benefit ratios.[4] River and harbor, reclamation, highway, and other public works projects may still be considered part of the public pork barrel and logrolled through legislatures. Nevertheless, coastal management legislation mandates the formation of balanced policies for both economic growth and the protection of environmental values. State responsibility for coastal management is not always assigned to agencies whose main purpose is engineering or public works. In Maine, Rhode Island, and Washington, coastal management is supervised by departments concerned with environmental protection and ecology or assigned to new councils that have no vested interests in construction.

What Are the Mechanics of Public Participation?

What obligation do public officials have to encourage public participation? Should they simply listen to self-identified interest groups, or should they try to organize other publics affected by their proposals and recruit them into the participation process? Should they even use public funds to do this? There is an even more fundamental question: Why in a representative form of democratic government is a separate public participation process needed anyway? Are not legislators and executives elected to govern and make decisions for the whole society? Is the political system designed by the founders of the republic inadequate to assure representation of all the publics concerned with public issues and to arrive at decisions truly in the public interests?

There has obviously been some dissatisfaction with representative government, and the political process that underlies it. Early reform movements invented the initiative, referendum, and recall procedures to replace representation by direct popular vote on issues when elected officials were regarded as unresponsive to social needs. In Washington and California, state coastal management legislation was the product of popular initiative. Why not simply govern by referendum rather than by representation? Many local and state issues, from school district budgets to constitutional amendments, are in fact decided by referendums. But the process is too cumbersome, expensive, and time-consuming to be used to settle all issues in jurisdictions with large populations. Perhaps this is why the direct democracy of the New England town meeting has not spread beyond that region's borders.

A Canadian politician, a member of the Legislative Assembly of the province of Manitoba, cites his own experience with representative government:

> The attitude [is] still held by many in public life that the conventional mechanisms of representative government are sufficient in insuring that the citizen will have a voice in decisions. While representative machinery is necessary and can often perform the function of registering people's concerns, it has its failings. The size of the administrative side of government is so large that elected members cannot keep all parts under surveillance. There is often a monopoly of information held by government agencies and they will act to protect their own vested interests. . . .
>
> Without the involvement of a citizen movement on behalf of the environment many issues will be ignored; many issues will receive only one side of an argument. . . . As one who is involved in the legislative arena, the citizen advocates working in our jurisdiction have added a qualitatively different dimension to the political process. . . . Without them politicians interested in environmental concerns would be highly circumscribed in being able to promote new legislation or opposing government on their environmental sins of omission or commission.[5]

Once it is recognized that representative government must be supplemented by direct citizen participation in decision-making, techniques must be devised not only to facilitate the process but also to encourage it. Perhaps the first step is to identify the relevant publics. Some organizations identify themselves, and they also help identify other organizations that should be involved. Two researchers used a survey to help the California Coastal Commission identify organizations that should be contacted in public information efforts on behalf of the Coastal Plan. The survey team tried to identify every possible national, state, regional, county and local organization interested in coastal management issues. Nevertheless, the questionnaire was mailed to only 127 organizations out of the total of five times that many that had been identified. Of these only 69 (54%) replied. The researchers found, as might be expected, that membership, staff size, and budget resources of these organizations varied widely. Their influence or representativeness, and presumably the amount of official credence that should be given to their positions, could not be easily quantified, however. The end product of the survey was a directory of interested organizations, which could be used as a mailing list for publications, hearing notices, etc. This method seemed to be an aid to public relations rather than public participation.[6]

A public participation technique that has long been used is the public hearing. It is a way to obtain information from the citizens and interest groups affected by a government proposal, but it has also been criticized as a means for manipulating the public. Hearings have a variety of objectives.

Information hearings are held:
1. to secure information and general opinions on a subject from experts before starting a major study that would lead to a report and recommendations;
2. for the expression of opinions on general policies or recommendations tentatively adopted;
3. to provide a forum for reactions to courses of definite action proposed in a government report or draft legislation; and
4. to obtain facts and opinions on plans for a specific project or activity.

Manipulative hearings are held:
1. to generate public support for action proposed by governments or private groups;
2. to find reasons for government inaction on a controversial issue. When the public is bored with an issue or confused by conflicting expert testimony, decision-makers may appear justified in delaying action; and

3. to sell a project as part of a public relations program under the
   guise of providing the opportunity to air opposing views.[7]

Public hearings have been criticized as being unrepresentative of
public opinion. Many citizens may be intimidated by the quasi-
judicial procedures and atmosphere of a formal hearing, but extre-
mists representing minority positions may use the hearings as a
platform to propagandize their own doctrines or counterproposals.
It is claimed that, "there has been a failure to recognize that public hearings are not valid methods of involvement in certain
circumstances."[8]

As a means to obtain a representative cross-section of public
opinion on coastal management and other issues, scientific surveys
are recommended. This is a passive rather than active form of
public participation, but it can be a useful component of a broader
program. Random samples are scientifically selected to stand a
very high probability of representing the entire population to be
surveyed. The manner in which questions are framed and asked
may introduce some chance of bias in the results, but survey findings are now conceded to be quite reliable. The survey is not
usually recognized as a communications medium, but it can provide
decision-makers with useful information. It can be used: (a) to
determine public awareness levels and concerns about particular
issues, (b) as a communications feedback mechanism to see if
public relations messages are reaching their target audiences, or
(c) as a means of measuring public opinion change regarding specific issues as discussion and debate develops between public and
private organizations.

A major difficulty of promoting public participation is the lack
of funding support for environmental organizations. Advocacy in
a technical field, such as coastal resources management, costs
money. It has therefore been proposed that public funds be made
available for this purpose, even though government officials may
not wish to pay costs for the opposition. Two bills have been introduced in Congress as S.1715 and H.R. 13901 to create a
"Public Participation in Government Proceedings Act." The Act
would permit or require government agencies to reimburse private
organizations for fees for attorneys and expert witnesses as well as
other costs of participation in public hearings or other proceedings.

It would also permit or require courts to award litigation fees to a citizen's group if: (a) it wins the case, (b) the case serves an important public purpose, (c) the group has no financial interest in the case, or (d) the group's financial resources are small compared to the legal costs. Citizen's groups usually depend on volunteer lawyers, scientists, researchers, economists and other experts. Corporations and government agencies can afford to hire the best law firms, fly in paid witnesses, and appeal to the courts again and again to wear out citizen groups and exhaust their resources. Public support of public interest advocacy groups is suggested as the way to make the public participation process more fair.[9]

What Do Citizen's Groups Expect From Public Participation?

Citizen's organizations appear to expect that the public participation process, now mandated in most federal aid programs for public works and resources management, will make up for what they consider to be inadequacies in the political process of representative government. Once legislation has been enacted, a bureaucratic organization is established to implement it. Citizens then find it difficult to observe or influence what the bureaucrats do. Citizen's organizations apparently also mistrust what they consider narrow-minded technical approaches to policy-making and project design. They seem to believe that the studies and conclusions of bureaucratic experts should be scrutinized and evaluated by the public and, where possible, by the citizen's group's own technical advocates.

Private interest groups want two kinds of roles in governmental policy-making. One is to influence directly the decisions of elected officials and bureaucrats in favor of one or another alternative. In this role, interest group representatives want access to the results of studies and investigations; and their own experts may offer data and information that may have been missed by the government staffs or consultants. These groups want to become informed so they can make their views known before final recommendations or choices are made. They consider that participation includes involvement in the technical phases of policy analysis and planning.

They do not want to be put in the position of simply reacting to agency proposals.

One constraint on this role for citizen's organizations is the reluctance of government agencies to make available the results of their investigations and analysis. If knowledge is power, those in government are not anxious to give up any of it, especially to those who pose the threat of informed opposition. This constraint is gradually being overcome by freedom-of-information laws, and especially by the requirement that government agencies prepare environmental impact statements for their projects that are open to public scrutiny. Several states, including New York, have enacted such legislation following the federal example.

The second kind of role that private organizations want to play is as advocates for or against a proposal in the political arena. This is the stage after agency recommendations have been made and before legislative action has been taken. Some interest groups may form an alliance with the agency and lobby for the proposal. Groups in opposition may take political action to try to defeat the proposal.

What Do Government Agencies Do With The Information?

What is the operational consequence of public participation? What would a coastal management agency do with the information obtained? The agency presumably ends up with a welter of conflicting opinions, demands, technical evaluations and political pressures. It could incorporate this information into its decision-making in a variety of ways: it could (a) simply "oil the squeaky wheel" and adopt the position of the loudest and most strident "public," (b) try to estimate the size of the various constituencies represented and adopt the position of the most numerous "public," (c) bargain its way to a position compromising the demands of various "publics," (d) search for good ideas and action alternatives that had not been previously identified, or (e) ignore all the information obtained and do what it had already decided before inviting public participation.

There are two aspects to the problem of aggregating citizen preferences as expressed in the public participation process. These have to do with the effectiveness of participation by different groups and the quantification of preferences.[10]

Processes Variables

These are variables that affect the impact that citizen groups make on public officials because of such factors as: (a) how much influence or prestige the organizations project, (b) how effectively they articulate and communicate their preferences, (c) how effectively the leaders and members communicate with each other, and (d) how much intensity is put into expressing preferences by such means as demonstrations and pressure on politicians. Minorities that have more resources of money, leadership, organization and communications skills can dominate the public participation process and make a greater impact on governmental decisions than weakly organized or unorganized majorities.

Aggregating Preferences

Leaving aside process variables, agency officials and politicians must have some means of determining how many citizens actually prefer specific project or program alternatives. Presumably a responsive government would make the choice that voters would make in a referendum; but voting is not part of public participation in the context of this discussion. Quantification of citizen preferences for one or another policy or action alternative is likely to be an impossible task. Where more than two alternatives must be considered the problem becomes more complex because clear majorities might not favor any one alternative. It has been noted that government water policy decisions formerly came out of a cozy relationship between government bureaus, congressional committees, and interest groups that profited from the construction projects. The "new" public participation aims at involving a wider spectrum of public and private interests. Nevertheless there are no guarantees that new rules and regulations for public participation will change the process of decision-making. Public officials may hear only what they want to hear, and use information inputs from public participation only if their usefulness is greater than the cost of using them. Information use costs and benefits have been summarized this way:[11]

Factors Affecting What Decision-Makers Hear. Decision-makers generally suffer from information overload, not scarcity. They therefore use a variety of considerations to screen what they hear. Agency bureaucrats tend to develop a particular fix on the issues with which they are involved. Information outside this framework may be viewed as irrelevant. Inputs from groups that have provided long-standing support will also likely be weighted more heavily than inputs from publics with little past contact or potential for future impact on the agency. Government organizations seek information that supports their inclinations and justifies their own decision process. A variety of points of view creates controversy. Coming out in favor of one or another position may, therefore, be politically costly whichever way the agency decides. Public officials, particularly professionals with engineering, economics, and other specialized backgrounds, experience, and professional indoctrination, are more receptive to information from sources whose values are most familiar to them. Another constraint on receptivity is that decision-makers are most open to new ideas during the earliest stages of planning, but formal public participation is usually solicited after the decision-makers have arrived at preferences on the issues and alternatives.

Information Costs. The money costs of obtaining information may be high. It diverts manpower from other activities and may delay politically urgent decisions. Information costs may also be high if much that is gathered is never used. Large amounts of information on conflicting public preferences have to be consolidated, but oversimplification may make it meaningless. Internal value conflict is also a cost to the agency. Information that conflicts with the bureaucrat's established values may be difficult to take into account and hence may be ignored or misunderstood. Agency officials may feel threatened by new publics, who may alienate their established constituencies and supporters. Using information obtained from these sources may be perceived as a political cost.

Given these problems of using information obtained from public participation, what benefit can be expected from deliberate efforts to encourage it? One obvious benefit is the public perception that the decision-making process has been open rather than secret, and that the opportunity has been provided for the public to express opinions and preferences. More substantive benefits may also be derived. Citizen's groups may identify action or policy alternatives that had not been considered by the official planners; they may provide data or information that might not have been available otherwise; they may put forward compelling reasons for rejecting official proposals. Once these information products have been made available through public participation, however, government officials and elected politicians can only take them into account in making judgements about administrative and legislative decisions. In the final analysis, then, government decisions are indeed made by the representative political process. Hopefully, however, public participation will make the process more democratic and more responsive to citizen preferences. It may even lead to technically better resolution of public issues.

REFERENCES

[1] 40 CFR 923.31 (b) (2) and 923.41, (January 9, 1975).

[2] Interview with Rob Elder, Maine State Planning Office, Augusta (July 19, 1976).

[3] Pierce, J. C. and H. R. Doerksen. "Citizen Influence in Water Policy Decisions: Context, Constraints, Alternatives," in *Water Politics and Public Involvement* (Ann Arbor, Michigan: Ann Arbor Science Publishers, Inc., 1976), p. 4.

[4] *Ibid.*, pp. 6-7.

[5] Axworthy, "Notes on Public Participation," in *Proceedings of a Workshop on Public Participation,* Patricia Bonner and Ronald Shimizu, Eds., Research Advisory Board, International Joint Commission, Windsor, Ontario (June, 1975).

[6] Ashbaugh, J. and J. Sorensen. "Identifying the 'Public' for Participation in Coastal Zone Management," *Coastal Zone Management J.* 2:383-409 (1976).

[7] Estrin, D. "Public Hearings: Comments on Their Use and Effectiveness," in *Proceedings of a Workshop on Public Participation,* Patricia Bonner and

Ronald Shimizu, Eds., Research Advisory Board, International Joint Commission, Windsor, Ontario (June, 1975).

[8]*Ibid.*, p. 46.

[9]Environmental Action. "Lobbying Assistance Alert," Washington, D.C. (July, 1976).

[10]Schneider, A. L. "Measuring Political Responsiveness: A Comparison of Several Alternative Methods," in *Water Politics and Public Involvement*, John C. Pierce and Harvey Doerksen, Eds. (Ann Arbor, Michigan: Ann Arbor Science Publishers, Inc., 1976), pp. 65–75.

CHAPTER XIX

MANAGEMENT EFFECTIVENESS

This investigation has been concerned with the formalities of coastal·resources management: its concepts, its laws, and its institutional structure. These are essential elements of resources management programs, and they vary considerably in form and details from state to state. It may indeed be useful to compare these elements to see what one state can learn from others. Nevertheless, laws and government processes are not readily transferable from one political milieu to another. In any case, what is important about coastal resources management is not the formalities of structure and process, but rather its effectiveness in facilitating economic growth while at the same time protecting and conserving environmental values.

It is not possible within the scope of this study to evaluate coastal management effectiveness. Nevertheless an approach to doing this may be considered here. Evaluation of management effectiveness would start with observation of the availability of inventories and analyses of the state of particular coastal resources and environmental systems. Information would also be obtained about problems of achieving resource management objectives and balancing economic development with environmental conservation. Observation of management operations would attempt to discover how the key factors of state and local laws, financial support of management agencies, implementation and enforcement procedures, and organizational structure actually facilitate or impede coastal zone problem solving and attainment of resource management objectives.

Evaluation of management effectiveness requires the identification of criteria, both qualitative and quantitative, by which to assess the condition of the coastal environment and the state of coastal resources. Should the application of these criteria to the coastal zone indicate some degree of ineffective management, its causes could be sought in the factors of legislation, financing, procedures, and organizational structure already mentioned. Information about management structure and operations in other states may suggest alternatives or innovations for improving management.

The Rhode Island and Washington programs point to ecological systems and seawater characteristics as examples of sources of quantitative indicators of the effectiveness of coastal resources management. More difficult is the identification and scaling of qualitative criteria. Enhancement or preservation of landscape, historical, scientific, recreational and educational values are included among coastal management objectives. Evaluation of their achievement, difficult though it may be, should also be part of the assessment of management effectiveness.

Rhode Island coastal management objectives are stated in the Act creating the Coastal Resources Management Council:

> It shall be the policy of this state to preserve, protect, develop
> and where possible, restore the coastal resources of the state . . .
> and that preservation and restoration of ecological systems shall
> be the primary guiding principle.[1]

The primary objective of preserving and restoring ecological systems could be elaborated and stated in operational terms. This would require first the complete scientific inventory and analysis of coastal ecologic systems in Rhode Island and an assessment of the conditions to which they should be restored. How successful the marine scientists in Rhode Island will be in describing the species varieties and populations in the various segments of the coastal zone and to what condition they should be restored remains to be seen. Nevertheless, this is one example of how an officially stated resource management objective could be translated into quantitative criteria by which to measure management effectiveness.

The Washington coastal zone management program also contains general statements of objectives relating to the development of economic values and the conservation of the natural, biologic, and physiographic characteristics of the state's shorelines. It also indicates a specific objective for which quantitative measures of management effectiveness may be formulated. This objective concerns the quality and characteristics of seawater.

The Washington program suggests that identification and regulation of permissible land and water uses within the coastal zone could be based on the kind and permanency of changes in seawater characteristics that these uses would cause. Having established a base line of desirable or acceptable characteristics of seawater along various segments of the state's shorelines, then variations could be measured. The Washington program suggests that permanency of change would be determined by whether it would be removed by natural processes within a reasonable amount of time. Measureable changes in seawater quality could be determined for these characteristics: chemical properties, depth, currents, tides, surface area, color, temperature, odor, sediment load, fresh-to-saltwater ratio, bottom configuration and patterns of movement.[2]

Although official statements of coastal zone objectives may be too general and vague to contain much operational meaning, they may nevertheless provide starting points for identifying criteria of management effectiveness. The Maine draft coastal program for the Mid-Coastal segment contained the global objective of simultaneously optimizing environmental values and maximizing economic and social benefits. Evaluating the Maine program will require greater specificity in the statement of objectives.

CRITERIA FOR EVALUATING
MANAGEMENT IN MAINE

Coastal zone planning and regulation of land and water use are not ends in themselves. These activities are important because they are expected to conserve environmental values. Having specific objectives in view, it should be possible to measure or evaluate the effectiveness of the management program in some way. The stated goal of the Maine coastal management program is:

> To develop a comprehensive plan providing for compatible and
> multiple uses of the coastal zone, optimizing those intrinsic and
> real values assuring the greatest long-term social and economic
> benefits for the people of the state of Maine.[3]

It is difficult to translate this statement into operational terms so
that the effectiveness of the program may be assessed. The output
of the program is said to be a "comprehensive plan," which in turn
is expected to benefit the coastal zone and the people of Maine.
It may be fair to say that this is a statement of an instrumental
objective rather than of the hoped-for environmental and social
outcomes of the management process.

The Maine program lists several objectives directly under its goal
statement. These are:

1. Inventory coastal resources and existing uses;
2. Develop a resource classification system with appropriate uses
   and development standards as a basis for regulating activities
   within the coastal zone;
3. Identify areas of major and impending conflicts and indicate
   priorities for immediate action;
4. Propose regulations and controls to ensure that coastal resources will be used in a manner that is consistent with their
   natural character and ecological relationships;
5. Elicit public views and interests through public hearings and
   other concurrent planning;
6. Coordinate efforts with other New England states; and
7. Propose institutional arrangements, state legislation, and local
   ordinances necessary to implement the Maine Coastal Plan.

Again it may be fair to say that these are statements of means
rather than objectives for some future desired state of the coastal
zone. Even though each intended output of the program planning
process may be successfully achieved, there is no indication in the
management program how they may in fact alter what is now
occurring in the coastal zone to produce a desired state that can
be described in operational terms. Such a description of an alternative desired future would provide the basis for an eventual
evaluation of the success of the management program in achieving
that future.

In some ways this observation on the stated goal and objectives of the Maine coastal zone management program is more semantic than real. In several sections of the program document there are in fact indications of what program implementation is intended to achieve in the coastal zone in terms that permit measurement or evaluation. It may also be unrealistic to expect a planning process to forecast a desired future state so explicitly as to be an exercise in science fiction. This is especially the case when information about the present situation is incomplete and inventories of the current state of environmental resources are still to be prepared.

Although the Maine coastal program is relatively advanced compared to many other states, it is too early to assess its effectiveness in terms of operational objectives that may be identified for it. It may, however, be appropriate to note some program objectives and criteria by which effectiveness may eventually be evaluated.

As in other states, the Maine coast is under development pressure. Population is migrating from Boston toward the northern end of the Northeast Megalopolis. Urbanization to accommodate new economic activities, new permanent residents, and new services parallels the development of new facilities for seasonal residents and tourists. Of particular significance for the Maine coast is the desirability of its deep water harbors for the accommodation of large tankers carrying imported petroleum products and the related demands for refining, storage and trans-shipment of these products.

Urbanization and industrial development are valued as sources of employment and income for Maine residents and as a tax base for state and local governments. Nevertheless, there are environmental costs involved that affect the land and water resources in the coastal zone. Degradation of these resources by pollution and destruction of plant and animal habitats or scenic values would affect such economic sectors as tourism and commercial fisheries, as well as deprive Maine residents of their environmental heritage. Development policy for the Maine coast must therefore balance private objectives for short-term economic gains derived from exploitation of the environment with long-term public values of environmental conservation. Some criteria for effectiveness in coastal management may therefore be summarized under the following headings.

Urbanization

Criteria would relate to the effectiveness of the guidance of the pattern of urbanization in the coastal zone to conserve land and environmental values. Population and economic growth are likely to exert greatest pressure in the coastal area. In the past, while energy resources were readily and cheaply available, low-density development requiring extensive transportation movements was the preferred pattern. As in other states, farms, wetlands, flood plains, and other environmentally valuable or hazardous areas were converted for urbanization. Objectives and criteria for future development will show greater concern for conserving land and achieving more efficient systems of transportation and utility services, without losing sight of the desirability to create an attractive man-made environment.

Water Supply

Urbanization to support population and economic growth depends on adequate sources of potable water. State and federal governments have established higher standards for drinking water. There is plenty of water for domestic use in Maine, but considerable capital expenditures and possible reorganization of individual water companies will be required to meet these standards. However, "the availability of water for certain nonconsumptive uses, such as industrial process water, may be limited, particularly in the southern part of the state."[4]

Environmental Quality

Efforts to reduce water pollution and achieve state and federal water quality standards will require careful investment of available financial resources. "The need for establishing carefully thought-out priorities for the use of these funds is one of the most eloquent

and fiscally compelling arguments for developing a more comprehensive approach to resources management and policy making in
the state."[5] Municipal and industrial discharges may be controlled
by investment in wastewater treatment facilities; but nonpoint
sources, such as soil erosion, fertilizer and other agricultural runoff,
urban stormwater runoff, and road salting are also important
sources of water pollution. Air contamination caused by industry,
energy production, transportation, and other concomitants of
urbanization, as well as the increasing volume of solid wastes will
be important problems for coastal management. They are all part
of the larger problem of guiding urban development to achieve an
acceptable balance between the objectives of economic advantage
and environmental protection.

Location of Facilities of State
and National Concern

Energy production is the focus of attention for this general resources management area. Maine's demand for power consumption
is expected to triple by the year 2000. Until new energy production technologies achieve large-scale contributions to the supply,
the power generation network will have to be expanded by fossil
or nuclear-powered steam plants and pumped storage or other
hydro-electric plants. Locating and designing these facilities to
mitigate environmental damage will be a serious test of coastal
zone management effectiveness.

Critical Environmental Areas

Once areas of critical environmental concern have been inventoried, it will be possible to measure management effectiveness in
terms of the relative success achieved in maintaining them in a
desirable or ecologically healthy state. Protecting fish and wildlife
habitats that contribute to recreation or commercial food production is matched by the need to prevent development in flood-prone
or other areas hazardous to life and property. Preservation of
historic sites and protection of scenic resources have both cultural

value as the heritage of the people of Maine as well as economic value as tourist attractions.

The fate of coastal areas of particular concern is one aspect of management for which quantitative criteria of effectiveness may be formulated. Wetlands, for example, may be included among such threatened areas. Maine has less than 17,000 acres of salt marshes along a coast with about 4000 miles of shoreline. About 4600 acres are under federal or state control or management.[6] A comprehensive survey of critical coastal areas was made by the Natural Resources Council of Maine, a public-interest conservation organization. It identified 2000 acres of scenic, historical or ecological significance. An eventual assessment of coastal management effectiveness could be based on a quantitative analysis of the future state of wetlands and other special areas.

Other operational objectives for coastal zone management may be identified for which detailed effectiveness criteria may be established. This task is beyond the scope of the present investigation. When completed at a later stage, however, it may be possible to evaluate state coastal zone management institutions to see how organizational structure influences management effectiveness.

REFERENCES

[1] "General Laws of Rhode Island," Section 46-23-1.

[2] *Washington Coastal Zone Management Program,* p. 36, (February 14, 1975).

[3] *Maine Coastal Zone Management Program, Mid-Coastal Segment* (February 18, 1976), p. 1.

[4] Maine State Planning Office and The New England River Basins Commission. *Management of Water and Related Land Resources in the State of Maine: Summary Report,* Augusta, Maine (March 1975), p. 5, which quotes from the report *Maine's Water Resources*, by the Maine Office of the Coordinator, Comprehensive Plan, Augusta (1967).

[5] *Ibid.,* p. 11.

[6] Maine Department of Environmental Protection. *Protecting Your Coastal Wetlands; A Citizen's Guide to the Wetlands Law,* Augusta (May, 1974).

CHAPTER XX

EPILOGUE

Coastal zone management is a young and dynamic program. This account of three early state efforts to establish coastal management on their own initiative and then try to take advantage of the later federal Coastal Zone Management Act offers no more than a snapshot taken during program infancy. The purpose of this epilogue is to provide a brief summary of major changes that were made in the federal program by the Coastal Zone Management Act Amendments of 1976. It will also describe recent developments in the preparation of the Rhode Island program.

More generous financial assistance is made available by the 1976 amendments for the program development stage. Depending on the amount of appropriated funds available, states may now receive each year up to 80% of the cost of developing coastal management programs.[1] Additional grants on the same matching basis may be made for assisting states "in the completion of the development and the initial implementation of its management program before such state qualifies for administrative grants under Section 306."[2]

Three major elements have been added to the requirements of a coastal management program:

1. A definition of the term 'beach' and a planning process for the protection of, and access to, public beaches and other public coastal areas of environmental, recreational, historical, esthetic, ecological or cultural value.

2. A planning process for energy facilities likely to be located in, or which may significantly affect, the coastal zone, including ... a process for anticipating and managing the impacts from such facilities.

267

3. A planning process for (a) assessing the effects of shoreline erosion (however caused), and (b) studying and evaluating ways to control, or lessen the impact of, such erosion, and to restore areas adversely affected by such erosion.[3]

The second of these tasks relates to the most significant amendments to the Coastal Zone Management Act. They contain this new Congressional finding:

The national objective of attaining a greater degree of energy self-sufficiency would be advanced by providing Federal financial assistance to meet state and local needs resulting from new or expanded energy activity in or affecting the coastal zone.[4]

In order to help attain this goal, the Act now includes a coastal energy impact program. The new Section 308 describes the kinds of assistance the federal government will give to state and local governments to deal with the impacts of energy development. Financial assistance may take these forms:

1. Grants to coastal states to plan and carry out projects and programs to deal with the impacts of energy development.

2. Grants to coastal states to plan for measures to deal with economic, social, or environmental consequences of siting, construction, expansion or operation of new or expanded energy facilities.

3. Loans to coastal states and local governments to assist them to provide new or improved public facilities and services required as a result of coastal energy activities.

4. Guarantees of bonds or other indebtedness issued by coastal states or local governments to provide new or improved public facilities or services required as a result of coastal energy activities.

5. Grants or other assistance to coastal states and local governments to enable them to meet obligations under loans and guarantees which they are unable to meet as they mature.

6. Grants to coastal states that have suffered or may suffer unavoidable loss of a valuable environmental or recreational resource as the result of coastal energy activities.

Economic, social and environmental impacts on the coastal zone
are likely to be caused by the search for new energy resources and
the construction of facilities to take advantage of them. The Department of the Interior has leased lands on the outer continental
shelf to private companies to drill for oil and natural gas. Explora-
tion itself may result in damage to the environment, but greater
danger from spills and blowouts may occur after the wells are in
production. At this stage pipelines must also be laid to convey the
crude oil and gas to tank farms on shore. Availability of these
products will encourage the development of industrial complexes
to refine the oil, process it for the production of chemicals, convert it to electricity, and store and transport the refined products
to other areas.

Even without new petroleum resources brought in from the
outer continental shelf, increasing demand for energy is likely to
be met by expanding port, storage and refining facilities for oil
brought from overseas. New power plants using oil or coal fuels
or atomic energy are also likely to be located in or near the coastal
zone.

Energy production and industrial use will have a direct environmental impact on the coastal zone, but there will also be economic
and social impacts on coastal communities. Some may be favorable, others unfavorable. The local government and state tax base
may be increased and the local and regional private sector of the
economy may be stimulated. Nevertheless, population would be
increased as workers and their families are attracted by new jobs.
This growth may take place more rapidly than additional fiscal
resources could become available for new schools, utilities, parks
and playgrounds, health facilities, public safety facilities, street and
highway improvements, and other public services and capital improvements. State and local governments will need extra funds
for planning, construction, and operation of these additional facilities. Without federal loans, grants, and guarantees on bond sales
they would probably not be able to raise the money in time to
meet the new needs.

INTERSTATE GRANTS

The new Section 309 in the amended Coastal Zone Management Act provides that the Secretary of Commerce may make annual grants of up to 90% of the cost of carrying out interstate coordination, study, planning, or implementation of coastal management programs according to approved interstate compacts or agreements. The coastal zone is no respecter of state boundary lines. Interstate coordination will be advantageous to Maine and New Hampshire where Portland Harbor and Piscataqua River activities affect both shorelines. Narragansett Bay is within the jurisdiction of Rhode Island, but Massachusetts communities also influence its shorelands and waters. Long Island Sound must be managed by both New York and Connecticut; and New Jersey must participate in dealing with the problems of the great New York Bight. Delaware and New Jersey both border on Delaware Bay, and Chesapeake Bay flows between Maryland and Virginia. On the west coast the Columbia River is common to Washington and Oregon, and its estuary requires coordinated management.

CRITIQUE OF THE RHODE ISLAND COASTAL MANAGEMENT PROGRAM

Chapter X, which describes the Rhode Island coastal zone management program, raises some questions about the compatibility of the Rhode Island approach to coastal resources management and the requirements of the Coastal Zone Management Act of 1972. The apparent discrepancies were noted in this paragraph,

> Rhode Island's flexible evolutionary approach to coastal resources management differs in some important respects from the management program visualized in the Coastal Zone Management Act and its related rules and regulations. The federal requirements visualize a complete and detailed program with a mapped coastal zone, mapped areas of particular environmental concern, categories of permissible uses and where they may be located, priorities for uses in various areas, and locations for uses of state and national interest. Rhode Island coastal resources management planners, however, followed their own legislative mandate, which was

enacted before the federal program came into being, regarding
management objectives, coastal boundaries, and regulation of
land and water uses. Whether this approach will be accepted by
the Office of Coastal Zone Management is uncertain at this time.
Nevertheless, Rhode Island is committed to it and is already
managing its coastal resources according to its own lights.

At the formal public hearing on the program in July, 1976,
attorneys for the Natural Resources Defense Council, the Conservation Law Foundation of Rhode Island, Ecology Action of Rhode
Island, the American Littoral Society, and the Audubon Society of
Rhode Island presented a detailed critique of the proposed state
coastal management program.[5] The spokesmen for these environmental organizations claimed that the proposed management program did not comply with the requirements of the federal Act,
that state legislation was inadequate, and that the Coastal Resources
Management Council was ineffective. They recommended that the
Rhode Island coastal management laws be repealed and new laws
enacted, that the Council be restructured, and that a comprehensive and detailed coastal management plan document be prepared
and adopted. Space does not permit repetition of all the fine legal
objections made by the attorneys. Some of the major ones go to
the heart of the Rhode Island approach to coastal management, as
may be noted by the following comments.

Coastal Zone Boundary

The Rhode Island legislature intended to limit the jurisdiction
of the Coastal Resources Management Council to a specific list of
activities and areas landward of the mean high water line. These
uses and areas are listed on page 131. Neither the law establishing
the Council nor the proposed management program define a geographically identifiable landward boundary for the coastal zone.
According to the environmental spokesmen, the Rhode Island program violates "the need for an 'effective and orderly boundary' (Section 920.11 Regulations) and identification of a coastal zone 'which
is easily regulated as a whole' (Section 923.11 Regulations)."[6]

Definition of Permissible Uses

By identifying specific uses and areas to which Council jurisdiction is limited, there are other activities and areas in the coastal zone that will not be regulated under the state coastal management program. The environmental organizations claimed that the federal law and regulations require the blanketing of a geographically defined coastal zone with land use regulations in a manner similar to a municipal zoning ordinance. It is their contention that the federal "language suggests the identification and mapping of areas with a system of permissible uses. The submission does not meet these regulations."[7]

The Impact Assessment Method of Regulation

Because the Rhode Island program has not divided the entire coastal zone into mapped areas with specific land use regulations for each one, as in a zoning ordinance, there is no legal foundation for deciding what are and what are not permissible uses. The Rhode Island approach is to use an illegal and ineffective environmental impact assessment method of deciding on a case-by-case method which permit applications to grant and which to deny.

> It is our contention that the use of this impact approach, without a set of comprehensive and specific regulations to guide the assessment of the impact, violates the letter and the intent of the Coastal Zone Management Act. This impact approach seeks to turn this Act into a completely different law similar to the National Environmental Policy Act. The impact approach vests too much uncontrolled discretion in the Coastal Resources Management Council. The approach makes the assessment of cumulative impacts difficult if not impossible. The impact approach is unfair to prospective developers because it gives them no guidance through pre-set regulations. The impact approach results in decision making with low public visibility, making citizen participation difficult if not impossible.[8]

Planning and Regulation

The Rhode Island legislature gave responsibility for both planning and regulation to the Coastal Resources Management Council.

The basic assumption of the Rhode Island approach to implementing the law establishing the Council was that planning and regulation should be carried on simultaneously. The threat to the state's
coastal resources was considered to be too immediate and serious
to delay regulation until management plans could be completely
worked out.

> The order in which management problems have been studied in
> depth and for which detailed policies and regulations have been
> formulated has been determined in large part by necessity. . . .
> The Plan, therefore, continues to grow in scope and detail as
> additional planning increments are studied, appropriate regula-
> tory responses are adopted, and existing plan elements are re-
> examined and modified to reflect evolving problems and priorities.[9]

The environmental organization critics of the Rhode Island management program did not accept this approach. They said that the
federal procedures required that a comprehensive and detailed
management plan must be prepared first and then regulations based
on the plan must be adopted and enforced. The critics also said
that the relationships between the University of Rhode Island
Coastal Resources Center, the Statewide Planning Program, and the
Coastal Resources Management Council were not clear. The University and Statewide Planning Program were supposed to provide
technical support for the Council, but the Council has not formally
adopted their studies, policy recommendations and plans.

> The adopted "Coastal Resources Management Council Plan:
> Policies and Regulations" is not a plan. It contains a general state-
> ment of goals. It sets forth policies and regulations in a few areas.
> There are no specific objectives, comprehensive policies, standards
> nor maps.[10]

The knowledge base for management decision making is incomplete. Studies of some significant coastal resources are missing.
Those studies that have been completed are resources inventories,
not plans. Nevertheless, even where excellent information and recommendations have been made by the University Coastal Resources
Center, their influence on Council policy and permitting decisions
is unclear; "several recommendations and conclusions of the Barrier
Beach studies . . . conflict with the CRMC's present policies."[11]

> The conclusion is that the uncertain status of existing studies, their
> admitted incompleteness, their failure to be specifically related to
> policies, objectives, and regulations, fail to provide an adequate
> basis for the plan required under the Coastal Zone Management
> Act.[12]

Because the plans are incomplete, the implementing regulations
are also incomplete. According to the Council's own procedures,
regulations have been adopted for sand and gravel extraction, commercial fisheries, and barrier beaches. There are no regulations for
the other elements to be included in the Council's *Plan, Policies,
and Regulations.* Still missing are regulations governing: (a) chemical and petroleum processing and storage, (b) power generating
and desalination plants, (c) cables and pipelines, (d) harbors, port
facilities, and marine transportation, (e) dredging and filling, (f)
fishing and agriculture, (g) marine recreation, (h) riparian rights,
(i) state-owned property, (j) shoreline protection facilities, (k)
natural areas of particular concern.[13]

The environmental organizations claim that without regulations
to control these activities, the Coastal Resources Management
Council cannot implement the federal law and regulations and is
unable to control development or resolve conflicts among competing uses. Moreover, the Council bases its regulatory decisions on
vague "criteria" rather than explicit "standards" that set forth
what is or is not acceptable.

> These criteria are discretionary to be used "where appropriate"
> and subject to "additional criteria." They are extremely vague:
> "effect on natural environment," "compatibility with nearby uses,"
> "capacity to support development." No indication of how impact
> will be measured, the amount of impact, or the specific impacts are
> identified. When one turns to the few areas where regulations have
> been adopted, these regulations are often deliberately vague to pro-
> vide complete discretion to the Council.[14]

THE COASTAL RESOURCES
MANAGEMENT COUNCIL

The harshest criticism made by the environmental organizations
was directed at the Coastal Resources Management Council. They

said that, "the current administration of the program raises serious questions as to whether this Council, if not altered, can protect coastal resources."[15] The Council has been in operation since 1971. It has had ample time to demonstrate its effectiveness as the agency with primary responsibility for protecting coastal resources. Its record has not been made public, however. The environmental organizations themselves, therefore, carried out a detailed review of Council activities. On the basis of this review they said, "It is our contention that this descriptive material raises serious questions as to whether the Council has the authority and is willing to exercise the authority it does have to protect the coastal zone of Rhode Island."[16]

Investigation indicated that early staff inadequacy that had caused delays in processing permit applications had been made up, but there was still insufficient staff to inspect activities resulting from past permits to insure compliance with Council rulings. Record keeping for the Council was also deficient. Records were incomplete and disorganized, making public accountability of Council operations impossible.

Statistics that could be compiled by the environmental groups about the Council permitting process showed that public hearings were infrequent (Table 1).

Table 1

Public Hearings in the Permitting Process

	Total Applications	Hearings	Percent
1973	135	6	5
1974	131	26	15
1975	190	28	15

Source: Presentation by Richard Brooks and Kenneth Payne, Public Hearing July 26, 1976, Providence, R.I., p. 94.

There have also been few denials of permits. There is insufficient information, however, to judge whether (a) the bargaining process between the Council and applicants results in better proposals and the withdrawal of applications that would obviously be denied, or (b) the Council has a strong development bias and approves applications without proper consideration of their environmental effects. Table 2 shows that only 9 out of 456 applications were denied between 1973 and 1975.

Table 2

Pattern of Coastal Resources Management Council Decisions

	Total	Approved	Denied	Incomplete	Other
1973	135	54	2	73	5
1974	131	93	4	9	8
1975	190	126	3	33	4
Total	456	273	9	115	17

Source: Presentation by Richard Brooks and Kenneth Payne, Public Hearing July 26, 1976, Providence, R.I., p. 96.

Most permit applications have been handled routinely by the Council and decisions handed down within six months. Nevertheless, in 1974 there was no action on 19 applications and no action on 31 applications in 1975. About two-thirds of those cases had gone to public hearings. This suggests that if an action is controversial or has had a public hearing, "the Council is very slow and cautious in making its decision."[17]

Court Cases

The Coastal Resources Management Council has been the defendant in 11 court cases in which plaintiffs sued to overturn Council permit decisions. Federal requirements for management program submissions include an analysis of relevant court cases. The Rhode Island program did not include this information. An analysis of the short history of the Council in the courts was made by the attorneys for the environmental organizations. Their conclusions were as follows:

These cases reveal serious problems with the Council's operations. First, note that the cases rarely involve permit denials. This failure to deny permits reflects the generally permissive attitude on the part of the Council. Second, the Council almost *never* prevails in court. The pattern of sloppy procedure, casual Council decision making, and the inadequate buttressing of its decisions has apparently antagonized the lower courts in their review of this agency. Third, it is fully apparent from the litigation that the Council has failed to provide a mechanism for settling disputes between different agencies of the city. Fourth, the cases raise many unresolved questions regarding the actual jurisdiction and power of the Coastal Resources Management Council.[18]

CITIZEN PARTICIPATION

It is perhaps to be expected that citizen environmental organizations would find deficiencies in arrangements for public participation. These organizations noted that the benefits of such participation include: (a) educating citizens about the problems of the Rhode Island coast and possibly solutions, (b) building a constituency for the coastal zone management program, (c) and improving planning by offering information about problems and ideas for action.

In-depth citizen participation was limited to five technical areas: barrier beaches, sand and gravel mining, commercial fisheries, coastal natural areas, and resource inventory. Citizen involvement in the other management responsibilities of the Coastal Resources Management Council may be organized in the future. But this kind of technical involvement is not broad citizen participation.

> Our experience and the testimony of citizens at "workshop" sessions convinces us that no effort has been made too give the citizenry an in-depth understanding of the management [program]. Moreover, full participation in the development of policy has been minimal. Last minute *pro forma* public meetings, held only at the insistence of our groups, turned into long and complicated presentations by the Council's staff. The draft document of the management program was virtually unreadable and incomplete . . . Citizens at the workshops complained about the vagueness of everything . . . Unfortunately, the Council has confused public relations with the sponsorship of true participation. The entire citizen participation effort has been aimed at informing the public, not involving the public. Reports to us from local planning board members and

staff indicate that the sessions of the CRMC held with local groups
were general presentations rather than in-depth consultations on
common problems.[19]

CONCLUSIONS

It has been noted in Chapter XIV that the Natural Resources
Defense Council raised similar objections to the Washington coastal
management program as it and other organizations did in the comments described above on the Rhode Island program. The Washington program was also considered to be incomplete, and that
program approval by the Secretary of Commerce would therefore
be premature. More work was suggested to refine and clarify the
Washington program in many of the same respects as those noted
for Rhode Island.

In the case of Washington, the federal response to such criticism
was that, "while the CZMA [Coastal Zone Management Act] requires that the management system be 'in place,' it does not require
nor can it be expected that a system is perfected or running at 100
percent efficiency at the time of approval."[20] In Rhode Island,
the response of the state and the federal Office of Coastal Zone
Management was to delay submission of the program until comments made at the public hearing could be studied. With close
attention by OCZM, the Rhode Island Statewide Planning Program
and the other participating agencies prepared extensive revisions
to the management program. Most of the comments on coastal
zone boundary definition, mapping of areas of particular concern,
and planning are being taken into account. The revised program is
scheduled for submission to Washington in the summer of 1977.[21]

In the seven years since the Coastal Zone Management Act became law only the Washington coastal zone management program
has been approved by the Secretary of Commerce. Even this approval acknowledged that the Washington program would need
further development during its implementation stage. It would
appear that Congress, the Department of Commerce, and the
Office of Coastal Zone Management greatly underestimated the
task of preparing coastal management programs. The Coastal Zone
Management Act of 1972 authorized only three annual grants to
the states to complete the task. It has turned out to be technically

more complex and more costly than anticipated to prepare the scientific and information base for planning and the regulatory process. And politics and public participation requirements are difficult to satisfy.

It was assumed by the drafters of the federal legislation and regulations that the prescribed elements of coastal resources management programs could be readily prepared without additional extensive and costly resources surveys and inventories. It was also assumed that adding new institutional structures for coastal management to the already complex patterns of state law and organization would be a relatively simple problem of administrative mechanics. Further, it was assumed that once resources inventories, plans, regulations, and a management structure were in place, there would be no extraordinary problems in applying plans and regulations to coping with real world demands for development in the coastal zone.

The Natural Resources Defense Council and the other environmental organizations that criticized the Washington and Rhode Island coastal programs appeared to subscribe to these same assumptions. NRDC had its own preconceived view of how coastal zone management should be structured. It had drafted a model coastal zone statute in 1974 and believed that it was suitable for all states.[22] Nevertheless, four states—California, Washington, Maine, and Rhode Island—had enacted coastal programs in 1971. Each took a different approach, and all were different from the NRDC model.

The Rhode Island Coastal Resources Management Council does not fit NRDC preconceptions. It has therefore been roundly criticized, along with the legislation establishing it and the state and University organizations that provide it with staff and technical services. The critique of the Rhode Island program was presented and presumably prepared by lawyers. They expected rigid compliance with federal laws and regulations, and they wanted a state program that in its turn had regulations amenable to rigid enforcement by state agencies. They seemed to assume that knowledge about coastal resources and processes is already available, and that it is only necessary to promulgate regulations based on this essentially complete knowledge to successfully protect the coastal environment. Some scientists upon whom we depend for such knowledge are more modest in assessing its availability or usefulness.

> Planners and politicians who must make decisions about estuarine resources are increasingly suggesting that ecologists prepare information in the form of a model of the system. The implication seems to be that since a model is an abstraction or apparent simplification based on what data is available, we can produce some kind of model immediately, as the time for management and administrative decisions is short, and the time required to obtain adequate data on ecological systems is long. . . .
>
> It is not possible to describe nature in any way that suits us and expect an explanatory and predictive theory to emerge. The description we choose may be "dynamically insufficient" in the system scientist's jargon. That is, the description may not reflect reality, and Lewontin suggests that "such is the agony of community ecology."
>
> From the foregoing discussion, we suggest that care should be taken in attempts to define management policies within the context of systems modeling . . . Ecologists might best contribute to resource management by stressing the ambiguities in our knowledge about natural communities, and induce managers and politicians to make decisions that openly acknowledge that they are sometimes based on tentative information.[23]

The authors of this extensive quotation might have wished to direct their good advice to lawyers as well as managers and politicians. Passing laws, adopting regulations, and even winning court cases do not necessarily resolve all the problems that may arise in understanding and coping with the consequences of action that may affect the natural environment. Lawyers might, therefore, wish to acquire better understanding of the technical, time, and cost constraints on producing reliable scientific information about coastal resources on which to base management decision making. Even generous federal grants under the Coastal Zone Management Act as amended may not guarantee it.

There are also obvious political constraints on repealing state laws and passing new ones. Even citizen participation, which is so strongly advocated by the critics of the Rhode Island program, might not produce general support for their views. The environmental organizations assume that the "public" is sympathetic to their own views. There are many different publics, however, and several attempts were required in the state legislature to assemble adequate public support for the 1971 Act that created the Coastal Resources Management Council. There is no way of knowing how well the spokesmen for environmental organizations represent the views of their own members, much less of the people of Rhode Island. There is not universal support for coastal zone management. In Maine and other states, segments of the public have succeeded in obstructing innovative coastal programs that were well on the way toward readiness for submission for federal review. Delay or even failure to win federal approval for the Rhode Island program might suit some citizens of that state very well.

REFERENCES

[1] *Coastal Zone Management Act of 1972* as amended, Sec. 305(c).

[2] *Ibid.*, Sec. 305(a) (2).

[3] *Ibid.*, Sec. 305(b) (7) (8) (9).

[4] *Ibid.*, Sec. 302(i).

[5] Presentation by Richard Brooks and Kenneth Payne, "In the Matter of: Public Hearing Under Sec. 308 of the Coastal Zone Management Act of 1972 to Determine Eligibility of Rhode Island's Proposed Coastal Resources Management Program," State House, Providence, Rhode Island, (July 26, 1976) (processed).

[6] *Ibid.*, p. 53.

[7] *Ibid.*, p. 45.

[8] *Ibid.*, p. 43.

[9] Rhode Island Coastal Resources Management Council. *Management Program* (Draft), Providence, Rhode Island, (March 3, 1976), p. 2.

[10] Presentation by Brooks and Payne, p. 80.

[11] *Ibid.*, p. 81.

[12] *Ibid.*, p. 82.

[13] *Ibid.*, p. 84.

[14] *Ibid.*, p. 86.

[15] *Ibid.*, p. 89.

[16] *Ibid.*, p. 90.

[17] *Ibid.*, p. 98.

[18] *Ibid.*, p. 102.

[19] *Ibid.*, pp. 130-131.

[20] U.S. Office of Coastal Zone Management. *Final Environmental Impact Statement, State of Washington Coastal Zone Management Program,* Department of Commerce, Washington, D.C., (April 9, 1976), p. i.

[21] Telephone interview with Susan Morrison, Statewide Planning Program, Providence, R. I., February 1, 1977.

[22] Smith, N., *et al.* "Model Coastal Zone Statute," *Coastal Zone Management Journal,* 1:209-226 (Winter 1974).

[23] Hedgpeth, J.D. and S. Obrebski. "Ecosystems Models and Resource Management," *The Coastal Society Bulletin,* 1:5-9 (November 1976).

INDEX

Critical Areas Advisory Board (ME)
51,205
Critical Areas Registry Act (ME) 81

Ecology, Department of (WA)
146-151,155-159,163-168,
171-179,185-190,202,208,219,
233,244
Master Application Center 178,
179
Economic Development, Department
of (RI) 95
ecosystems 3,4,133-137,260
eminent domain power 20,24,25
energy production 265
Enforcement, Division of (RI) 113,
116,122
environment
classification 159-163
conservancy 161,184
natural 161,184
rural 161,184
urban 162,185,264
Environmental Coordination Procedures Act (WA) 148,151
environmental impact statements
244,253
Draft (DEIS) 187
Final (FEIS) 188,189
Environmental Protection, Department of (ME) 44,47,48,51,61,73,
205,219
executive department 53-60

federal land 131,132,158
federal review of state programs 16
Forest Practices Act (WA) 150
freedom-of-information laws 253
Freshwater Wetlands Act (RI) 110

General Assembly (RI) 104,107,
117,129
government, *See* intergovernmental
coordination; local government
governor 24-26,28,35,38,39,53-55,
58-60,89,99,101,112,145,245
Governor's Advisory Committee on
Coastal Development and Conservation (ME) 35,55,58-60,85,
233,245
growth policy 227-229,232

Health, Department of (RI) 94,96,
126
Health, Department of (WA) 150

initiative 43-46
intergovernmental coordination 7,
8,11,20,21-28,33-36,93,96,102,
116,147-151,195-197,211-224,
245
Intertidal Salt Marsh Act (RI)
107-110
investment subsidies 229

Kumekawa, G. 106

Lake Chelan 145
land use 79,135-138,200
control 36,125,157,160,165,
181,190,201,212-224,261
national policy 227-229
priorities 81-84,133
Land Use Regulation Commission
(ME) 47,61
lead agency 25-28,124,127
legislation 38,43-51,71